To See Jesus

Text copyright © 2017 remains with the Australian Province of the Society of Jesus

All rights reserved. Except for any fair dealing permitted under the Copyright Act, no part of this book may be reproduced by any means without prior permission. Inquiries should be made to the publisher.

ISBN   978-1-925486-66-7 paperback
978-1-925486-67-4 hardback
978-1-925486-68-1 epub
978-1-925486-69-8 Kindle
978-1-925486-70-4 pdf

Cover design Yvonne Ashby. Layout by Astrid Sengkey

Text Minion Pro Size 10 &11

Published by:

An imprint of the ATF Press Publishing
Group owned by ATF (Australia) Ltd.
PO Box 504
Hindmarsh, SA 5007
ABN 90 116 359 963
www.atfpress.com
Making a lasting impact

To See Jesus

By Tom O'Hara SJ

ATF Theology
Adelaide
2017

Abbreviations

References to the text of *The Spiritual Exercises* are given in the customary way, according to the numbering of the paragraphs of the text (for example, SE 124).

The Spiritual Exercises appears in italics when it is the book that is indicated. In all other cases plain text is used (for example, to make the Spiritual Exercises).

Translations from *The Spiritual Exercises* are from the text of Louis J Puhl (St Paul, Allahabad, 1981), except where some particular point of translation is being made.

Translations of Scripture are from the NRSV (New Revised Standard Version), except where some particular point of translation is being made.

Volumes of the *Monumenta Historica Societatis Iesu* are referred to by their traditional numbering in order of publication. Following are the full names of the volumes referred to in the footnotes:

MHSI 26: Monumenta Ignatiana Series Prima: *Sancti Ignatii de Loyola Epistolae et Instructiones Tomus Secundus*

MHSI 27: *Epistolae P Hieronymi Nadal Tomus Quartus*

MHSI 28: Monumenta Ignatiana Series Prima: *Sancti Ignatii de Loyola Epistolae et Instructiones Tomus Tertius*

MHSI 42: Monumenta lqnatiana Series Prima: *Sancti Ignatii de Loyola Epistolae et Instructiones Tomus Duodecimus*

MHSI 57: Monumenta Ignatiana Series Secunda: *Exercitia Spiritulia et eorum Directoria*

MHSI 63: Monumenta Ignatiana Series Tertia: *Tomus Primus Monumenta Constitutionum Praevia*

MHSI 66: Monumenta Ignatiana Series Quarta: *Scripta de S Ignatio Tomus I Fontes Narrativi Vol I*
MHSI 73: Monumenta Ignatiana Series Quarta: *Scripta de S. Ignatio Tomus II Fontes Narrativi Vol II*
MHSI 76: Monumenta Ignatiana Series *Secunda Exercitia Spiritualia Sancti Ignatii de Loyola et Eorurn Directoria Tomus II Directoria*
MHSI 90: *Epistolae et Monumenta P Hieronymi Nadal Tomus V*
MHSI90A: *P Hieronymi Nadal Orationis Observationes*
MHSI 100: Monumenta Ignatiana Series Secunda: *Exercitia Spiritualia*

Contents

Abbreviations	v
Introduction	ix

Chapter One   1
a) Basic principles for understanding the Spiritual Exercises   1
   1. Continuity and discontinuity   3
   2. Flexibility and adaptation   4
   3. Process and content   6
   4. The role of desire   8
   5. Generosity   8
b) The dynamic of the Spiritual Exercises   10
c) The problem   14
d) Terminology of Ignatius   28
   Meditation and contemplation   33

Chapter Two   41
a) Natural contemplation   41
   The use of imagination   46
b) Universality of contemplation and mysticism   48
c) Contemplative prayer   51
   The kataphatic and apophatic ways   65
d) Catechism of the Catholic Church   67

Chapter Three 83
a) Ludolph of Saxony 83
b) Lectio Divina 98
c) Use of the gospels according to modern exegesis 115
d) The depth of Ignatius's Trinitarian and Christological
    conversion 123
    1. Personal reminiscences 124
    2. Testimony of Ignatius's companions 129
    3. The Spiritual Diary 133

Chapter Four 149
a) The conversion-discipleship dynamic 149
b) Contemplation of the mysteries of the life of Christ 160
    1. What is not involved 160
    2. Use of the imagination 161
    3. Essence of this form of contemplation 165
    4. Contemporaneity of the mysteries 181
    5. To know, love and follow 185
    6. The Imitation of Christ 186
    7. Presence to the humanity of Christ 199
    8. The mysteries chosen for contemplation 205
c) Contemplation and the goal of the Spiritual Exercisess 224

Conclusion 229

Index of Biblical References 233

Index of Names and Authors 237

Introduction

Immediately after the account of the triumphant entry of Jesus into Jerusalem for his last Passover, in the twelfth chapter the Gospel of John relates the story of an encounter of Jesus with some Greek visitors to Jerusalem: 'Now among those who went up to worship at the festival were some Greeks. They came to Philip, who was from Bethsaida in Galilee, and said to him, 'Sir, we wish to see Jesus.' Philip went and told Andrew; then Andrew and Philip went and told Jesus.'[1] Two words to which John gives a double meaning are the words 'come' and 'see'. Each conveys the ordinary sense of the verb, but on a deeper level signifies coming into a relationship with Jesus through believing. John deals with belief by using the verb πιστυειν (to believe) which he uses 98 times, never the noun πιστὶ (faith). When it is Jesus or God, who is the object of this believing, John follows the verb with the preposition εισ (into). A few examples of the numerous instances of this usage are:

2:11—Jesus did this, the first of his signs, in Cana of Galilee, and revealed his glory; and his disciples believed in him.

3:16—For God so loved the world that he gave his only Son, so that everyone who believes in him may not perish but may have eternal life.

6:29—Jesus answered them, This is the work of God, that you may believe in him whom he has sent.

14:1—Do not let your hearts be troubled. Believe in God, believe also in me.

17:20—I ask not only on behalf of these, but also on behalf of those who will believe in me through their word.

---

1. Jn 12:20–22.

This language of John's at least hints at the dynamic character of the act of believing which brings a person into union with Jesus and with God. It is through the act of 'believing into' that one responds to divine grace and enters into the kind of union with Jesus and with the Father that becomes a central theme of the Johannine writings, especially in the discourse at the Last Supper and in the First Letter of John.

John uses the request to see Jesus very creatively. It is the occasion for Jesus to expand on what is implied in the deeper meaning of 'see'. Union with him through believing can only come about through his 'hour'. So this leads Jesus, here for the first time, in the twelfth chapter of John to announce that now the hour has come. To see Jesus, i.e. to be a disciple, a person must follow him into the hour (verse 26). So, here John gives the conditions of discipleship, including losing one's life in order to find it, which the synoptic writers repeat more than once as Jesus is making his way up from Galilee to Jerusalem. John goes on to write of the initial disturbance of Jesus at the prospect of the hour (v 27) and to show Jesus praying to the Father to be saved from or through the hour, as in the Gethsemane accounts of the synoptics. As in the Transfiguration of the synoptics, there is a voice from heaven, 'not for my sake but for yours' (v 30), to strengthen prospective disciples in face of the coming scandal of the cross. The simple request of the Greek visitors to see Jesus has led John to go right to the depth of what is required really to see Jesus; it is only possible by entering with him into the hour of death and glorification.

In the first chapter of the Gospel John tells the story of the two men, one of them Andrew,[2] who had first followed Jesus after he was pointed out to them by John the Baptist. When Jesus sees them following, he asks the very penetrating question: 'What are you looking for?' To which they reply, equally at depth: 'Where are you staying?',[3] a theme (stay, remain, abide) that John will take up later[4] in the profound discourse of Jesus about his relationship with those who believe. The reply of Jesus to the question about where he abidesis:

---

2. Jn 1:40.
3. Jn 1:38.
4. Jn 15:4–10. The theme of 'abide in' dominates Jesus' image of the vine and the branches, and will be taken up again in 1 John.

'Come and see.'[5] These first two followers are being invited to spend the afternoon with Jesus, and simultaneously to begin the journey of relationship with him through believing that will transform their existence.

The theme of 'come' in this sense is repeated by John in the words: 'Yet you refuse to come to me to have life.'[6] 'Everything that the Father gives me will come to me, and anyone who comes to me I will never drive away.'[7] 'No one can come to me unless drawn by the Father who sent me.'[8] 'For this reason I have told you that no one can come to me unless it is granted by the Father.'[9] 'Let anyone who is thirsty come to me, and let the one who believes in me drink.'[10] The same kind of union with the believer is indicated when the coming is reversed, when Jesus says: 'I will not leave you orphaned; I am coming to you.'[11] and: 'Those who love me will keep my word, and my Father will love them, and we will come to them and make our home with them!'[12] From our part there is belief, from God's part presence.

The theme of 'seeing' for John reaches its climax in the fourteenth chapter when Jesus declares: 'If you know me, you will know my Father also. From now on you do know him and have seen him.'[13] To Philip's request, 'Lord, show us the Father, and we will be satisfied', Jesus replies, 'Have I been with you all this time, Philip, and you still do not know me? Whoever has seen me has seen the Father.'[14] Speaking of his approaching death, Jesus announces: 'In a little while the world will no longer see me; but you will see me; because I live, you also will live.'[15] That is to say, the world in the Johannine sense of the enemy of the Christian community is not intimately united with Jesus through believing, but the disciples will be. The disciples gathered round Jesus for this last discourse will have two different

---

5. Jn 1:39.
6. Jn 5:40.
7. Jn 6:37.
8. Jn 6:44.
9. Jn 6:65.
10. Jn 7:37.
11. Jn 14:18
12. Jn 14:23.
13. Jn 14:7.
14. Jn 14:9.
15. Jn 14:19.

experiences: the experience of giving up and being scattered[16] and the experience of receiving the gift of the promised Paraclete, and enjoying the union with Jesus and the Father foretold in the same discourse.

The experience of seeing Jesus and so being in intimate union with him comes to its fruition in the life of the community of the First Letter of John, where the prologue announces:

> We declare to you what was from the beginning, what we have heard, what we have seen with our own eyes, what we have looked at and touched with our hands, concerning the word of life—this life was revealed, and we have seen it and testify to it, and declare to you the eternal life that was with the Father and was revealed to us—we declare to you what we have seen and heard so that you also may have fellowship with us; and truly our fellowship is with the Father and with his Son Jesus Christ. We are writing these things so that our joy may be complete.[17]

Six times in just three verses the author draws upon the sense of sight to indicate the community's union with the Word who is life. This union is brought about also through the senses of hearing and touch. The object of the senses is Word and life, something clearly beyond sense-knowledge as commonly understood. But the author is not writing about merely metaphorical 'spiritual' senses, though this will be a legitimate development of later spiritual theology. The experience that is recounted is the experience of the community. Even if, as is most likely, there are none of those who had actually walked with Jesus of Nazareth still alive at the time of the writing of this prologue, the community is the recipient of the living tradition from those who had actually seen, heard and touched Jesus with their bodily senses.

When God chose to enter the human race through the incarnation, the way of mediation, between God and humankind was established forever. The man, Jesus, is not some optional extra for those who

---

16. Jn 16:32.
17. 1 Jn 1:1–4.

find it convenient or suited to their temperament to approach God through an intermediary, 'For there is one God; there is also one mediator between God and humankind, Christ Jesus, himself human'.[18] All justification, all grace, every gift of God is mediated to human persons, whether or not they realise it, through our Lord, Jesus Christ. This leads to the privileged way of entry into union with God, Father, Son and Holy Spirit through the kind of knowledge of the Word made flesh that the author of 1 John was writing about. This does not imply that the only way to union with God is a presence to the humanity of Christ. Great non-Christian traditions of meditation and mysticism lead into such union those who are scarcely, if at all, aware of the name of Jesus. For the Christian, as the tradition of the church has amply witnessed, apophatic ways of contemplation, which do not attend explicitly to the humanity of Christ, have led many to profound union with God. While this is true, the fact remains that objectively the man, Jesus, Christ and Lord, is sole mediator and that to know him in a human way, person to person, is the privileged mode of entry into union with the Trinity.

While the mode of union with God in Christ written about in the prologue of 1 John is through sense knowledge, there are obviously questions to be asked about how this operates. It is clearly not a simple, corporeal exercise of the senses that is implied. For one thing, this would require presence in place and time. For the writer, at one or two generations after the death of Jesus this was clearly not possible. Second, the apostle Paul declares that an 'exterior' knowledge of Christ (regarding him 'according to the flesh') is of no avail in the matter of salvation. 'So from now on we regard no one according to worldly standards; if indeed we have regarded Christ according to worldly standards, now we no longer regard him in that way.'[19] It was on the road to Damascus when Paul asked 'Who are you, Lord?' and

---

18. 1 Tim 2:5.
19. 2 Cor 5:16. The translation is by Victor Furnish, *Anchor Bible* Volume 32 A (New York: Doubleday, 1984), 306. James D Dunn, *The Theology* of *Paul the Apostle* (Grand Rapids: Eerdmans, 1998), 184, points out that the correct translation and exegesis of this verse does not favour an opinion that Paul was writing here about having known Jesus during his 'public life'. The qualification 'according to the flesh' belongs with the verb 'regard' rather than the noun, 'Christ'. The context is rather one of no longer judging anyone by any other standard than that of the cross and resurrection of Christ.

the Lord replied: 'I am Jesus whom you are persecuting,'[20] that God chose to reveal God's Son to Paul.[21] Writing to the Corinthians, Paul professed that he 'decided to know nothing among you except Jesus Christ, and him crucified.'[22] Indeed from the time of his conversion onward Paul's whole life of prayer and apostolate was dominated by his desire 'to know Christ and the power of his resurrection and the sharing of his sufferings by becoming like him in his death.'[23]

The disciple of the Johannine community hears through that community the stories about Jesus. These are handed on, as they are today in the gospels, in a form that is concrete and personal. They are spoken and received in faith, a faith nourished through the sacraments of baptism, confirmation and Eucharist. The same Spirit, present in the heart of the believer through faith and the sacraments, is present in the Word of scripture and is active whenever that Word is read in liturgical or in private, personal prayer. As the stories are relived in the imagination, the presence through faith of Christ in the heart of the disciple is activated. There is a real sense of seeing, hearing and touching, and, as will be developed in later spiritual theology, of smelling and tasting the person of the Word made flesh. The imagination is at work, but not just the imagination. It is the imagination, and through it the use of the inner senses that give the benefit of immediate presence to the person of Christ. The quality of that presence requires the union of all the intentional faculties of the person. In modern terms, the whole person, both conscious and unconscious, will be intentionally present to the person of Christ.

This is the kind of prayer that Ignatius of Loyola recommends as the main way of praying in his Spiritual Exercises. One who has undergone a radical conversion away from sin to the person of Christ crucified is ready to take up the gospels in discipleship, and to listen to the personal call of Christ to spend their life in his service for the coming of the Kingdom. Hearing this call will involve a continuation of the dynamic of healing and conversion through presence in faith via all the intentional faculties to the Christ of the gospel, together with a formation according to the mind and heart of Christ, the

---

20. Acts 9:5.
21. Gal 1:15.
22. 1 Cor 2:2.
23. Phil 3:10.

activation of baptismal grace, so that being 'another Christ' is not simply a theological formula, but determines the way that person lives, relates, thinks, feels, wills and chooses.

The scope of this work is to examine what is involved in the contemplation of the person of Christ in the gospels, as recommended by St Ignatius for those making the Spiritual Exercises. The study will confine itself to the Second Week of the Exercises, what Ignatius calls 'the life of Christ our Lord up to Palm Sunday inclusive.'[24] The contemplation of the Lord's Passion and the contemplation of his risen life together with the Contemplation to Attain the Love of God have their own specific character that would require a separate treatment.

---

24. SE 4.

Chapter One

The scope of this work is to explore the meaning of contemplation in the Second Week of the Spiritual Exercises of St Ignatius of Loyola.

Basic principles for understanding the Spiritual Exercises

The Spiritual Exercises are, as the name implies and as Ignatius points out in his very first paragraph, a series of prayer exercises; they are not a treatise on the spiritual life. The author does not begin by careful definition of terms. So, when we look at contemplation in the Second Week of the Exercises, we find that Ignatius is largely silent on what he understands by the use of the word 'contemplation' in this context. In the book of the Exercises he simply gives a series of practical instructions that the one giving the Exercises may use and adapt in working with the one who is making them. Unlike Teresa or John of the Cross, Ignatius does not offer psychological or theological analyses of what may occur during the course of prayer. In seeking after his meaning, therefore, we need to proceed by precisely locating the particular part under consideration in the movement of the Exercises as a whole. The dynamic, as understood by Ignatius, is revealed by constantly keeping in mind the goal of the Exercises, and by applying to the whole process the basic ways of proceeding that are outlined, especially in the Annotations and the Rules for the Discernment of Spirits.

Ignatius's way of writing in presenting the text of *The Spiritual Exercises* leaves itself open to many misunderstandings. If one attends only to the meaning of the words, without careful attention to their context, it is an obvious and natural temptation to regard contemplation as presented by Ignatius as one among many 'methods of prayer'. Doing this, and following the 'method' as outlined in the text literally, step by step, one runs the danger of missing the deeper and true significance. If we move beyond a literal understanding of the 'method', questions that arise are: What are the fundamental goals of the Spiritual Exercises that throw light on the kind of prayer intended here? What is the relationship between God, as giver of all grace and the one making the Exercises? How is Ignatius's meaning influenced by his own conversion, following of Christ and familiarity with the Trinity? What were the influences that shaped the content of that conversion? Did he intend to share that experience, or, as some contend, simply provide in *The Spiritual Exercises* a book for beginners? How, in fact, did Ignatius understand the word 'contemplation'? What is the relationship between contemplation as presented by Ignatius and the understanding of that word in Spiritual Theology today? What is the role of imagination in this process? Is it necessary, when talking of the Second Week of the Spiritual Exercises, to qualify the word 'contemplation' by calling it 'Ignatian contemplation' or 'imaginative contemplation'? Or, should it be referred to simply as contemplation, with the implication that it belongs in the mainstream of what is understood by that word in traditional spiritual theology?'

The tone of the first paragraph of the Spiritual Exercises indicates that Ignatius takes a very broad view of what may be appropriate ways of praying in the Exercises. 'By the term "Spiritual Exercises" is meant every method of examination of conscience, of meditation, of contemplation, of 'vocal and mental prayer; and of other spiritual activities that will be mentioned later.'[1] What determines the kind of prayer that takes place in the Exercises is the twofold end of 'preparing and, disposing' the soul to rid itself of all inordinate attachments, and, after their removal, 'of seeking and finding the will of God in the disposition' of our life for the salvation of our souls.'[2]

An even more fundamental determinant of the way of prayer at any stage in the Spiritual Exercises will be the particular gift of God given to the individual making them.

---

1. SE 1.
2. SE 1.

Underlying the Annotations of the Spiritual Exercises are a series of basic principles which must be kept in mind in order to be in touch with the kind of movement that Ignatius anticipated a person would experience in making the full Exercises. Some of these fundamental presuppositions that will throw light on the text of Ignatius are:

Continuity and discontinuity

Ignatius presupposes that a person coming to make the Exercises already has a history. The opening words of the First Principle and Foundation, 'Man was created'... already point in this direction. The person who enters on the spiritual enterprise of making the Exercises has been created and preserved in life by God up to this present moment. Their whole personal history is relevant to the possibilities of what God will do for them during the time of the Exercises. The guide of the Exercises must listen carefully to the key elements of the person's life story in order to be able to propose spiritual exercises that will be appropriate for this person here and now. The whole process will then become a dynamic one in which each stage builds on what has gone before. This principle will have many implications for the guide. It is clearly inappropriate, as Ignatius points out, to expect all retreatants to move through the different phases of the spiritual experience at the same rate.[3] Moreover, it is quite inappropriate to encourage a person to move to a new phase of the Exercises when the fruit of the current phase is insufficiently obtained. Ignatius insisted that for some there is no point in going beyond the first week of the Exercises. All that they require is the gift of repentance for sin, a significant celebration of the sacrament of reconciliation, reception of the Eucharist, and taking up their life again in serving God through the keeping of the commandments.[4]

---

3. SE 4.
4. 4 SE 18: 'Hence one who wishes no further help than some instruction and the attainment of a certain degree of peace of soul may be given the Particular Examination of Conscience (24–31), and after that the General Examination of Conscience (32–43). Along with this, let him be given for half an hour each morning the method of prayer of the Commandments and on the Capital Sins, etc (238–248). Weekly confession should be recommended to him, and if possible, the reception of Holy Communion every two weeks, or even better, every week if he desires it.'

While the guide of the Spiritual Exercises must show great discernment in respecting the principle of 'continuity', at the same time there is a fundamental 'discontinuity' at the heart of human nature that will also be always operative. It would be a mistake, for instance, to expect that at every step of the way in the Spiritual Exercises there will be a precise text of scripture that will speak to the need of this retreatant at this time and phase of spiritual development. While allowing for the individual needs of different retreatants in terms of remaining for longer or shorter periods in each 'week' of the Exercises, Ignatius also directs that the whole of the Exercises should be completed in approximately thirty days.[5] This wisdom of Ignatius has been borne out abundantly in the modern experience of giving the Spiritual Exercises. Retreatants report repeatedly that shorter experiences of the Exercises, like twenty days for instance, do not allow them to come to grips fully with the insertion of the mystery of their lives into salvation history. At the same time, the investment of time and of psychic energy is such that the common experience is that to continue much further than thirty days at the level of intensity required would not be feasible.

This principle of 'continuity and discontinuity' is a philosophic one, going right to the heart of human nature. As enfleshed spirits, human persons can never take possession of their whole being in one simple act. Spread out in space and time, they will always be involved in the struggle to bring order, unity and continuity into lives that are subject to disorder, multiplicity and discontinuity. For an understanding of the Spiritual Exercises this needs to be borne in mind at every step of the way.

Flexibility and adaptation

In many places Ignatius refers to the need to adapt the Spiritual Exercises to the particular needs of the individual engaged in making them.[6] This principle is so essential to Ignatius's way of proceeding

---

5. SE 4. Jerome Nadal, for instance, made his Spiritual Exercises from November 5 to 29, 1548. William V Bangert & Thomas M McCoog, *Jerome Nadal SJ 1507–1580* (Chicago: Loyola University Press, Chicago, 1992), 22–26.
6. This principle of flexibility and adaptation is so fundamental to the Exercises that references to it can be seen in SE 1, 4, 6, 8, 18, 129, and it underlies the whole series of the Annotations.

that its influence can be detected in virtually every one of the twenty Annotations. We are dealing here not only with a whole spectrum of possible human differences, revealed in the persons making the Exercises, but also with God's self-communication. In this God is sovereignly free, and communicates precisely as God chooses to communicate. Fundamental to Ignatius' understanding and process is that God acts directly with the person who is making the Exercises.[7] Quite apart from the sovereign independence of God's self-communication to each one, the fact that persons in their uniqueness are all different means that adaptation must be practised throughout the giving of the Exercises.

The universality and importance of the principle of 'flexibility and adaptation' is brought out by Ignatius in his writing about those who are making the Exercises. He adopts a whole series of different 'models'. He starts out presupposing a person who is spiritually rather illiterate and needs to have explained the difference between mortal and venial sin, as well as the very simple ways of approaching examination of conscience. The model of the person engaged in the First Week is that of a rather gross sinner. This is the obvious meaning of the phrase: 'the number of times I have deserved to be condemned forever because of my numerous sins.'[8] More is implied here than the sensitivity of a conscience awakened to the horrendous reality of any sin; Ignatius is pointing to the real situation before God of a sinner who has merited hell because of numerous mortal sins. 'Consider also countless others who have been lost for fewer sins than I have committed.'[9] Within a week the model has shifted drastically to one of being invited to 'smell the infinite fragrance and taste the infinite sweetness of the divinity.'[10]

The flexibility of Ignatius himself in switching from one model to another is a clear indication that he is not endeavouring to write a programme of Exercises that can be followed systematically and literally by all persons. Indeed, in the 'autograph' directory he makes it clear that the book of *The Spiritual Exercises* is for directors, not for those making the Exercises. 'The director should not bring the

---

7. SE 2, 15, 16.
8. SE 50.
9. SE 52.
10. SE 124.

text of the Exercises in with him to read to the retreatant. Rather he should have studied diligently the points he is to give.'[11] The essential Ignatian flexibility points to something that is central to the thesis of this book namely, the great restraint of Ignatius in refraining from spelling out what the possibilities are for different retreatants in the different Exercises; and, specifically relevant to our purpose, what are the possible depths in the contemplation of the mysteries of the life of Christ.

Process and content

Closely allied to the above principle of 'continuity and discontinuity' is the dialectic that exists in the Spiritual Exercises between the poles of process and content. This is of capital importance for addressing our question of the nature of contemplation in the Second Week of the Exercises. Ignatius is concerned throughout with what he refers to elsewhere as a 'way of proceeding'. The whole enterprise is one of discerning the divine action in the life of the one making the Exercises. Simply to take the words of the book, to analyse them and to attempt an exegesis of their meaning would be useless for arriving at their profound significance. Because it is process rather than content that Ignatius is primarily concerned with, it is absolutely determinant of meaning to bear in mind throughout the goal or end of the enterprise. 'By the term 'Spiritual Exercises' is meant every way of preparing and disposing the soul to rid itself of all inordinate attachments, and after their removal, of seeking and finding the will of God in the disposition of our life for the salvation of our soul.'[12]

The whole enterprise is a discerning response to the leading of the good spirit and a turning away from the prompting of the evil spirit. While Ignatius uses various terms for this good spirit (just as he does for the evil spirit), like the good spirit,[13] God and His Angels,[14] God alone,[15] the good angel,[16] God our Lord,[17] in terms of modern

---

11. MHSI 57, 780: 'El que da los ejercicios no deue lleuar ellibro dellos para de alli leer solos, sino que tenga bien estudiado lo que ha de tratar.'
12. SE 1.
13. SE 314, 315, 318.
14. SE 329.
15. SE 320.
16. SE 331.
17. SE 336.

spirituality the same movements are expressed in terms of initiatives of the Holy Spirit, the third Person of the Trinity.

Here we have a typical example of the way in which the 'incomplete treatise' of Ignatius lends itself to theological understanding in the light of development of doctrine since his time. All the ways of proceeding suggested by the author, the instructions he gives and the meanings of his words must be interpreted in terms of the basic principles of spirituality underlying Ignatius's writing and of his understanding of the dynamic at work in the course of making the Exercises. Such meaning is legitimately filled out in a language of modern theological development that is not foreign to his thought, although not explicitly expressed by him. In this respect the Spiritual Exercises are often said to be open-ended. While Ignatius did not spell out a complete theology of the spiritual life, he enunciated its basic principles in a way that was sound and open to further understanding and development. The underlying psychology of Ignatius, for instance, is so sound that people trained in modern psychology often find that in making the Exercises there is no conflict between the experience and their professional training. This open-endedness is an underlying principle that will be central to our method in this work. Ignatius gives in the book of the Spiritual Exercises a vast array of practical instructions on prayer and other matters, and refers in the Annotations to their need to be adapted to the one making the Exercises by the one who is giving them. It follows that we will not be able to penetrate the depth of his thinking by a simple analysis of the words that Ignatius uses. The words must always be interpreted from the background of Ignatius's own experience, as we reflect in the light of the divine-human dialogue going on between God and the one making the Exercises.

We must always bear in mind the dynamic of the spiritual life as Ignatius came to understand it through his experience, his dialogue with others who seriously committed themselves to the development of their relationship with God, and his later studies. This experience began from the time of God's first taking hold of him as a convalescent at Loyola, and was continued principally through his own making of 'spiritual exercises' at Manresa. Throughout Ignatius took note of and reflected carefully upon all these experiences. Through listening to many others and further reflection in the light of his own experience he was gifted with an accurate understanding of what happens in the divine-human dialogue when persons commit themselves to opening up the whole of their inner life to God. It was impossible for him to include all of this in the pages of a book. Ignatius could not write about all the possible different experiences persons would have in entering on a prolonged time of prayer in response to God's call. Rather, in the very small book known as *The Spiritual Exercises* Ignatius chose the way of providing a summary of the general dynamic to be filled out by the one giving the Exercises through careful listening to the way that the overall dynamic is being realised for the one who is making them.

The role of desire
While giving detailed prescriptions for many activities of the one making the Exercises, Ignatius is eminently clear that it all takes place in response to divine initiative. It is all in the realm of grace; hence the importance, at every step of the way, of petitionary prayer. In the First Principle and Foundation Ignatius affirms the goodness of all creation, and in the first place, of man. Though the time to deal with betrayal of God's love through sin will come very soon, the basic truth is that we are good, so that, if we can get in touch with what we really want, with our deep desires, these will reveal to us the way in which God will lead us. At the same time, in the Spiritual Exercises Ignatius distils the wisdom coming from his personal experience and that of the many others with whom he was in dialogue, so that he spells out clearly what desire is appropriate to each part of the dynamic of his Exercises. Though the specific grace that is sought after will vary with the different exercises of the different weeks, it will always be under the rubric of 'what I want' *(lo que quiero)*.

Generosity
The persons who are to make the Spiritual Exercises necessarily present themselves 'just as they are', with all their personal history and background up to this time in their life. However, the making of these Exercises is no ordinary undertaking. It is a major investment of time, of spiritual and psychic energy, in short, of self. The person is well aware of being open to the possibility of a most profound encounter with God. Spontaneously, great expectations are aroused.

Ignatius takes account of this in Annotation 5, concerning the initial disposition of generosity that ought to be brought to making the Exercises: 'It will be very profitable for the one who is to go through the Exercises to enter upon them with magnanimity and generosity towards their Creator and Lord, and to offer Him their entire will and liberty, that His Divine Majesty may dispose of them and all they possess according to His most holy will.'[18] Correspondingly, the one who enters on the Exercises does so in response to the divine initiative. All that happens in the course of these exercises will be determined through the ongoing dialogue between the Creator and the person engaged in them. Hence, the importance of the fifth annotation.[19] Already, at the start a complete self-offering to God in magnanimity and generosity is needed if the full fruit of the Exercises is to be obtained. Indeed, the language in which the fullness of that fruit is expressed in the Contemplation to Attain the Love of God: 'Take, Lord, and accept all my liberty, my memory, my understanding and my entire will, all that I have and possess.'[20] is the very same as the language of this fifth annotation: 'and to offer him their entire will and liberty, that his Divine Majesty may dispose of him and all he possesses according to His most holy will.'[21]

This supremely important Annotation is given by Ignatius in the language of understatement: 'It is very profitable' *(mucho aprovecha)*. At this moment of desiring to face up to the whole of their relationship with God and respond totally, a person is in the situation of one who takes to heart the words of Deuteronomy 6:4–5 'Hear, O Israel: the Lord is our God, the Lord alone. You shall love the Lord your God with all your heart, and with all your soul, and with all your might.' This is more than 'very helpful'; it expresses the deepest reality and whole dynamism of the life of the rational creature before God. In the context of the Spiritual Exercises, all the fruit which follows will be a function of this initial response of magnanimity and generosity.

---

18. SE 5.
19. The importance of this Annotation among the twenty given by Ignatius is underlined by the earliest version of the Spiritual Exercises we have, namely that of John Helyar (Paris, 1535). He begins his text with the fifth Annotation (SE 5), followed immediately by the First Principle and Foundation (SE 23) and the Presupposition of Ignatius (SE 22).
20. SE 234.
21. SE 5.

The 'magnanimity and generosity' are themselves God's gift, so that there is nothing voluntaristic about this initial attitude. Perhaps the understated language of St Ignatius is a help to a prospective retreatant to avoid an initial attitude of stress and striving.

The dynamic of the Spiritual Exercises

A clear priority of process over content and the key role of the twofold goal of the Spiritual Exercises are expressed in the first Annotation and the title: 'Spiritual Exercises'. 'These exercises have as their purpose the conquest of self and the regulation of one's life in such a way that no decision is made under the influence of any inordinate attachment' (SE 21). This has led to a most important feature of the modern understanding of the Exercises, namely, the focus on their dynamic or movement. The first part of the twofold goal is expressed in the first Annotation as 'disposing the soul to rid itself of all inordinate attachments' and in the title as the 'conquest of self'. Positively, in modern terminology, this is what we understand by 'conversion'. The second part of the goal Ignatius expresses as 'seeking and finding the will of God in the disposition of our life for the salvation of our souls' (first Annotation), and 'the regulation of one's life in such a way that no decision is made under the influence of any inordinate attachment' (title).

It hardly seems necessary to state that the whole of this process takes place in response to the divine initiative. It is the will of God that is being sought. The Creator and Lord in person is communicating with the devout soul (Annotation 15).

The one who is making the Exercises comes before 'God our Lord' as creature, that is, as one totally loved. In his powerful statement of the First Principle and Foundation Ignatius does not mention the word love, or faith or hope. This is characteristic of his style in *The Spiritual Exercises,* often to leave the theological and pneumatic background unstated, in order not to obscure the force of the practical implications for the one engaged in the essentially practical task of making the Exercises. It is unthinkable that Ignatius, the man of great trinitarian, mystical experience, should regard God as an impersonal deity. Yet without referring to the divine persons or the loving act of creation, conservation and redemption, he simply states in the passive that man was created to praise, reverence and serve God our Lord. The latter expression opens the way to discussion about who is the God our Lord here intended. Elsewhere Ignatius refers to Jesus Christ; as 'our God and Lord'.[22] An instance from *The Spiritual Exercises* where it seems that Ignatius is referring to Jesus in his use of 'God our Lord' is the colloquy of the fifth exercise of the First Week: 'Enter into colloquy with Christ our Lord ... Thereupon, I will give thanks to God our Lord that He has not put an end to my life and permitted me to fall into any of these three classes.'[23] Harvey Egan discusses the various possibilities of understanding different formulae Ignatius applies to God.[24] He concludes that in some places Ignatius *probably* means Jesus when he writes 'the Divine Majesty', and that in other places he *seems to mean* Jesus when he writes 'God, our Lord'. What is certain is that Ignatius did sometimes refer to Jesus by both these titles. In the greeting at the start of two of his letters he used the expressions: 'Christ our Creator and Lord'[25] and 'Jesus Christ, our God and Lord'.[26]

The praise, reverence and service of God our Lord, while remaining an end in itself, is also the means to the salvation of our soul. Once again Ignatius does not spell out any meaning for this dense expression, and it can be legitimately understood today as coming to the fullness of life, both in this world and the next. So, at the opening of the Spiritual Exercises, at this time of looking at the purpose of one's creation, the one who makes the Exercises is to be encouraged to gather together the whole history of the revealed God, Father, Son and Holy Spirit's dealing with them throughout the story of their life up to this time. Rightly, the modern approach to giving

---

22. In the introduction of Ignatius's letter of October 1547 to Teresa Rejedella, for instance, in H Rahner, *Ignatius of Loyola Letters to Women* (New York: Herder & Herder, 1960), 341.
23. SE 71.
24. H Egan, *Ignatius Loyola the Mystic* (Wilmington, Delaware: Michael Glazier, 1987), 77
25. Ignatius of Loyola, Letter to Peter de Soto, of 20 February 1546 in William Young, *Letters* of *St Ignatius* of *Loyola* (Chicago: Loyola University Press, 1959), 89: 'May the sovereign grace and everlasting love of Christ our Creator and Lord greet your paternity and bring an increase of His gifts and graces for His greater service, praise and glory.'
26. Ignatius of Loyola, Letter to Teresa Rejadell, 341: 'The grace and love of Jesus Christ, our God and Lord, live ever in our souls. Amen.'

the Spiritual Exercises commences with the most fundamental truth of all, that God is love, inviting the one making the Exercises to reflect upon the story of God's love throughout their own life, to 'drink in', to 'bask in' the love of God. Not only is this not foreign to the thinking of Ignatius, it is precisely how he sees God in our regard. Ignatius always sees God in trinitarian terms, sometimes as Father, sometimes as Son, sometimes as the Holy Spirit, sometimes the three persons. Writing to Teresa Rejadell, he expressed his complete confidence in the initiating and efficacious love of God in these words: 'As to your personal troubles, it is certainly inevitable that whoever knows himself should find troubles and necessities in himself. He will never lack such things until in the forge of the eternal love of God, our Creator and Lord, all our sinfulness is entirely consumed. Then we shall be penetrated by him, our souls wholly possessed by him and our will wholly conformed, or rather transformed, into that which is essential holiness and perfect goodness.'[27]

When Ignatius comes to consider 'the other things on the face of the earth', once again he is not interested in spelling out a theology of creation or of mankind's environment. What he focuses on is the inner attitude of the one making the Exercises in the light of the need for a total response to the creative act of God, when faced with the challenge of making that response in and through the world of creation. We need to attain a freedom that will allow us to desire and choose only what leads more to the end for which we were created.

Whatever about Jesus Christ being the one intended by Ignatius in the formula 'Man was created to praise, reverence and serve God, our Lord', it is certainly true that our quest after the necessary freedom or 'indifference' is only possible through co-operation with the redemption received in Christ, and in response to the grace of Christ. The relationship of the retreatant to Christ does not have to wait for the Second Week or for the colloquy with Christ crucified in the First Week. It runs right through the Spiritual Exercises from their very start.

The First Principle and Foundation serves, then, as a theological overview of the program of the Spiritual Exercises. The author does not assign to it a time of meditation: in the first week of the Exercises,

---

27. Letter to Teresa Rejadell, 341.

but simply places it as a foundational statement before beginning the first exercise of the First Week.

Clearly the goal of the First Week of the Spiritual Exercises corresponds to the first part of the twofold overall goal of the Exercises: 'disposing the soul to rid itself of all inordinate attachments' (SE 2) or 'the conquest of self' (SE 21). Though conversion is always an ongoing reality in the life of the Christian, the fruit of the meditations on sin is to open oneself to the redeeming grace of Christ, to experience a turning away from sin, a genuine conversion of heart, a new freedom.

Some who have achieved 'the fruit of the First Week' will fall into the category of those mentioned in the eighteenth Annotation, and should be encouraged to continue their lives in striving to keep the commandments, examining their conscience regularly and frequenting the sacraments.

But then there are those for whom greater fruit is possible. These are seen in contradistinction to those who will 'not go on further and take up the matter of a choice of a Way of Life.'[28] To these 'all the Spiritual Exercises should be given in the order in which they follow below.'[29]

Those who go on to the Second Week of the Spiritual Exercises will be drawing dynamically all the time on the grace of Christ of the First Week and building upon it. This is of capital importance for our thesis on the nature of contemplation in the Second Week and will be spelt out in detail in chapter Four. Sufficient to remark here that the following of Christ, built upon heart-knowledge and love, is the way to a radical evangelical freedom, allowing a person not only to make a truly free choice of a way of life, but to make that choice in intimate response to God's election of them in Christ.

The choice of a way of life made in this manner will unite the person permanently to the personal love of Christ that has been revealed to them in the election. The living out of that love will be done in profound union with the paschal mystery of the crucified and risen Lord, so that the contemplation of the Lord's sufferings, death and resurrection will be a confirmation of the 'rightness' of the election that has been made, as well as strengthening the one who has made it to live it out authentically and generously.

---

28. SE 18.
29. SE 20.

Ignatius completes the dynamic of the Spiritual Exercises with the Contemplation to Attain the Love of God, through which the one making this contemplation is invited to make an ever-deeper response to the all-embracing love of God, and to grow in the facility to find the presence of God in all things in living out the state of life to which they have been elected. The love of God, implied but not stated in the First Principle and Foundation, has now completed its circle. Love was the person's starting-point; it is now clearly their end, both in the ongoing pattern of their life and their final end.

The problem

Since the time of the International Conference on the Spiritual Exercises at Loyola in 1966, there has been a whole spectrum of different attitudes to the contemplations of the Second Week adopted by writers on the Exercises. A look at some of these writings throws light on our problematic of the precise nature of contemplation in the Second Week of the Spiritual Exercises.

At one end of the spectrum we have the work of Luis Bermejo. Bermejo writes:

> . . . they have possibly been influenced by the Spiritual Exercises, for in them Ignatius recommends the exercitant to make himself present and take active part in the biblical scene, to act as if he himself were there, at the crib of the nativity or in Gethsemani or on Calvary or wherever.[30]

I am aware that some find this method really profitable. I have to confess, however, that in spite of my cherished Jesuit training and heritage, I have for a long time entertained serious reservations about this method of prayer, which may be very devotional, but is based on fiction. The retreatant who takes the various scenes of Jesus' life for prayer was *not* present in Bethlehem, he was *not* next to the suffering Christ in the garden or speaking to the dying Christ on the cross. Hence to act as if he had been there strikes me as highly imaginary and devoid of a sufficiently solid foundation. One may certainly

---

30. *Thirsting for the Springs* (Anand: Gujarat Sahitya Prakash, 1990), 111.

contemplate those various episodes which are so meaningful in themselves, but at the same time he should never forget that he is only a spectator, not an actor. To leap backward over the centuries and place oneself in first-century Palestine, unobtrusively or prominently, mixed with Jesus' followers, is purely fictional and therefore unreliable. I do not think you will ever reach the prayer of quiet by following such a flimsy method.

In the book from which this quotation is taken, Bermejo is concerned with disposing retreatants to have psychologically contemplative experiences which he identifies with Teresa of Avila's Prayer of Quiet and Prayer of Union. He does not see contemplation of the mysteries of Christ as proposed by Ignatius in the Second and following Weeks of the Exercises as promoting such experiences. So be it. That the Spiritual Exercises lead to the reality of Quiet and Union is shown in chapter Four below.

Without going into a detailed critique of all the presuppositions involved in this quotation from Bermejo, it is sufficient to make the following three points:

1. We are not concerned here with merely a *method* of prayer, but with a living contact with the person of Jesus Christ revealed in the Word of God, especially in the Gospels. This contact is here experienced by a person who has handed over their whole being to union with Christ through the experience of conversion in the First Week of the Exercises. The prayer is already in its essence contemplative. This is far from being *highly imaginary and devoid of a sufficiently solid foundation*. It is a matter of entering into the contemplation, not of being involved with a flimsy *method*.

2. The opening part of the quotation, to *act as if he were there*, draws attention to a frequent problem for writers in this area: the failure to distinguish between the essentially past character of the historical event as history and the essentially present character of the same historical event as mystery. It is the latter on which Ignatius focuses in the contemplations of the Second and following Weeks.

3. The meaning of contemplation in the Second Week of the Spiritual Exercises is that one is indeed involved as an *actor* (in the sense of participant), not just as a spectator. But this acting, or rather action is in no sense a pretence. The basis of this participation is union with Christ through faith and baptism. A person opens himself

or herself to the Word of God, not as an outsider, but as one already in union with Christ; and that union will be nourished and developed through their openness to the Word.

Another strange understanding of Ignatius is given by Frank Houdek, in an article in *The Way Supplement*, entitled: 'The Limitations of Ignatian Prayer'.[31] Houdek sees the Spiritual Exercises as having two main limitations: their limitation to discursive prayer techniques, and their excessive Christocentrism. He writes that Ignatius provided a well-organised series of techniques, methods and strategies, all of which are 'subordinated to the service of the neighbour'. 'By Ignatian prayer we mean the techniques or methods of prayer contained in the Spiritual Exercises of Ignatius of Loyola. This is an ordered set of strategies to assist anyone who is intent on familiarity with God, but under a particular modality.'[32]

In the same issue of *The Way Supplement* Joseph Veale begins an article with the very perceptive remark: 'It is not at all certain that St Ignatius would recognise himself in the term 'Ignatian Prayer'. What he tried to make clear is that the only teacher of prayer is the Holy Spirit.'[33]

Houdek asserts: 'Almost all of the techniques of prayer in the Spiritual Exercises are forms of discursive prayer. This reality is of the essence of discursive prayer: it is active, cognitive, imaginative prayer. This style of prayer best describes the strategies and techniques of the Spiritual Exercises. This implies limitation in the Ignatian strategies of prayer. These methods would be ill-suited to a person whose gift of prayer was more passive or non-discursive.'[34] Referring to Ignatius at Manresa, Houdek writes that 'he exercised himself very actively in prayer of self-examination, meditation, imaginative gospel contemplation, and prayer of repetition.'[35] In reality, rather than provide a 'method', a 'strategy' or a 'technique', Ignatius points to a variety of different ways of praying that enable a person to receive God's personal gift of prayer for them. Among these different ways,

---

31. F Houdek, 'The Limitations of Ignatian Prayer', in *The Way Supplement* 82 (Spring 1995): 26.
32. Houdek, 'The Limitations of Ignatian Prayer', 27.
33. J Veale, 'Manifold Gifts', in *The Way Supplement* 82 (1995): 44.
34. Houdek, 'The Limitations of Ignatian Prayer', 28.
35. Houdek, 'The Limitations of Ignatian Prayer', 29.

entry through the gospel mysteries into the presence of Christ, in order to know, love and follow him has the pre-eminent place. Should this be seen as a method or technique, it is a simple matter to apply to it the words of the Principle and Foundation: 'to use them in so far as they help towards one's end and to free oneself from them in so far as they are a hindrance to it.'[36]

What Houdek has done here is to read the text of the Second Week contemplations outside their context in the dynamic of the Spiritual Exercises, and to conclude that they provide a 'method of discursive prayer'. Moreover, it hardly seems appropriate to apply the terms 'technique' and 'strategy' to something that is an attempt to respond to the initiating love of God. A similar criticism can be made of Houdek's remarks about subordinating' prayer to the service of one's neighbour. Houdek wrote: 'In discussing the limitations of Ignatian prayer, it is important, therefore, to keep in mind that, for Ignatius, prayer is not an end in itself. It is rather subordinated to a larger goal: the service of the neighbour motivated by love of Jesus Christ.'[37] If, rightly, we understand prayer in this context as union with God, this union can be subordinate to nothing other than itself. But subordination is not what Ignatius intends here. It is rather that the prayer of the Exercises leads to service of the neighbour, which is in its turn a means to union with God. Prayer and service are mutually interdependent. Prayer is not subordinated to service. The goal of all prayer and service is the coming of the Kingdom of God.

The second major limitation that Houdek finds in 'Ignatian prayer' is that it is too Christocentric: 'Though for many people this Christocentrism of the Exercises is one of their most endearing features, it is nevertheless a limitation of Ignatian prayer.'[38] The limitation, he finds, is experienced by those who prefer 'a more Spirit-centered prayer'. 'Though the person of Christ remains important for such Christians, their prayer and spirituality is dominated by the person of the Holy Spirit. For them Ignatian prayer is too limited and therefore less useful than other prayer forms or techniques.'[39] To make the Holy Spirit the explicit focus of one's prayer is not to move away from an

---

36. SE 23.
37. SE 26.
38. Houdek, 'The Limitations of Ignatian Prayer', 31.
39. Houdek, 'The Limitations of Ignatian Prayer', 31.

implicit Christocentrism. The same Holy Spirit is the Spirit of the risen Lord. The ways of praying outlined in the Spiritual Exercises are not the only legitimate, Christian approaches to God. But it remains true that all Christian prayer is prayer through Christ, to the Father, in the Spirit.

The 'excessive Christocentrism' of prayer in the Spiritual Exercises also makes it unsuitable, according to Houdek, to many women, who are seeking more feminine images of God, and to those who 'wish to use eastern spiritual discipline and practice'. Whatever the style of prayer of an individual, it remains true that all grace is the grace of Christ, so that theologically it is impossible for Christian spiritual exercises to be too Christocentric in this sense of the word. Houdek clearly does not intend such an unorthodox understanding of 'excessive Christocentrism'. Given the acceptance of the truth that all Christian prayer is at least implicitly Christocentric, the style of prayer must always be adapted to the individual way that God leads each person. As Ignatius wrote to Francis Borgia: 'But for each individual that part will be much better where God our Lord communicates more of Himself in revealing His most holy graces and spiritual gifts, because He sees and knows what is best for each one and, as one who knows everything, He shows each one the way. For us to find it with the help of His divine grace, it is very helpful to search and to try many ways, so that we may advance by the one which for each of us is clearest, happiest and most blessed in this life, which is all guided and ordered towards that other everlasting life, embraced and united as we are with such holy gifts.'[40]

A less radical position on the contemplation of the mysteries of the life of Christ in the Second Week of the Spiritual Exercises with some similarities to Houdek's position is taken by Dermot Mansfield, in an article entitled 'The Prayer of Faith, Spiritual Direction and The

---

40. MHSI 26, 236, Letter of Ignatius to Francis Borgia of 20 September, 1548: '. . . aquella parte es mucho mejor para qualquier indiuido, donde Dios NS mas se comunica mostrando sus santissimos dones y gracias spirituales, porque veey y saue lo que mas le conuiene, y como quien todo sabe, le muestra la via; y nosotros para hallarla, mediante su gratia diuina, ayuda mucho buscar y prouar por muchas maneras para caminar por la 'que es las mas declarada', mas felice y bienauenturada en est a vida, toda guiada y ordenda para la otra sin fin, abracados y unidos con los tales 'santissimos' dones.'

Exercises'.[41] Mansfield is dealing with the case of those retreatants in whom 'there is a change from a relatively active, sensible phase to one where the emphasis will be more on faith, on receptivity, and on God's part.'[42] He sees a need to provide a structure within the structure of a retreat, outside times of formal prayer, for the retreatant to meditate and reflect in a way that is more active. Out of this will arise 'a situation where the director may have a role in discussion and elucidation.'[43] 'First of all', writes Mansfield, 'I take it that the method of prayer outlined by Ignatius is generally 'meditative' - and this includes even what Ignatius terms 'contemplation' from the Second Week onwards, as one looks towards Christ, though there is an expected process of simplification in the prayer and over each day. Therefore, if the prayer of faith has become the habitual way of the exercitant, it follows that he or she cannot use the method outlined in the Exercises, and should not be expected to do so.'[44] But, Ignatius himself would not expect such an exercitant, or anyone, for that matter, to 'use the method outlined in the Exercises'. He expected, as was quoted above, that the director of the Exercises would have fully absorbed their spirit, as well as mastered the text, and so would be able to adapt his guidance to each unique person. Moreover, it is our contention that Ignatius did not 'outline a method', but here in the Second Week gave some indications of a way to approach the contemplation of Christ in his mysteries.

George Ganss comments upon contemplation in the Second and subsequent Weeks of the Exercises.[45] Before coming to the contemplations of the Second Week, Ganss has an endnote (49) on a most important remark of Ignatius in the Directives given after the First Week. In the fourth of these directives Ignatius concludes by writing: 'Second, if in any point I find what I am seeking, there I will repose until I am fully satisfied, without any anxiety to go on.'[46] Ganss calls this 'another key principle of great importance in

---

41. Dermot Mansfield, 'The Prayer of Faith, Siritual Direction and The Exercises', in *The Way* 25/4 (1985), 315.
42. Mansfield, 'The Prayer of Faith', 315.
43. Mansfield, 'The Prayer of Faith', 321.
44. Mansfield, 'The Prayer of Faith', 320.
45. George Ganss, *The Spiritual Exercises* of *St Ignatius, A Translation and Commentary* (St Louis: Institute of Jesuit Sources, 1992).
46. SE 76.

all Ignatian methods of prayer'.[47] In reality it is far more than this; it is a key principle for the understanding of the whole process of the Exercises. 'Through its prudent application any portion of an Ignatian prayer period may, with God's grace, lead to increasingly simplified mental prayer. For example, the satisfying pause in a contemplation (according to Ignatius's meaning in 101–107) may become the gateway into acquired contemplation and even into infused contemplation if God should grant it!'[48] It is clear from this quotation that Ganss accepts as normative the classical terminology of simplification in mental prayer, leading to 'acquired' and 'infused' contemplation. It is a strange remark that the gateway into deeper prayer may open in 'the satisfying pause in a contemplation.' In other words, it is not the contemplation of the mystery itself that is the truly effective prayer in the journey of the retreatant, but rather the higher gifts of acquired and infused contemplation that may be granted when the contemplation of the mystery pauses or ceases for a time. The thesis of this work is the contrary. It is precisely through the presence of the retreatant in faith to the mystery being contemplated that union with God in Christ is happening, even at the greatest depth, if this should be God's particular gift.

In another relevant endnote (61), on the first contemplation of the Second Week of the Exercises, Ganss discusses directly how he understands contemplation in the exercises of this Week. It is noteworthy that he puts the heading 'Contemplation' in quotation marks, already hinting that he regards it as not quite 'the real thing'. Once again contemplation for Ignatius is categorised as a 'method of (mental) prayer'. 'Since this method leads to reflection it can be and often is discursive mental prayer.'[49] This sentence would be unarguably correct, were Ignatius concerned with nothing other than a systematic, clearly defined method. But what Ignatius is directing the retreatant to is the contemplation of Christ in his mysteries. If reflection should emerge from such contemplation, this does not have the effect of somehow downgrading the contemplation itself into the category of discursive mental prayer. A correct understanding of contemplation here can only be gathered from the end to which it

---

47. Ganss, *The Spiritual Exercises* of *St Ignatius*, 158.
48. Ganss, *The Spiritual Exercises* of *St Ignatius*, 1 58.
49. Ganss, *The Spiritual Exercises* of *St Ignatius*, 162.

leads, and from its whole function within the dynamic of the Spiritual Exercises.

'Contemplation in this sense prepares for but is somewhat different from what many writers on mystical theology term 'acquired contemplation' or 'infused contemplation'.[50] There is no argument with the fact that Ignatius is using a different terminology; hence there is a difference between what he writes and the 'classical' understanding of contemplation. What is not acceptable in Ganss' approach is to regard contemplation as presented by Ignatius in the Exercises as something inferior to what has been classically accepted as if there were only one way of understanding the fullness of the gift of contemplation.

A very common stance taken by commentators on the Spiritual Exercises is that of H Coathelem in his *Commentaire du Livre des Exercices*. When writing of the nature of 'Ignatian contemplation', he commences by saying that it is not a matter of contemplation in the Teresian sense of the word, that is of supernatural or mystical contemplation.[51] Coathelem is asserting not only that Ignatius had not used terminology similar to that of Teresa, but also that there is something involved here less deserving of the adjectives 'supernatural' or 'mystical'. While he goes on to make some good points about the possibility of the past mystery being present to the praying person now, it is the role of the imagination that is the stumbling block. 'Its part and its role vary according to psychological types.'[52] That is indeed true, but any part or role of the imagination can be sufficient for entry into contemplation of the Lord's mysteries. Coathelem then quotes Achille Gagliardi's opinion that 'the activities of inferior faculties can help the superior faculties to pray, but they themselves do not pray.'[53] The 'most' that can be said about the contemplations of the mysteries of the life of Christ is that they are oriented towards the affections of the will: 'But contemplation is usually affective. So, what was said above about the orientation of meditation towards the

---

50. Ganss, *The Spiritual Exercises* of *St Ignatius*, 162.
51. H Coathelem, *Commentaire du Livre des Exercices* (Paris: Collection Christus, 1964), 168.
52. Coathelem, *Commentaire du Livre des Exercices*, 170: 'Sa part et son role varient suivant les types psychologiques'.
53. Coathelem, *Commentaire du Livre des Exercices*, 170: 'les acitivites des facultes inferieures peuvent aider les superieures a prier, elles-memes ne prient pas!'

affections of the will is equally true of contemplation of the mysteries of the life of Christ.'[54]

A more open position on this question is taken by another French commentator on the Exercises. On the 'Contemplation of the Mysteries' Alexandre Brou wrote: 'The second method indicated in the Exercises is entitled 'contemplation'. It is not a matter of contemplation in the strict sense of the word, that is of the prolonged gaze of love upon God, still seen through the veils of faith, God being the proper object of this prayer, and this gaze being a sort of simple intuition, without multiple acts. We still have here a discursive prayer, but having as its matter some Gospel events, so that one can easily stop there, remain there, and satisfy there the gaze of the soul. It is contemplation in this sense, that one gazes rather than reasons. But discursive procedure is not excluded. This prayer will be reasoning or affective in different cases, and more strictly contemplative, and even mystical if God so wishes. For we know that the humanity of Jesus is not excluded, as the quietists wanted, from the highest prayer.'[55] After 'defining' contemplation as 'a prolonged gaze of love upon God', Brou describes a prayer in which one gazes long and lovingly upon Jesus. Such prayer, he declares, will be more strictly contemplative and even mystical, if God so wishes. This prayer can also be discursive and reasoning or affective, which is, of course, what it must needs be, if the 'higher' gift of contemplation is not received on a particular

---

54. Coathelem, *Commentaire du Livre des Exercices*, 170: 'Mais la contemplation est généralement de nature affective. Des lors, ce qui a ete dit plus haut de l'orientation de la méditation vers les affections de la volonté vaut également de la contemplation des mystères de la vie du Christ.'
55. A Brou, *Saint Ignace Maître d'Oraison* (Paris: Spes, 1925), 159: 'La seconde methode indiquée dans les Exercises est étiquetée 'contemplation'. Il ne s'agit pas de contemplation au sens technique du mot, c'est-à-dire du regard d'amour proloné sur Dieu lui-même, vu encore à travers les voiles du foi; Dieu étant l'objet propre de cette oraison, et ce regard étant une sorte d'intuition toute simple et sans actes multiples, C'est une oraison discursive encore, mais ayant pour matière des episodes de l'Évangile, tels que facilement pourra s'arrêter, s'y prolonger, s'y complaire le regard de l'âme, Contemplation en ce sens, qu'on regarde plus qu'on raisonne. Mais le précéde discursif n'est pas exclus. Cette oraison sera raisonnante ou affective selon les cas et plus strictement contemplative, et mystique même si Dieu le veut. Car nous savons que l'humanité sainte de Jesus n'est point bannie, comme le voulaient les quietistesv de la plus haute oraison.'

occasion. But, the whole orientation of this way of praying with gospel mysteries is towards a genuine contemplation. Even in inviting us to pray in a way in which we gaze upon Jesus, who is the Son of God, Ignatius cannot guarantee that the gift of contemplation will always be given or received, but in the context of the dynamic of the Spiritual Exercises, the reception of this gift is what one should normally expect in the Second and following Weeks.

In 1973 John English published a book on the Spiritual Exercises entitled *Spiritual Freedom*. In 1995 he published a revised and enlarged edition with the same title. In both he treats at some length contemplation in the Second Week of the Exercises. Here we are dealing with the later edition. In the chapter entitled: 'Contemplation: The Hidden Life' English writes that, in presenting the contemplation of the infancy and hidden life of Jesus, Ignatius is not dealing with contemplation in the strict sense. 'Contemplation, strictly speaking, carries a person into the presence of God, or into one of the mysteries of Christ. At this point, Ignatius is not dealing with contemplation in that strict sense, but merely presenting a method of prayer.'[56] But it is precisely in order to allow a person to be 'carried into the mysteries of Christ' that Ignatius presented contemplation of the infancy and hidden life; and always for Ignatius presence to Christ in his mysteries is at the same time presence to Father, Son and Holy Spirit.

English addresses the difficult process of explaining how a past event can be present to a person at a later time in a meaningful way. He then draws on the powerful effect that literature can have on a person, claiming that 'this ability to enter personally into a novel, a movie, or a stage production is what Ignatius wants us to exercise in contemplating the mysteries of Christ's life. If a particular retreatant is unable to do this, at least to some degree, then the one who gives the Exercises should introduce the retreatant to another method of prayer.'[57] But there are no grounds for suggesting that Ignatius was interested in a person's literary skills; and there is far more at stake here than a method of prayer; it is rather a retreatant's personal involvement with Christ through his mysteries, in order to know, love and follow him. One incapable of this kind of involvement should have been gently sent away after doing the First Week exercises.

---

56. J English, *Spiritual Freedom* (Chicago: Loyola University, 1995), 131.
57. English, *Spiritual Freedom*, 134.

English then attempts an answer to the 'fascinating theological question' of 'how and why we can actually re-enter the mystery of Christ's life'. First, very rightly, he draws upon our baptism, through which 'Jesus' Spirit enlivens in us 'experiential memory'.[58] The effect of this memory is to return us to the events of Christ's hidden and public life in Israel two thousand years ago. But we are not being returned to something past. The events of Christ's hidden and public life are present to us *here* and *now*, as the whole Christ, the now risen Lord, is one with us through our baptism.

When he draws on the mystery of the Eucharist, English rightly says that 'in the resurrected state, Christ is able to represent the mysteries of Jesus' life just as the paschal mystery is represented in the Eucharist'.[59] This leads English to conclude that 'when we are 'in' the mystery we receive the gift of contemplation, strictly speaking. Ignatius suggests a method of opening ourselves up to the mystery; but when we are actually in the mystery, this is the result of further action by God'.[60] Now, while it remains true that the whole of this exercise of contemplation is received as a gift from God, who will gift us with varying depths of union at different times, it is also true that from the beginning of the exercise we are, to use English's phrase 'in the mystery'—by virtue of faith and baptism, or, to put it another way, as an outcome of the conversion experience of the First Week of the Spiritual Exercises.

In the concluding part of this chapter on 'Contemplation: the Hidden Life' English gives three examples of what may occur in the course of praying according the instructions of the Second Week.

The first concerns the experience of praying with 'the effort of the imagination with its accompanying reflection', and then a second movement occurring 'when we find an hour has gone by, and only during the prayer review do we notice that there has been an experience of God's presence. When we reflect on the prayer period, we become aware that we picked up and kissed the infant Jesus, held the child in our arms, or performed some similar action. We have come to a new awareness of Jesus in this mystery'.[61] It would be quite

---

58. English, *Spiritual Freedom*, 135.
59. English, *Spiritual Freedom*, 136.
60. English, *Spiritual Freedom*, 137.
61. English, *Spiritual Freedom*, 138.

wrong to conclude that only the 'second movement' is worthy of the name 'contemplation', or that in the 'first movement' of effort of the imagination and reflection we have not received a new (though hidden) awareness of Jesus in his mystery.

The second example concerns the Application of the Senses. English writes as follows: 'The fifth contemplation is the Application of Senses. It should be done at the end of the day after the retreatant has contemplated five times; the soul is then full and able to apply the senses.'[62] Now, while it is true that Ignatius puts this exercise in the schematic presentation of the Exercises at the end of the day, and many see the quiet time of evening as particularly suitable for this kind of prayer, there is no guarantee that the retreatant's experience will be one of arriving at the end of the day with 'the soul full and able to apply the senses.' All the contemplations of the gospel mysteries involve seeing the persons, hearing what they are saying or might say and watching their actions. Perhaps the grace will be given to smell the infinite fragrance and taste the infinite sweetness of the divinity at some other time of day, in some other contemplation.

Finally, English gives us a possible shape for the development of a retreatant's day:

> During each day's prayer (five exercises) on a single mystery of Christ's life, the following development may occur at first, we tend to stand outside the mystery, reading and reflecting on the scriptural event; then we use our imagination to see and hear the persons and actions in the mystery; we then feel ourselves actually present at the mystery, and even becoming part of the mystery (as a servant) finally, as the presence and involvement deepen, we are carried beyond the external to an experience of the person or persons present in the mystery.[63]

Such neat, orderly developments, hardly ever, if at all, happen in the course of the unpredictable experiences of those making the Spiritual Exercises. This way of approaching the Exercises is really the opposite

---

62. English, *Spiritual Freedom*, 142–143.
63. English, *Spiritual Freedom*, 144.

of that of Ignatius. One of his very few presuppositions about 'what might happen' is that he believes it is impossible to give one oneself seriously to prayer over an extended period without experiencing the movements of the good spirit and the evil spirit.[64] God brings about God's purposes more often in spite of our efforts to find a neat and orderly development in our prayer-life. The danger in writing of such possible developments is that of leading some retreatants to produce a neat and orderly review of their day's prayer that is in truth an illusion. It would be far better to encourage the retreatant, drawing on the grace of conversion of the First Week, and the grace of baptism and the Eucharist, to endeavour to be open through taking up the gospels to whatever gift of presence and contemplation God should grant.

In an excellent article Brendan Byrne argues for a broadening of scriptural interpretation from the confines of simply the historical-critical method to give proper place to the use of the imagination as proposed in the contemplations of the mysteries in the Spiritual Exercises.[65] If anything, he over-stresses the role of the imagination for Ignatius in the statement: 'Ignatius believed very strongly that in achieving the conversion and freedom which are the main aim of the Exercises, the imagination was where the contest was chiefly engaged. The more active and less passive the retreatant could be in this process, so much the better.'[66] It would be very difficult to reconcile the last statement with the importance Ignatius gives to the first time of election, or to consolation without preceding cause. More importantly, the whole of the Exercises are to be made as a response to the Creator communicating directly with the creature, so that a God-given passivity can be far more important than any activity on the part of the retreatant.

While stressing the role of the imagination in the Second Week of the Exercises, Byrne in different places refers to the prayer involved as 'meditation', 'the Ignatian method of contemplation' and 'imaginative contemplation'; he always stops short of calling it simply

---

64. SE 6.
65. Brendan Byrne 'To See with the Eyes of the Imagination. Scripture in the Exercises and Recent interpretation', in *The Way Supplement*, 72 (Autumn 1991): 3–19
66. Byrne, 'To See with the Eyes of the Imagination', 6.

'contemplation'. He mentions the bias many exegetes have towards the importance of intellectual understanding over the fruit of personal contemplation when he quotes the words of 'a distinguished biblical scholar' at a conference on the Exercises: 'As long as they remember that it's the fruit of their imagination and not the inspired meaning for all time.'[67] The person making the Exercises is not engaged in trying to work out 'the inspired meaning for all time', but in responding to God's personal self-communication to them through God's Word. Certainly it is of capital importance to avoid illusion and flights of imagination not grounded in the salvation history revealed in Christ and the personal history of the praying person, but the retreatant is not seeking 'the inspired meaning for all time.' Later in the same article Byrne himself answered the difficulty he had raised here when he wrote: 'What a retreatant discovers in imaginative contemplation is primarily a message for his or her own conversion. It is not something for public proclamation.'[68]

Authors who take a somewhat rational, analytic approach to the understanding of the Spiritual Exercises rather than a more pneumatic, dynamic one could find some support in an authority like Joseph de Guibert. In *The Jesuits Their Spiritual Doctrine and Practice* he wrote in a footnote: 'It is not a mere accident that the words *meditation* and *contemplation* are employed in the *Exercises*. A scene from the life of Christ is never 'meditated' but 'contemplated'. Assuredly, the Ignatian contemplation of these scenes is discursive prayer, but in its movement it is less reasoning and abstract, and more direct, concrete, restful and affective. Too much overlooking of this fact has sometimes caused the *Exercises* to be regarded as a mere office-machine for reasoning.'[69] This is certainly an advance on a way of thinking that did see the essence of the 'Ignatian method' as consisting in reasoning and abstraction, but it is only a small advance. The tone of this footnote is in keeping with an analytic approach in seeing the contemplations of the Second Week as 'discursive prayer'. On the same page de Guibert declared: 'If Christ appears less in the First Week (than in the Second Week of the Spiritual Exercises), He

---

67. Byrne, 'To See with the Eyes of the Imagination', 6.
68. Byrne, 'To See with the Eyes of the Imagination', 15.
69. J de Guibert, *The Jesuits Their Spiritual Doctrine and Practice* (Chicago: Institute of Jesuit Sources, 1964), 135, footnote 41.

is there nevertheless.'[70] Christ may be explicitly named less often in the First Week than in the Second Week, but the truth is far more than his merely being 'there nevertheless'. The First Week has no meaning at all apart from exposure of the one making the Exercises to the redemptive love God made available in Christ Jesus. For Hugo Rahner the First Week of the Spiritual Exercises can only be understood in terms of Christology. As he put it: 'For sin is essentially a Christological event, and has been so ever since the first sin was committed.'[71]

Terminology of Ignatius

There is certainly confusion over the appropriate terminology to apply to the prayer recommended by Ignatius in the Second Week. Gilles Cusson, who has an eminently clear exposition of the dynamics of the Exercises in *La Pédagogie de la Expérience Spirituelle Personelle* once in that book called contemplation of the mysteries 'meditations on the life of Christ.'[72] and also referred to his (Ignatius's) 'method of contemplation.'[73] In a later work, Cusson refers consistently to contemplation of the mysteries, and in doing so gives a very concise and accurate description of what is meant by this contemplation: 'By means of contemplation, which is presence in faith, the retreatant welcomes the content of the revealed mystery, in order to learn to communicate at depth with the reality it offers.'[74]

One of the more unfortunate usages is the constant application of the word 'method' to prayer, as in 'the Ignatian method', 'the method of contemplation', and 'the Three Methods of Prayer'[75] presented by Ignatius in the Exercises after the Contemplation to Attain the Love

---

70. Guibert, *The Jesuits Their Spiritual Doctrine*, 135.
71. H Rahner, *Ignatius the Theologian* (San Francisco: Ignatius Press, 1990), 67. In chapter 2, 'The Christology of the Spiritual Exercises' Rahner devotes pages 59—93 to the discussion of the Christology of the First Week.
72. G Cusson, *La Pédagogie de l'Expériénce Spirituelle Personelle* (Bruges: Desclée de Brouwer, 1968), 269: 'fondement des meditations sur la vie du Christ'.
73. Cusson, *La Pédagogie*, 270: 'explique sa methode de contemplation'; again, on page 278: 'la methode ignatienne de contemplation'.
74. G Cusson, *The Spiritual Exercises Made in Everyday Life* (St Louis: Institute of Jesuit Sources, 1989), 72.
75. SE 238-258.

of God. Method implies a clear, rational understanding of a goal, and the systematic adopting of appropriate and systematic means to achieve that goal. Method is well thought out; it is dominated by the rational, and it is perfectly logical to expect that if the method is carefully followed, the desired goal will be achieved. This is at variance with what must take place in the life of prayer. The use of the word 'method' with respect to prayer can at least give the impression of a hint of Pelagianism. The person at prayer must be constantly ready to follow the leading of God's Spirit, which cannot be planned and anticipated. The Spirit must be allowed to blow as the Spirit wills. Certainly there are times during prayer, and, as we will see later, the most contemplative writers stress this, when the person at prayer is not conscious of the *divine* gifting and needs to fall back on some way of attempting to come to such awareness. In the Spiritual Exercises, which have a clearly defined goal, and in which the author has been privileged to be able to understand the dynamic of the way God generally works in leading people to that goal, there are clear instructions about how to follow a way that will lead to God. But this should not be called a 'method'. A parallel is the reaction of Benedictines on hearing the *lectio divina* described as 'the Benedictine method of prayer', as in Tony de Mello's *Sadhana, a Way to God*.[76] The *lectio* is not a method of prayer; it is the Benedictine way of life.

Towards the end of the book of *The Spiritual Exercises* Ignatius presents three ways to pray.[77] In the Spanish autograph these are *tres modos de orar*, in the Latin vulgate translation *modi tres orandi*. The normal English translation of *modo* is 'way'. The Italian and French translations, which have the words *metodo* and *methode* available if they choose to use them (as does the Spanish with *metodo*) use the words: *modo*[78] and *menière*[79] In each case *orar* is translated by a corresponding infinitive *orare* or *prier*. Similarly, Hans Urs von

---

76. A de Mello, *Sadhana A Way to God* (Anand: Gujarat Sahitya Prakash, Anand, 1976), 103.
77. SE 238–260.
78. P Schiavone, S *Ignazio de Loyola Esercizi Spiritueli Ricerca sulle fonti* (Milan: San Paolo, 1995), 321.
79. Ignace de Loyola, *Ecrits* (translated under the direction of Maurice Giuliani) (Paris: Desclée Cusson, De Brouwer, 1991), 174–5; Francois Courel, *Les Exercices Spirituels* (Paris: Collection Christus, 1960).

Balthasar gives the German translation *Drei Weisen zu beten*.[80] Unfortunately, English translators 'got into the habit' of rendering *modos de orar* as 'methods of prayer'. This usage became almost universal.[81] The degree to which the word 'method' became associated with the Spiritual Exercises is illustrated in George Ganss's translation of the Constitutions of the Society of Jesus. Though, in every other instance, he renders Ignatius's *modo de proceder* as 'manner of proceeding', when he comes to the unique place where it refers to the Spiritual Exercises, he translates it as *'method* of proceeding'.[82]

In the first half of the twentieth century very many religious were subjected to having three points for *meditation* read at ten minute intervals; they were told to apply their memory, understanding and will to these, and were informed that this was 'the ignatian method of prayer'. Spectres of Illuminism and Protestantism had induced a wariness of contemplation, and even affectivity in prayer. Despite the progress from this position, the temptation to have a clearly identifiable 'ignatian method of prayer' has continued, and 'imaginative contemplation' is now commonly taken to be *'the* ignatian method

---

80. Hans Urs von Balthasar, *Ignatius von Loyola Die Exerzitien* (Einsiedeln: Johannes Verlag, 1965).
81. Among translators of *The Spiritual Exercises* into English, Thomas Corbishley (Wheathampstead: Burns & Oates, 1963) translates the heading of SE 238 *(Tre modi de orar)* as 'Three ways of praying', as do Joseph Munitiz and Philip Endean in *Saint Ignatius of Loyola: Personal Writings* (London: Penguin, 1996). 'Three methods of prayer', which became the generally accepted English translation, appears in the translations of John Morris (London: Burns & Oates, 1900), Elder Mullan (New York: PK Kenedy & Sons, 1914), WH Longridge (London: Robert Scott, 1919), Aloysius Ambruzzi (Mangalore: Codiabail Press, 1931), Louis Puhl (Chicago: Loyola University Press, 1951), Anthony Mottola (New York: Image Books, 1964), and Elizabeth Meier Tetlow (Lanthan MD: University Press of America, 1987). Charles Seager (London: Charles Dolman, 1847), David Fleming (St Louis: Institute of Jesuit Sources, 1978) and George Ganss (St Louis: Institute of Jesuit Sources, 1992) at least preserve an active verb and write of 'Three Methods of Praying'. Lewis Delmage (New York: Joseph F Wagner, 1968) gives the translation: 'Three Modes of Prayer'. Joseph Tetlow (New York: Crossroad, 1992) heads his commentary on this part of *The Spiritual Exercises*: 'Three further ways to pray' (148); but when he come to translate the text of the *Exercises* Tetlow reverts to 'Three Methods of Praying' (150). The old Italian translation of Pio Biondolini (Milan: Vita e Pensiero, 1928) refers to 'Tre metodi di Orazione'. Far more common is *Tre modi di orare*, as in Pietro Schiavone.
82. Saint Ignatius of Loyola, *The Constitutions of the Society of Jesus*, (translated by G Ganss) (St Louis: Institute of Jesuit Sources, 1970), (409), 203.

of prayer'. Such narrow perspectives were adopted in the name of the man who states in the first paragraph of his Spiritual Exercises: 'By the term 'Spiritual Exercises' is meant *every* way of examining one's conscience, of meditation, of contemplating, of praying vocally and mentally, and other spiritual operations, as will be mentioned later.'[83] In all the writings of Ignatius the word 'method' *(metodo)* occurs only once.[84] That occurrence is of doubtful authorship, and the word is not used about prayer, but about organising one's preparation for general confession. In the directory 'dictated' to Fr Vitoria are the words: 'and to instruct him that that he should use some method in writing down his sins and remembering them.'[85] In the introduction to this directory the editor comments: 'Therefore Ignatius did not always dictate these words, but, as the title itself indicates 'their major part or substance'."[86]

Despite the absence of the word 'method' *(metodo)* from the writing of Ignatius, his use of 'way' *(modo)* could at times be legitimately rendered in English as 'method', as for instance in the second Annotation, where Louis Puhl translates *la persona que da a otro modo y orden para meditar o contemplar* as 'the one who explains to another the method and order of contemplating.'[87] It remains true, however, that Ignatius always preferred the gentler word *modo* to *metodo*, and that the English 'method' can convey unsatisfactory overtones of a prayer that is too well organised to allow for the freedom of the Spirit. Ignatius's well-ordered approach to spirituality and to prayer resulted in the repeated use of the word 'method' by those commenting on *The Spiritual Exercises*. This was particularly true of French writers of the early twentieth century. The attitudes of commentators to the idea of method in *The Spiritual Exercises* cover a whole spectrum from those who find these methods stifling to those who find them simply a framework at the service of freedom. Joseph

---

83. SE 1.
84. I Echarte (ed), *Concordancia Ignaciana* (Biblbao: Ediciones Mensajero, 1996; Milano: Sal Terrae, 1996), 783.
85. MHSI 76, 104: 'y darle orden que use de metodo en el escrivir los peccados y accordarse dellos'.
86. MHSI 89: 'Non ergo ea verba semper S. Ignatius dictavit, sed ut ipse titulus indicat "eorum maximam partem vel substantiam".'
87. SE 2 in L Puhl, *The Spiritual Exercises* of *St Ignatius* (Allahabad: St Pauls, 1981), 15.

de Guibert was quite ambivalent in his attitude to method in the Spiritual Exercises. On the one hand he wrote: 'More than once the use of methods has been given as a distinguishing characteristic of ignatian spirituality. This, of course, is tantamount to judging the type of locomotives by the colour they are painted.'[88] But he followed this immediately by declaring: 'It is perfectly true that a goodly number of methods of prayer or reform are taught in the *Exercises,* and that the *Exercises* themselves constitute a method.'[89] De Guibert went on to say that not much space in his writing would be devoted to methods, and that Ignatius was rather a simplifier of methods in prayer and spirituality than a creator of them. In a strange understatement he declares that 'he (Ignatius) allows the one meditating to control what remains in accordance with the subject matter and the impulses of grace.'[90] Rather, Ignatius always respected the freedom under grace of the one meditating and his whole aim was to facilitate the free response of the person to divine grace. It is a case of 'damning with faint praise' to assert that Ignatius 'allows' the person at prayer to use their God-given freedom.

Alexandre Brou was another who wrote much about ignatian methods. In his book, *La Spiritualité de S Ignace,* he devoted a whole chapter (ch. 4) to 'Methods of Prayer'. He commenced the chapter by broadening the idea of 'the ignatian method': 'people speak of *the method* of St Ignatius, when, if you count properly, you can find five: meditation, contemplation, application of senses, second and third way of prayer; ... and even six, seven or eight, with the methods of examination of conscience and 'the contemplation for divine love'.'[91] But, with his typical breadth of understanding he goes on to add: 'On the contrary, and without much paradox, one can say that these methods are as little methods as possible, and that they do not

---

88. J de Guibert, *The Jesuits Their Spiritual Doctrine and Practice,* p 167.
89. Guibert, *The Jesuits,* 167.
90. Guibert, *The Jesuits,* 168.
91. A Brou, *La Spiritualité S. Ignace* (Paris: Beauchesne, 1914), 42: 'on parle de *la methode* de saint Ignace, alors que, en comptant bien on en pourrait trouver chez lui jusqu'a cinq: meditation, contemplation, application des sens, seconde et troisième manière de prier . . . et même six, sept, huit, avec les methodes d'examen de conscience, et 'la contemplation pour l'amour divin'.

belong to him (Ignatius). In what is essential to them they belong to everybody.'[92]

An indication of the fixation on the 'method' of Ignatius in the writings of authors in French of the early twentieth century is given in a comment of Louis Peeters on the Bull, *Pastoralis Officii*, of Pope Paul III (31 July, 1548) approving *The Spiritual Exercises*. Peeters wrote: 'But what Pope Paul III praises specially in the *Exercises* is 'the order and method' which invest all the catholic ideas with a singular efficacy to arouse pious sentiments in the souls of the faithful.'[93] In the text of the Bull the word 'method' is not even mentioned; what Paul III actually wrote was: 'Ignatius of Loyola has composed certain documents or Spiritual Exercises, drawn from Sacred Scripture and experience of the spiritual life, and arranged them in an order most suitable for moving the minds of the faithful.'[94]

Meditation and contemplation.

In the First Week of the Exercises Ignatius proposed meditation as the initial form of prayer, using the classical Augustinian psychology of the three powers of the soul: memory, understanding and will. As William Peters has pointed out, Ignatius, while distinguishing clearly between meditation and contemplation is his Exercises, already introduces contemplation in the Exercises of the First Week. In the fourth exercise, or summary, the intellect is to think diligently over and recall, without any digression, the matter contemplated in the previous exercises. This is in keeping with the whole purpose in performing spiritual exercises, namely of progressing to greater and

---

92. Brou, *La Spiritualité S. Ignace*, 42–3: 'Par contre, et sans beaucoup de paradoxe, on peut dire que ces methodes sont aussi peu methodes que possible, et qu'elles ne sont pas de lui. En ce qu'elles ont d'essentiel, elles appartiennent à tout le monde.'
93. L Peeters, *Vers l'Union Divine par les Exercices de S. Ignace* (Bruges: Museum Lessianum, 1924), 54: 'Or ce que le pape Paul III loue specialement dans les *Exercices*, c'est 'l'ordre et la methode' qui révèrent des données catholiques d'une efficacité singulière pour exciter dans les âmes des fidèles de pieux sentiments.'
94. MHSI 57, 216: 'Ignatius de Loyola . . . quaedam documenta sive Exercitia Spiritualia, ex Sacris Scripturis et vitae spiritualis experimentis elicita, composuerit, et in ordinem ad pie movendos fidelium animos aptissimum redegerit'

greater depth. This leads Peters rightly to conclude that it is through the experience of consolation that the movement from meditation to contemplation takes place. The same obtains in the Second Week of the Exercises when the meditation of The Two Standards leads in the subsequent repetitions to contemplation.[95]

Already we are getting some indication of what Ignatius understands in using the terms 'meditation' and 'contemplation'. The one making the Exercises starts out by using memory, understanding and will, but is then led through the movements of different spirits to respond to the leading of the Creator and Lord, to leave behind the search through memory and understanding for more material to propose to the will, and simply to experience at depth and savour what is now given. This is the thrust of the second Annotation of Ignatius 'that it is not to know much that fills and satisfies the soul, but to feel and taste things interiorly'.

The primary goal of the First Week of the Exercises is clearly the first of the two ends proposed by Ignatius in his first annotation, 'preparing and disposing the soul to rid itself of all inordinate attachments' (in other words, 'basic conversion of heart'). Often this has been seen as the first of the three classical stages of the spiritual life, that of purgation. The Second Week will then correspond to the phase of illumination, and the Third and Fourth Weeks to the phase of union. Classically contemplative prayer has always been seen as proper to the second and third phase, especially to the third, or unitive way. However, the divine operation cannot be restricted to fitting these analytical categories. Not only is it God's prerogative to gift a person with contemplation during the time of purgation should God so choose, but it is necessary that there be some contemplative experience even during this phase, or a thorough purgation will not happen. It is only through faith that conversion of heart can happen, specifically through that faith which brings a person into union with the gift of redemption given in Christ Jesus. So, already we must expect a person making the Spiritual Exercises to be gifted with contemplative prayer, even in the First Week.

William Peters remarks that 'Ignatius must have been quite familiar with Cisneros' opinion that contemplation is intimately connected with the unitive way'.[96] This is perfectly in harmony with

---

95. SE 156.
96. W Peters, *The Spiritual Exercises of St Ignatius Exposition and Interpretation*

Ignatius' asking the retreatant, even in the First Week of the Exercises, to return in contemplation to the points where they experience consolation. Ignatius does not confine 'repetition' merely to points of consolation, but includes also desolation. Though desolation, for Ignatius, is a sign that the evil spirit is at work, it is always under the providence of the loving God. So, the exercise of contemplation in the presence of that loving God is the way not only to be freed from the attack of the evil spirit, but to grow in union. Far more significant for the thesis of this book is Peters' next remark: 'He (Cisneros) distinguishes three ways of contemplating, which are really three stages. They are: to be present, to meet the Father in the Person of Christ, and to become united with Christ himself.'[97] There is general agreement among commentators that, through his association with the Benedictine monastery of Montserrat during his stay at Manresa, Ignatius would have been exposed to and probably given a copy of Cisneros's *Ejercitatio de la Vida Espiritual*. While he may have been influenced by the title (though for Ignatius 'to exercise oneself' is a favourite expression in many other contexts), there is no literary dependence, as is clearly proven in the *Monumenta Historica Societatis Jesu*.[98] But Cisneros's three stages of contemplation are exactly what Ignatius invites the retreatant to in the Second Week of the Exercises: by use of all the faculties, including the imagination, to be present, through this presence to the Person of Christ to meet the Father, and to become united with Christ himself.

Very strikingly Peters draws attention to the fact that in the whole book of the Spiritual Exercises 'there are only five meditations, namely, in the first week, the first two exercises and the meditation on hell; in the second week the exercises on Two Standards and Three Classes of Men ... All the other exercises belonging to the thirty-day retreat are contemplations.'[99] In the Spiritual Exercises Ignatius uses the word *contemplacion* 52 times, and the verb *contemplar* 25 times whereas *meditacion* and *meditar* appear 15 and 8 times, respectively.[100] When referring to the mysteries of Christ Ignatius *always* uses 'contemplation'

(Program to Adapt the Spiritual Exercises, Jersey City, 1967), 38.
97. Peters, *The Spiritual Exercises of St Ignatius Exposition*, 38.
98. MHSI 57, 99–123
99. W Peters, *The Spiritual Exercises*, 38.
100. I Echarte (ed), *Concordancia Ignaciana*, 235–7, and 769–70.

and 'to contemplate'. There are only two apparent exceptions. When giving the points for the Mysteries of the Life of Christ our Lord, Ignatius writes: 'In each mystery for the most part three points are given in order to meditate and contemplate on them with greater facility.'[101] Here Ignatius is giving 'points' outside the text for the thirty day retreat, to be used according to the way of praying appropriate for each person, be it meditation or contemplation. This situation is different from that of the person who has become involved through the experience of the First Week in the dynamic of the Spiritual Exercises. The second apparent exception on the part of Ignatius is in the 'autograph directory' concerning the elections, where there is the remark 'the way this takes place is by proceeding in one's meditations on Christ our Lord.'[102] This is far less a reason for believing that the meticulous Ignatius has departed from his consistent usage than it is an argument for the hand of others in the production of the 'autograph directory'. This is especially true of Polanco, who, as Peters points out, took little if any notice of the distinction in the Exercises between contemplation and meditation.[103] A third possible, but by no means certain deviation by Ignatius from his normal terminology occurred in the draft of the *Examen Generale,* prepared by Ignatius and Polanco. Salmeron, knowing the thinking of Ignatius, made the following recommendation: '(meditating and contemplating his sins and the life and passion). It seems it would be better to say: meditating his sins, and contemplating (the events) and mysteries.'[104] This change was accepted by Ignatius and incorporated into the final text, which reads: 'meditating upon his sins, contemplating the events and mysteries of the life, death, resurrection and ascension of Christ our Lord'. The incident, if anything, shows the consistency of the thinking of Ignatius on the appropriate terminology.

It has also been remarked that Ignatius himself used the Vulgate translation of the Exercises which curiously in one place, the first

---

101. SE 261.
102. MHSI 57, 781
103. W Peters, *The Spiritual Exercises,* 187.
104. MHSI 63, 392. Salmeron wrote in 1551 or 1552: '(meditando y contemplando sus pecados, y los pass os de la uida y passion). Parece seria mejor dezir: meditando sus pecados, y contemplando (los passos) y misteros)'. See the footnote to The General Examen and its Declarations (65) in St Ignatius of Loyola, *The Constitutions,* 96.

contemplation of the first day of the Second Week, makes the change from 'contemplation' to 'meditation'.[105] It seems strange that the writer of the Vulgate translation, André des Freux (generally referred to by his Latinised name, Frusius) should have made this change from contemplation to meditation in only one of the Second Week exercises. But Frusius was intent on providing a literary rather than a literal translation. His stylistic concerns often lead to his changing of Ignatius's wording simply for variety. For instance, he finds Ignatius's repetition of the blunt phrase 'what I want' (*lo que quiero*) in the preludes unsatisfactory. Where Ignatius uses this phrase unchanged in 8 of the 11 examples of prayer given in the text of the Exercises, Frusius provides a variant translation in every one of these exercises.[106] In the light of this, it is perhaps surprising that Frusius changes 'contemplation' to 'meditation' in only the one instance. The preference of Ignatius for using the word 'contemplation' for the exercises of the Second Week is abundantly clear. It is not the translation of a single word in this isolated case that is important, but the powerful dynamic of conversion and seeking and finding the will of God for one's living. Ignatius was so devoted to 'thinking with the Church' that he treasured the Vulgate translation, not as his personal piece of work, but as a document approved by the Holy See.[107]

Perhaps surprisingly, Ignatius's use of the word 'imagination' in the Spiritual Exercises is quite sparing. It appears as a noun four times, as a verb four times, and as an adjective twice. Of these usages six occur in those five exercises which are the only examples of meditation in the book of the Exercises, one in the Rules for the Discernment of Spirits, and only three in the contemplations of the life of Christ. This is not to

---

105. MHSI 100, 222: 'Primae diei meditatio prima erit de Incarnatione Iesu Christi, complectens oration em praeparatoriam, tria praeludia et puncta tria cum uno colloquio.'
106. Where the words of the autograph in each of the eight instances referred to are: 'lo que queiro', Frusius translates as: 'quod hic quaerimus, postulationem gratiae, ad gratiam petendam, optatae rei petitio, ex optatae rei petitione, pro voti consecutione poscere, continet gratiam petendam, ut gratiam Dei efflagitem.'
107. PH Kolvenbach drew attention in 'Linguaggio e Spiritualita' in *Gli Esercizi Spirituali di Sant'Ignazio Linguistice-Storie-Spiritualite* (Rome: Pomel, 1998), 12, to the comment of Luis Gonçalves da Câmara that Ignatius regretted corrections that were made to the Vulgate according to a Spanish text in 1553, given that the Latin text had been approved by the pope.

deny that the activity of the imagination is of key importance in these exercises, but Ignatius uses very concrete language: contemplate, see, listen, hear, be present, consider, and serve. The imagination is not to be thought of as putting the praying person at one remove from these very concrete activities, in the immediacy of relationship with Christ through contemplation.

To understand the Spiritual Exercises, it is absolutely necessary to enter into the mystical experience of St Ignatius and his mystical perspective in writing the book, In 1924 Louis Peeters put it this way: 'The work is understood through the author. Anyone who loses sight of the mystical life of St Ignatius will have only a remote, inadequate understanding of the *Exercises*. For the wonderful thing about this modest, little book is that it is a guide to the spiritual life from its beginnings right through to its climax.'[108]

In writing on the vision of St Ignatius in the chapel at La Storta, Hugo Rahner makes a very similar, perceptive remark about understanding the Spiritual Exercises. Rahner wrote: 'It is not surprising, then, (looking at the mystical 'finding of God in all things' from a human point of view) to find reflected in the book of the Spiritual Exercises what had been in Ignatius's soul since the experience at the Cardoner. One could even go so far as to say that we will really understand the structure and wording of the book of Exercises only if we place ourselves in the mystical position of Saint Ignatius, especially in this trinitarian contemplation of all things from God's viewpoint. The grace of Ignatius' life was to see the coherence of all the mysteries of faith in the light of the trinity—to see in one glance from God's side all that is outside God. Hence this mystical overview can be found in a survey of the individual meditations of the Exercises.'[109] In a footnote at this point Rahner remarked: 'It is one thing for a book to teach mysticism and another for it to be written by a mystic. This origin can also be attributed to a 'non-mystical' book. Yet it is quite clear that Ignatius not only does not exclude mystical

---

108. L Peeters, *Vers l'union divine par les Exercices de S. Ignace*, 25: 'L'auteur explique l'oeuvre. Qui oublie la vie mystique de S. Ignace, n'aura des *Exercices* qu'une idee lointaine, inadequate. Car la merveille de ce modeste petit livre est d'etre un guide de la vie spirituelle depuis ses débuts jusqu'a sa consommation.'
109. H Rahner, *The Vision of St Ignatius in the Chapel of La Storta* (Rome: Centrum Ignatianum Spiritualitatis, 1975), 79.

ways in the Exercises but in many places hints at them with prudence and reserve.'[110]

What is especially relevant here is the remark that understanding the wording of the Exercises requires an insertion into Ignatius's mystical viewpoint. At the very least this understanding requires careful attention to the overall purpose of Ignatius in writing the Spiritual Exercises, to their twofold end or goal; it demands careful attention to Ignatius's bald statement of basic principles. He refrains from spelling these out at length, but requires that they illumine all reflection on his small book if it is to be understood. It requires also that we see in the book of *The Spiritual Exercises* a 'prudent and reserved' attempt to share the richness of the author's own contemplation and mysticism.

The authors mentioned above who qualify Ignatius's writing about contemplation in the second week of the Exercises by calling it 'Ignatian contemplation' or 'imaginative contemplation' or 'a discursive method' or 'meditation' or 'a strategy or technique' are not unaware of the quality of the mysticism of Ignatius. The difficulty arises from taking as normative a terminology about contemplation which was general in the first half of the twentieth century. John of the Cross and Teresa have given careful analyses of the psychological experiences of passivity in contemplation. This does not require us to accept their terminologies and approaches as the only ones in this field. The Spiritual Exercises of Ignatius also lead praying persons to the heights of contemplation. Ignatius points the way for the one making the Exercises through contemplation of the mysteries of the Word make flesh. Is such contemplation truly worthy of the name? This is the question we must now address as we look at traditional and contemporary understandings of this word 'contemplation'.

---

110. Rahner, *The Vision of St Ignatius*, 80

Chapter Two

Natural contemplation

The word 'contemplation' has a long and varied history. To understand it in modern terms, one must begin with that natural gift of contemplation which is an essential part of humanness and, as such, is given to everyone on this planet. The origins of the word are of a religious nature: to contemplate etymologically means to be 'together with' in the *'templum'* or sacred space. This was a sacred piece of ground within which the soothsayer gave his pronouncements before it came to mean the sacred building which we understand by the word 'temple'. What the soothsayer pronounced was not something belonging to another, ethereal world, but of very practical use in this world. In other words, the result of the contemplative pronouncement was to put the receiver in touch with truth or reality in the world of human concerns. Contemplation is a way of knowing. It is a way of knowing that is concrete. Whereas intellectual knowing usually operates through abstraction, at one remove from reality, contemplative knowing implies an immediate grasp of reality. This knowledge is not the same as the immediate, concrete contact with reality that is had in sense knowledge. It is on a different level. It is neither abstract, intellectual knowing nor sense knowledge, but belongs to both sense and intellect, and is often understood in terms of intuition or the use of the 'higher' faculties of the human spirit. By the nature of the case there is something about contemplation which defies rational categorisation. It seems to involve all the knowing faculties in an act which is essentially simple. Such an act may be instantaneous or spread out in time, without seeming to lose its essential simplicity. Sense knowledge, imaginative knowledge, reminiscence and intellectual knowledge may all be involved in the act of contemplation, but the word conveys to us a dimension of the way of knowing that is beyond all of these. The term 'experience' is often used to indicate this kind of knowledge which is too mysterious to fit into any common epistemological category.

It is a basic human experience common to those of all religions and of no professed religions to be able to be still, attentive, alert and aware. Very commonly, these attitudes are those considered appropriate for human persons in the presence of some grand, natural wonder or when experiencing some deeply moving personal event. There is a silence, a sense of awe or wonder, a desire to stay with the object of the experience, to prolong the encounter, to be as open and receptive as possible, to exercise the senses, especially by looking and listening, to get in touch with the feelings that are evoked by the experience, to savour and delight in these feelings.

Contemplation, as a gift, is not the preserve of any special group or class of people, but is given to all. Not only is the possession of such a gift independent of the age and life experience of the recipient, but it is particularly clear in the case of children. The child is free of the kind of economic, technological and political concerns that loom so large in the thinking of the adult. Hence, it is able to accept reality as it is, without an effort to control it, manipulate it, to make it subservient to some personal goal, or to relativise the real in terms of its own ego. While it does not take long for the effects of original sin to become evident in children, the child displays a basic innocence in which the sophisticated concerns of adults about their own ego are not present. The infant already begins to show the adult something of what is involved in the kind of knowing called contemplation. Though its span of attention is very limited, it will focus on something like its own toes, and begin to explore through the senses the reality of this strange other it perceives at the end of its cot. The exploration takes place primarily through the senses of sight and touch. It will even pick up the toes and place them in its mouth. There is a response of the whole young person to the experience of coming to know the toes. There is a clear delight, easily observable in the eyes and the whole facial expression. The sense knowledge is associated with an affective reaction which is not just of a passing nature. The infant knows, non-conceptually, that there is an important activity going on here. It will return again and again to the loved object, seemingly never tiring of exploring this new-found reality. Here we see contemplation already at work. It gives the recipient a kind of knowledge that may not involve having a lot of knowledge about the object. The knowledge is not quantitative, but qualitative. There is an immediate contact in depth with the object being contemplated. There is an absorption in it. As the infant develops, anything may capture its fancy and become the object of affection and contemplation, be it an old sock or a saucepan lid, much to the frustration of the parents who have provided expensive presents, which *seem to them* likely to win and hold the child's attention.

As a child grows and becomes mobile, it will delight in repetitive activity, such as chasing seagulls on the beach. Though experience soon teaches it that it will never catch these flying others, the child seemingly never tires of repeating the contemplative activity of relating to the immediate reality of the birds in this way. Even though the attention span of children is notoriously short, the desire to return and explore again and again is so strong that children are capable of displaying remarkable endurance and patience.

Here we begin to see some of the qualities of infantile contemplation that must be present in any exercise of this gift. It is gift not only as an ability; a contemplative faculty, but the particular occasions when contemplation becomes available and possible cannot be planned. Many factors beyond the control of the individual human being seem to be required to allow contemplation really to occur.

To contemplate requires remaining in the presence of the object of contemplation, staying with it, being 'silent', listening, waiting, and so being patient. A passing glance is not contemplative; what is required is a prolonged gaze. There is the ever-present temptation to 'run away'. Unable to 'endure' the pain of focusing all their inner resources, the person wants to be somewhere else. Simultaneously they experience the attraction and the promise of satisfaction to be found in the act of contemplation. So there is a continuing struggle between attraction and resistance. At times either pole of this dialectic may seem to disappear. Resistance is hardly operative when one becomes rapt in contemplation, experiencing ecstasy or delight. Attraction seems to be minimal when the experience is one of restlessness and inability to remain focused.

In order to focus on the other, a human person must b~ sufficiently free of their own ego to let go of self-preoccupation and allow the other to occupy the whole field of their consciousness. Through the exercise of this natural gift of contemplation one experiences communion with the reality contemplated. One is receptive of the reality of the other, the non-ego, and at the same time one surrenders the ego as one becomes absorbed in what is received. This surrender of the ego is evident in the *apatheia* of the Stoics, the *nirvana* of the Buddhists, or the experience of ecstasy.

The kind of knowledge being described in this 'natural contemplation' puts one in touch with the *reality* of the object of contemplation. So does abstract, intellectual knowledge, right judgment about the object of knowing. But there is a further dimension in contemplative knowing. This is the dimension of *mystery*. Contemplation is, in fact, the mode of knowing which is appropriate in the face of mystery. Pierre Voulet made this point, equally applicable to natural contemplation, when writing about contemplation of the gospel mysteries: 'The idea of contemplation is associated with that of mystery. It is mystery that contemplation must penetrate and deepen.'[1] The word 'mystery', from the Greek *mysterion*, meaning a secret doctrine, is used to indicate the quality of reality that is not revealed in the intellectual knowing of right judgment. Reality is never exhausted by such judgment. It cannot be dismissed as simply 'known'. If one returns after looking and judging to *gaze at*, one can be gifted with a new kind of awareness with relation to the object of knowledge. In fact, the prolonged looking that is called *gazing* is often what is most spontaneously evoked by the use of the word contemplation. Words commonly used to describe such an awareness are: absorption, communion with, and, in the case of relation to other persons, intimacy.

Intimacy may be experienced in a one-to-one relationship or in a group situation. One of the basic characteristics of this prized human experience is a heightened awareness and ability to stay in presence

---

1. P Voulet, 'La Contemplation Évangelique', in *Christus* 5 (1958): 459: 'L'idee de contemplation est associée à celle de mystère, C'est le mystère que la contemplation doit pénétrer et approfondir.'

of another and remain focused upon them. There is a forgetfulness of self. As intimacy occurs, ease and relaxation in the situation increase. Generally the desire to be elsewhere, to 'run away' diminishes, though such reluctance may still be experienced. As conversation develops in a situation of intimacy, the persons become comfortable with pauses and silences. Generally the experience is quiet, gentle and joyful.

Intimacy is experienced as gift. It is generally unexpected and unpredictable. It cannot be forced to happen. There can even be a fleeting moment of intimacy with a total stranger, occurring in a shared glance as people pass one another in the street. Intimacy belongs more appropriately in a relationship with a partner or long-term friend. Such intimacy has a distinctive quality different from that of intimacy with a new friend or a stranger. Human persons require time to grow in relationship The depth of relating can be built up slowly and at leisure. The deeper the knowledge of the other, the further one realises (what renains to be revealed). There is a vague awareness of the infinite dimension of the other that can never be exhausted in human knowing. Over and against this, there remains the possibility of the 'love at first sight' experience, which immediately possesses a quality of completeness and commitment that will never be revoked.

When intimacy develops in a group situation, each one seems to be keenly aware of each of the others. A surprising sensitivity develops. The sense of competitiveness seems to disappear. Nobody seems anxious to break in to have their say. All listen carefully, allow the development of times of silence in which to savour the contribution of the others, and then they speak in a way which continues to promote the sense of intimacy that is occurring. There is a true empathy, an entering into the experience of the other.

If intimacy and contemplation are gifts, is there anything that can be done to facilitate their happening? Having gained some initial insight into the possibility of such gifts, one needs to value and desire them. This will lead to a willingness to exercise the discipline required to be present and available, should the gift occur. Part of this discipline is a moving out from the confines of one's 'own ego. This demands a break with habits that are enemies of contemplation.

A person needs to move away from being too busy, too hectic, too objective, scientific, technological, economically focussed, political and task-oriented. There is a need to be able to leave aside work and really to play. By 'play' is not meant devoting time to a sport or game in which the rules are clearly defined and the main objective is to win. To play is to be child-like, to allow the rules of the game constantly to change, to be challenged to continual adaptation to the other players and the shifting circumstances of the game, to leave oneself behind, to be caught up into the adventure of providing a joyful experience for all the other participants.

When one has recaptured this childhood capacity really to play, there is a further step required in order to be ready for intimacy. One needs to be willing to leave play aside, and simply to be with the other person, to do nothing together. There is a 'wasting of time' in the presence of the other. One is now ready for the gift of intimacy, should it be given.

The lessons about what is required for intimacy can never be learned once and for all. They need continually to be re-learned, because the capacity for intimacy is unlimited.

The use of imagination

If we endeavour to apply the above reflections on natural contemplation to the contemplation of something or someone that is removed from the one doing the contemplating by space or time, or both, we seem to be facing a problem. When the essence of the contemplative experience is mediated through presence, how is it possible to have such an experience when one is in actual fact absent? To solve this problem there is need to have recourse to the inner nature of the type of experience under consideration. Is it possible through the use of the imagination to escape the limitations of space and time in such a way that the contemplative experience can still occur? If it is possible, can the experience avoid being necessarily impoverished? When one of the key concepts of contemplation as outlined above is to be in touch at depth with the inner reality of the object of contemplation, how can this be possible through use of the imagination?

Unfortunately much of education has tended to downplay imagination. Children are taught to believe that what is most real is what is most materially solid. Firmness to the sense of touch becomes a criterion for reality, so that what is regarded as most truly real is steel or concrete. In this kind of thinking, dreams and visions are dismissed as being *only* imagination. The deeper, fully human truth is the opposite. Imagination is more real than steel and concrete, because it gives entry into a more meaningful world, the inner world of the person, in which dreams and visions take a person beyond their limitations to live a fuller and more authentic life.

Through the use of imagination a person can enter the world of any great character of history, or even of fiction. They can recognise the looks of such a person, the sound of their voice, the whole complex of qualities that go to build up a personality. True personal relationship with someone absent becomes a possibility.

Quite apart from the natural contemplation of something striking in the world of nature, or in the fields of art, music or literature, one can visit in imagination a scene or an event and experience what it means to participate. It is helpful to take a concrete example. In 1992 a veteran of the naval battle of the Coral Sea takes the opportunity of the fiftieth anniversary to revisit the scene of that battle, which was decisive in the defence of Australia from Japanese invasion. He goes already armed with a cluster of memories. But, as soon as he arrives at the scene, more memories and images flood in. In imagination he sees again the position of the ships, the faces of his comrades, the bombs dropping through the air, the exploding vessels. He hears the sound of it all. He touches again the dying friend whom he had held in his arms. He grasps again the hands that had reached out to pull him from the water. He smells the explosives, the dead bodies and tastes again the blood, sweat and tears. Powerful feelings are aroused in him. He weeps again. He experiences being carried beyond imagination and emotion into deeper feelings, like loss, grief, gratitude and love. He knows that he has entered into his heart, and remains a long time in profound silence. This experience will remain with him always and influence him for the rest of his life.

Here we have a striking example of the exercise of the natural gift of contemplation. It takes place in the absence of the external event, within the 'inner life' of the contemplating person. Objectively, the battle of the Coral Sea was over fifty years earlier. Subjectively, for the one who revisited it, it took place again. Historical events do not lose their reality as they pass into eternity. They retain their significance in a way that makes them the subjects of possible contemplation.

From this basic description of the common human experience there emerges a series of words that become applicable to contemplation whether it be a purely natural activity or a religious one. Such words are: attraction, reluctance, discipline, waiting, patience, presence, attention, gazing, listening, awareness, experience, immediacy, intimacy, communion, ecstasy, truth, reality, mystery. All of these must be expected to be applicable to any spiritual activity that is called contemplation.

When we come to consider contemplative prayer, it is not as if we are leaving aside the natural gift of contemplation and turning to a completely new concept. The gift of contemplative prayer is always realised in, with and through the natural gift of contemplation. This understanding of contemplation is strongly expressed by Karl Rahner:

> And so in my opinion there is no purely natural mysticism. What is called by that name is simply the 'basis in nature' aspect of man's total constitution, and it is this constitution which (through the supernatural existential) puts to man the inescapable question whether he will accept in immediacy to God the fact that he is ordered to him, or will fail to do so, and how he will mediate this Yes or No to the supernatural finalisation of his existence through the categorical objects of his choices. 'Consolation' therefore consists in this supernatural dynamism's remaining open to the immediacy of God without being distorted by a particular object of choice.[2]

Universality of contemplation and mysticism.

If contemplation is a natural gift, and it is true that as Rahner claims there is no purely natural gift of contemplation without the involvement of the 'supernatural existential', then it follows that contemplative prayer and mysticism, far from being extremely rare gifts as was generally taught in Ascetical and Mystical Theology in

---

2. 'Comments by Karl Rahner on Questions Raised by Avery Dulles', in Friedrich Wulf (ed), *Ignatius of Loyola His Personality and Spiritual Heritage* 1556–1956 (St Loius: Institute of Jesuit Sources, 1977), 290.

the first half of the twentieth century, are universal gifts, given to all persons on the planet. It remains necessary, of course, to make distinctions in terminology to describe gifts of mysticism that are rarer and very highly developed, but contemplation is, at least occasionally and inchoatively, a gift for all.

The assertion of universality with regard to contemplation and mysticism has become increasingly common in modern Spiritual Theology. Harvey Egan cites the influence of 'Karl Rahner, Hans Urs von Balthasar, Thomas Merton, William Johnston, and others' in giving as one definition of mysticism 'the implicit or explicit experience of faith, hope and love that is rooted in all authentic human experience.'[3] Egan goes on to say: 'Radical fidelity to the demands of daily life, even if only through implicit, hidden, or anonymous faith, hope, and love—in short, self-surrender to the Mystery that haunts one's life—grounds the mysticism of everyday life.'[4]

The mysticism of everyday life was a favourite theme of Karl Rahner, who regarded mysticism as far more common than earlier, 'classical' teaching would allow: 'If these older mystics are to be able to help us in this task, we must of course assume for our part that in every human being (as a result of the nature of the mind and of the grace of the divine self-communication offered to everyone) there is something like an anonymous, un-thematic, perhaps repressed, basic experience of being oriented to God, which is constitutive of man in his concrete make-up (of nature and grace), which can be repressed but not destroyed, which is 'mystical' or (if you prefer a more cautious terminology) has its climax in what the older teachers called infused contemplation.'[5] Commenting on this, Egan adds: 'This means that *everyone* experiences, even if only vaguely and implicitly, a holy, loving mystery who communicates its very self. God's self–communication, grace, does not invade the human situation in an extrinsic way, but is intrinsic to human nature itself.'[6] In the *Encyclopedia* of *Theology* Rahner wrote: 'Man's deification and possession of uncreated grace cannot, in the real sense of the words, be surpassed by anything that

---

3. H Egan, *Ignatius Loyola the Mystic*, 21.
4. Egan, *Ignatius Loyola the Mystic*, 21.
5. K Rahner, 'Teresa of Avila Doctor of the Church', in *Opportunities for Faith* (London: SPCK, 1974), 125.
6. H Egan, *Ignatius Loyola the Mystic*, 22.

is not glory. Moreover, it cannot be assumed that mystical experience leaves the sphere of faith and becomes an experience that is not faith. Mysticism occurs, on the contrary, within the framework of normal grace and within the experience of faith.[7]

Already in 1926 Dom Cuthbert Butler had hinted at this universal understanding of mysticism when he concluded his work *Western Mysticism* with the words: 'We learn that mysticism, like religion itself, is within the reach of all: 'It is not too hard for you, nor is it far off. It is not in heaven, that you should ask, who will go to heaven to bring it down for us? It is very near to you, in your mouth, and in your heart, that you may do it.'[8] Butler applies to mysticism the words of Deuteronomy 30:11-14.

William Johnston cites Bernard Lonergan on the universal call to mysticism: 'The original and almost shocking thing in Lonergan is that he looks on mystical love as the goal and climax of human living. This love is the peak-point of the thrust towards self-transcendence and authenticity that is rooted in the minds and hearts of all human beings. There is nothing elitist about it. It is not a gift offered to Christians alone. It is not offered to religious people alone. It is offered to all men and women who would be fully human. Can we not conclude that for Lonergan there is a universal call to mysticism?'[9]

Several years earlier William Johnston had taken a similar position towards the universal call to mysticism, at least for the people about whom he was writing at the time, Christians: 'Mystical contemplation is not extraordinary; it is very ordinary. All Christians, I believe, are called to it; and when they follow this path, they become their true selves, their very ordinary selves.'[10]

What is true of Lonergan's approach to the universal call to mysticism is also true of Reginald Garrigou-Lagrange's. Following on Juan Gonzalez Arintero and Auguste Saudreau, Garrigou-Lagrange emphasised the universal call to holiness and saw the call to mysticism as the normal way of Christian perfection. This led him to deny the distinction between 'acquired' and 'infused' contemplation.

---

7. K Rahner (ed), *Encyclopedia of Theology* (London: Burns and Oates, 1975), 1010.
8. Cuthbert Butler, *Western Mysticism* (Dublin: Arrow Books, Dublin, 1960), 272
9. W Johnston, *Mystical Theology* (London: Harper Collins, 1996), 114–115.
10. W Johnston, *Being in Love* (Collins, London, 1988), 48.

For Garrigou-Lagrange all contemplation was 'infused', and he cited St Bonaventure, St Francis de Sales and Louis de Blois to this effect.[11] Though there are 'degrees' of infused contemplation, none of these is to be regarded as 'extraordinary' but the ordinary working of divine grace.

Contemplative prayer

Grace not only perfects nature, but is operative in, with and through nature. In the light of this principle one must expect all that has been said about the natural gift of contemplation to apply to a consideration of the supernatural activity of contemplative prayer.

A parallel can clearly be drawn between the experience of the two great religious leaders, Siddhartha Gautama (the Buddha) of the sixth century B.C. and St Ignatius of Loyola of the sixteenth century A.D. Each had an experience which he described as enlightenment. Exhausted by many spiritual exercises performed over several years in quest of enlightenment, the Buddha sat down under a bodi tree and was unexpectedly gifted with *enlightenment*. Suddenly he saw all of reality in a new light, at, a new depth, with a new sense of communion. Ignatius relates in his autobiographical reminiscence that after a few months of spiritual exercises following his conversion

> he sat down for a little while with his face towards the river which was running deep below. And as he was seated there, the eyes of his understanding began to be opened; not that he saw some vision, but understanding and knowing many things, spiritual things just as much as matters of faith and learning, and this with an *enlightenment* so strong that all things seemed new to him. One cannot set out the particular things that he understood then, though they were many: only that he received a great clarity in his understanding, such that in the whole course of his life, right up to the 62 years he has completed, he does not think, gathering together all the helps he has had from God and all the things he has come to know

---

11. R Garrigou-Lagrange, *Perfection Chretienne et Contemplation* (Editions de la Vie Spirituelle, Saint-Maximian, 1923), 285.

(even if he joins them all into one), that he has ever attained so much as on that single occasion.[12]

It would be quite incorrect to try to categorise the Buddha's experience as a natural one and Ignatius's as supernatural. Both were gifted by the same God in strikingly similar ways. What distinguishes the two is that the content of the experience of Ignatius is expressed in terms of Christian revelation and that of the Buddha is not. For the Buddha salvation must come about through one's own effort, independent of the intervention of any gods. Ignatius belongs to a tradition that will see salvation in terms of personal response to the triune God revealed in Jesus Christ. This salvation is appropriated through the sacramental life of a community, and personally through the exercise of prayer, contemplation and mysticism in ways already defined in the tradition. Ignatius inherited the catholic faith of the Basque country of the fifteenth century. Juan Alfonso Polanco describes him as up to the time of his conversion 'very much attached to the faith' though 'he did not live in keeping with his belief.'[13] Through his reading at the time of his convalescence of *The Life of Christ* of Ludolph, the Saxon Carthusian and the *Flos Sanctorum* of Jacopo da Varazze, he exposed himself to the full force of the contemplative tradition of the Church via the *lectio divina* and the influence in the lives of the saints. These influences he carried with him into his own personal retreat of about eleven months in Manresa, and so into the writing of *The Spiritual Exercises*. From the time of the writing of the Exercises to the present day, the language of prayer, contemplation and mysticism within the Church has not ceased to develop through the personal experience, reflection and attempt to articulate that experience by persons of an extraordinary variety of cultures and spiritual traditions. Through all of this there remains a language of contemplative prayer as used by Ignatius and developed to the present day in a manner that is both consistent with and can throw much light on what Ignatius of Loyola intended when he invited people making the Spiritual Exercises to contemplate the mysteries of the life of Christ.

---

12. J Munitiz and P Endean, *Reminiscences* or *Autobiography* of *Ignatius Loyola* in *St Ignatius* of *Loyola Personal Writings* (London: Penguin, 1966), (30) 27.
13. MHSI 66, 154, Juan Alfonso Polanco: 'Hasta este tiempo, aunque era aficionado a la fe, no vivia nada conforme a ella'.

Through the experience of conversion, initiated during his convalescence at Loyola and carried on during his time of intensive prayer at Manresa, Ignatius was inserted into a long tradition of contemplative prayer and mystical experience. However, he makes no attempt to draw explicitly on the writings on contemplation of those who went ahead of him. Far more important to him is simply to record his own experience, reflected upon and authenticated through his dialogue with confessors and others throughout this time. 'At this time God was dealing with him in the same way as a schoolteacher deals with a child teaching him;'[14] but this schooling proceeded through the mentality of the spiritual culture to which Ignatius belonged and into which he found himself progressively more inserted. His account of his conversion was only given with great reluctance after repeated urgings from his companions, especially Jerome Nadal, and he finally agreed to give a verbal account of his story only in 1553, within three years of his death.[15] Because for Ignatius the contemplative and mystical experience is a matter of the direct, personal schooling of God dealing with the individual soul, he sees no advantage to be gained by attempting to outline the possible psychology of the contemplative experience of one who responds to the divine initiative in a complete surrender and a consistent effort to put their whole life at the disposal of God and God's service.

As a result of this ignatian approach, there is no 'school' of contemplation into which Ignatius can be slotted. Any attempt to understand what the word 'contemplation' might mean for Ignatius must rest upon the influence of his time of convalescence, as revealed in his understanding of Ludolph of Saxony's *Life of Christ* and the *Flos Sanctorum* of Jacopo da Varazze, together with his developing spirituality at Manresa and after, revealed in his *Reminiscences*, the fragments of his *Spiritual Diary* that are extant and in the book of *The Spiritual Exercises*. The latter clearly does not concern itself with any description of the possible experience of contemplative prayer undergone by one who makes the Exercises. Rather, it provides an instrument for opening up the person to the action of God through meditation upon their own personal life history, and

---

14. J Munitiz and P Endean, *Reminiscences*, (27) 25.
15. C Dalmases, *Ignatius of Loyola Founder* of *the Jesuits* (St Loius: Institute of Jesuit Sources, 1985), 279.

through a contemplative meeting with the Christ of the Gospel, so that more and more the former is inserted into the dynamic of the latter. The personal history of the one making the Exercises takes on progressively more of the delineation of salvation history as revealed through God's presence in Christ. This presence becomes something that is not happening outside the retreatant, but the unfolding of the divine plan takes place within God's election of this person. That election will involve primarily the choice of a state of life, as in the election of the Second Week of the Exercises, but will also reveal itself in every practical detail of a life given over to the living out of that election.

Though Ignatius did not give a definition of terms he was using in the Spiritual Exercises, like 'contemplation' and 'meditation', he was clearly inserted into the history of catholic, Christian spirituality. The basic influence of Ludolph's *Life* of *Christ* upon him during his conversion experience led him to incorporate into his Exercises many elements of the *lectio divina*. Ludolph himself drew heavily upon Bernard for his understanding of the *lectio*, and was influenced by the leading current writings in the area like the *Meditaciones Vite Christi* of John de Caulibus, which were for a long time attributed to St Bonaventure, and the *De Jesu Puero Duodenni* of St Aelred of Rievaulx, similarly for a long time attributed to St Bernard. There was for Ignatius no problem in proposing contemplation in the Second Week of the Spiritual Exercises as set out in these truly contemplative works.

There is no doubt that Ignatius and his contemporaries were clear about a distinction between meditation and contemplation, even if Ignatius himself made no attempt to give definitions. The distinction drawn by Ignatius between the two was clearly shown by William Peters, as treated in chapter One, above. That such a distinction existed and was a real problem to be addressed is shown in the very early (1541) text of *The Spiritual Exercises* known as the text of Master John. This text was for a long time taken to be by Polanco, but he had scarcely joined the Society, and had not yet begun his Philosophy studies, so he was certainly not a 'Master'. The text is probably the work of one of Ignatius's first companions, Master John Codure.[16] One

---

16. MHSI 100, 510: Candido Dalmases, 'Juan Codure autor probable del texto de los Ejercicios atribuido a Polanco' in *Archivum Historicum Societatis Jesu*, 37

of the main characteristics of this text of *The Spiritual Exercises* is the addition of explanations of the ignatian text. Master John adds to the text of Ignatius a new Annotation, to which he evidently gives great importance, as he 'assigns it the very prominent place of Annotation 2. This is devoted to explaining the difference between meditation and contemplation:

> Second (Annotation). Meditation and contemplation can be understood in three ways: First, that they mean the same, as meditation and contemplation both belong without any distinction to acts of the intellect and will. Second, as different from each other, each having its own proper meaning. In this sense meditation is defined as follows: Meditation is a vehement and salutary application of the mind to something to be investigated or known experimentally. Understood in this way, meditation is taken to be an operation of the intellect only: not any evil or curious operation, but a salutary one; and not every salutary one, but one which is done with vehemence, because of the difficulty which those who first begin to experience in the beginning. Hence David says in Psalm 118 (v 97): 'How I have loved your law, Lord; it is my meditation all day.' In this, meditation differs very greatly from contemplation which, properly understood, is done with facility, and therefore it is said that one progresses from meditation to contemplation, when all the difficulty is removed from the vehemence of meditation, and the birth having now occurred [there is evidently an error in the Latin here: *'parto iam habitu'* for *'part iam habitu'*) the way is opened for contemplation, which embraces the operations of both intellect and will. Undoubtedly this was .what David was speaking of in Psalm 38 (v 4): 'In my meditation a fire will break forth.' Hence, as far as it concerns the operations of the intellect, it is defined to be a free and uncumbered intuition of the mind for perceiving things (embracing everyting); as far as it concerns the operations of the will, it is usually defined as follows: Contemplation is as it were death of fleshly desires through the uplifting exaltation of the mind.
>
> To these two meanings is added a third, by which the acts of the intellect can be better distinguished from the acts of the will; namely, as we take it that meditation is an act of the

---

(1968): 145.

intellect, constituted in itself, whether this act is made with difficulty or with facility, so we take contemplation to be especially an act of the will, which the act of the intellect serves, and to which it is directed, as to its end. If we take the words in this sense, it means that whenever anyone meditates, there is also contemplation included, both because the will rouses the person to meditation, and because as a result of meditation the will is moved to its own acts; likewise, whenever anyone is free to contemplate, they do not rashly take it up so that meditation is absent, because the act and operation of the intellect always necessarily precedes the act of the will; nevertheless, the words, thus understood, are most often thought to differ, and this for various reasons: First, because just as the more proper function of the intellect is to meditate, so that of the will is to contemplate; second, because it more properly belongs to meditation to discourse and to look around, to roam around many things with the mind and intellect; but it belongs to contemplation in rest, quiet, tranquillity and the sweetest taste and fruit of the things meditated to delight and. refresh oneself; finally, as meditation, which tends to contemplation as to its end, looks towards the beginning of the desired effect and end, so contemplation joins and unifies the mind with the goal of the same effect. I call the 'effect' that which we wish to acquire by meditating and contemplating, for example great and vehement grief over sins committed, abundance of tears, most fervent desire of eternal goods, and most ardent love, in short, the taste and the sense of the sweetness of anything spiritual. Therefore the name of meditation is more aptly applied to the exercises of the first week, and contemplation to those of the second, third and fourth weeks.'[17]

---

17. MHSI 100, 518–520: 'Secunda. Meditatio et contemplatio tribus modis accipi possunt: Primum, ut idem significent, sicut meditatio et contemplatio promiscue ac citra discrimen ad intellectus et voluntatis pertineant; deinde ut inter se differant, et proprium utraque significatum habeat, iuxta quem modum meditatio sic deffinitur: Meditatio est vehemens et salubris animi applicatio ad aliquid investigandum vel experimentaliter cognsocendum. Hoc autem modo meditatio capitur pro operatione intellectus solum, nec pro quavis operatione mala et curiosa, sed salubri, nec utcumque salubri, sed que cum vehementia fiat, propter difficultatem quam in principio experiuntur ii, qui primo incipiunt meditari. Ideo David ait, *Ps.* 118: *'Quomodo dilexi legem tuam, Domine, tota die meditatio mea est.'* Qua in re potissimum differt a contemplatione, que proprie sumpta fit cum facilitate, et ideo dicitur

After grappling with the style and content of this Annotation, perhaps we are grateful that Ignatius did not attempt such clarifications. The explanation, as given by Master John, is scarcely an adequate one. Many points, such as the 'vehemence' of meditation and the great 'facility' of contemplation lay them open to severe criticism; but the author is clear that meditation belongs more to the intellect and contemplation more to the will. Without saying precisely why, he declares that meditation belongs more properly to the First Week exercises and contemplation to those of the other three Weeks.

Ignatius wrote his Spiritual Exercises within a history of Christian prayer and spirituality that had developed over a millennium and a half, with countless different shades of meaning given to the words 'meditation' and 'contemplation', as well as to 'the three ways of the spiritual life'. In the succeeding half millennium these subjects continued to be debated among spiritual theologians. During this debate neo-scholasticism intervened, with its highly intellectual, structured and systematised exposition of the whole of reality, so that by the early part of the twentieth century great efforts were being

---

quod a meditatione pergitur ad contemplationem, quando ex vehementia meditationis tollitur omnis difficultas, et [part iam habitu], via sternitur ad contemplationem, quae tam intellectus quam voluntatis operationes complectitur, de qua procul dubio David dicit, Ps. 38: 'In meditatione mea exardescet ignis.' Porro quatenus ad intellectus operationes spectat, definitur esse liber et expeditus mentis intuitus in res perspiciendas, usquequaque diffusus; quatenus vero ad voluntatis operationes pertinet, sic diffiniri solet: Contemplatio est mors quedam carnalium desideriorum per sublevantem mentis iubulum. His duobus significandi modis tertius adiungitur, quo actus intellectus a voluntatis actibus melius discerni possint; nimirum, ut meditationem accipi amus pro actu intellectus sicut in sese constat, sive cum facilitate, sive cum difficultate fiat; contemplationem autem praecipue pro actu voluntatis, cui actus intellectus subservit, et ad quem ceu scopum dirigitur. Et quamquam sumptis ad hunc modum vocabulis fere fit, ut quoties quispiam meditatur, etiam contemplationem admisceatur tum quia voluntas ad meditandum excitat, tum quia ex iam meditatis voluntatem ad exercendos actus, acquirere cupimus, verbi gratia, magnum ac vehementem de perpetratis sceleribus dolorem, gemitum, lachrimarum affluentiam, ferventissimum eternorum bonorum desiderium et flagrantissimum amorem, in summa, quemvis spiritualis dulcedinis gustum aut sensum. Proinde meditationis nomen prime hebdomadis exercitiis, contemplationis vocabulum secunde, tertie et quarte aptius accommmodabitur.'

made to systematise Ascetical and Mystical Theology and provide a clear, rational exposition of the life of Christian prayer.

A summary of where this effort had led by the time of Second Vatican Council, in terms of providing a clear terminology through which to understand contemplative prayer, was given by George Ganss, as follows:

> 'DISCURSIVE MENTAL PRAYER (also termed meditation) is characterised by many acts of reasoning, affection, resolution, and communion with God. It is especially suitable for 'the beginners' *(incipientes)* in the 'purgative way' or stage of growth in the spiritual life. Such persons still need to acquire solidly established convictions and motives. In this form of mental prayer the acts of reasoning have a prominent or often predominant part, though if they were not supplemented by affectionate communion with God they would remain study rather than prayer. It is natural that as a person becomes more and more familiar with the basic truths which motivate him in living the spiritual life he finds less and less need of multiplied acts of reasoning.
>
> AFFECTIVE MENTAL PRAYER is that in which there are many devout affections or acts of love. In fact, these now have the predominant part. This prayer is especially suitable to those classified as 'the advancing' *(proficientes)* who are in the 'illuminative way' or stage of spiritual growth. With their basic convictions now fairly well established, they are earnestly striving to advance in the practice of the Christian virtues, especially by imitating Christ.
>
> CONTEMPLATIVE MENTAL PRAYER is a steady, loving gaze on God or some spiritual object or truth in which the intellect and will repose with complacency. The multiplied acts of love characteristic of affective prayer have now become simplified into one protracted gaze. This prayer is also called the prayer 'of recollection', or 'of simplified gaze' (in French *simple regard),* or 'acquired contemplation'. Such simplified prayer is especially suitable to those who are highly developed in the spiritual life, 'the perfect' *(perfecti)* in the 'unitive way' or stage of growth. They are living in intimate union with God through charity, and love of Him motivates all their other acts.
>
> In ACQUIRED CONTEMPLATION the simplified intellectual and affective act is the result both of the person's activity and of grace. He can take a certain initiative, insofar

as he, aided by God's grace which is always present to the just man, turns his loving gaze now, for example, on God's goodness rather than his omnipotence, or on Christ engaged in preaching rather than in healing, or on Mary's admirable kindness at Cana, or on the apostolic zeal of St Paul.

In INFUSED CONTEMPLATION (also termed mystical prayer) the act of gazing lovingly on God or some holy object is a gift which God infuses into the soul by a special operation of grace. A man cannot by his own activity bring this special operation upon himself. Only negatively can he prepare himself to receive it, by removing impediments or by freely acquiescing in the gift if God grants it. God gives or withdraws the gift as He pleases, and that for a short or a long duration. Thus the initiative is with Him and the gift cannot be acquired by the activity of the free will coupled with that grace always present to the just man, but is a completely gratuitous gift of God. He too gives it its various forms or characteristics in different persons, or in the same person at different times. Many theologians now hold the opinion that infused contemplation comes within the normal development of the supernatural life in such wise that if a person faithfully cooperates with the graces received in acquired prayer, God will surely give him the grace of infused contemplation. This opinion, however, is controverted by other theologians who think that it has not yet been proved, even though it is an interesting but still rather speculative hypothesis.[18]

Many of the presuppositions and modes of expression of this way of writing about contemplation can be open to severe criticism, the basic problem being the attempt to offer a thorough, systematic, rational categorisation of prayer, which necessarily (especially in its higher expressions) transcends the rational. A detailed criticism of this summary is not relevant to our present scope. It is sufficient to note that very often failure to understand Ignatius's use of contemplation in the Spiritual Exercises comes from attempts to fit the words of parts of the Spiritual Exercises into these kinds of categories.

In general, within this schema three ways of mental prayer were distinguished: meditation or discursive prayer, affective prayer

---

18. G Ganss, 'Supplementary Notes to J de Guibert, *The Jesuits Their Spiritual Doctrine and Practice*', 605.

or prayer of simple regard, and contemplation, strictly so called. There was a gradual progression from thinking to experiencing, going via affectivity. The main characteristic of contemplation was its passivity, so that even the affectivity was silenced. This fitted neatly with those schools of contemplation which could be termed apophatic, so that gradually the term 'contemplation' came to be confined to the paradoxical experience of faith in the God who is beyond all experience. Where did contemplation in the Second Week of Ignatius's Spiritual Exercises fit into this scheme of things? Clearly it went further into the divine mystery than meditation, yet it had not reached that passivity which was the domain of contemplation. So, it came to be identified as 'affective prayer'. It belonged to the intermediate rung of the ladder: meditation—affective prayer—contemplation. So, Alexandre Brou, for example, could write about the prayer of Jesuits: 'It will be what the Holy Spirit grants it to be, if the soul is generous. But, discursive, affective or contemplative, it should be practical. It does not have its goal in itself, in the heavenly repose of contemplation.'[19] It may seem strange to many a contemplative to identify contemplation with 'heavenly repose', but this became the customary way of describing contemplation among Jesuit authors, in their eagerness to argue for the need in ignatian spirituality to go beyond contemplation to action. The identification of contemplation of the mysteries of the earthly life of Christ with affective prayer gave a nice buffer between this contemplation and 'contemplation strictly so called'. As Brou wrote elsewhere about the contemplations of the life of Christ: 'It is not a question of contemplation in the strict sense of the word, that is to say of the prolonged gaze of love on God himself still seen through the veils of faith; in that kind of prayer God is the proper object of the prayer, and the gaze is a totally simple kind of intuition without multiple acts.'[20] Our argument is that taking up the

---

19. A Brou, *La Spiritualité de Saint Ignace*, 29: 'Elle sera ce que le Saint-Esprit lui donnera d'être, si l'âme est genereuse. Mais, discursive, affective ou contemplative, elle doit etre pratique. Elle n'a pas sa fin en elle-même, dans le repos celeste de la contemplation.'
20. A Brou, *Saint Ignace Maître D'Oraison*, 159: 'Il ne s'agit pas de contemplation au sens technique du mot, c'est à dire du regard d'amour prolonqe sur Dieu lul-même, vu encore a travers les voiles de la foi; Dieu étant l'objet propre de cette oraison, et ce regard etant une sort d'intuition toute simple et sans actes multiples.'

gospels in order to gaze at Jesus is precisely a 'prolonged gaze of love on God himself, still through the veils of faith.'

In recent years there has been a reaction against attempts like the above to categorise contemplative prayer. Certainly, it hardly seems appropriate to fit people's prayer life into preconceived categories, as de Guibert did in *The Jesuits: Their Spiritual Doctrine and Practice*. Repeatedly he summed up the prayer life of a person as being 'infused contemplation'. The tendency to make neat judgments about contemplative prayer was well illustrated when de Guibert wrote: 'We shall not understand Ignatius if we do not keep this fundamental fact before our eyes: Right from the start he is a mystic in the strongest sense of the term, and that to the same degree as a St Francis of Assisi or a St John of the Cross.'[21] One can only wonder what meaning the words 'to the same degree' could possibly have, and what criteria could exist for making such a judgment. It is far better to adopt the modern approach of Charles Bernard, for instance. He introduced his work 'Contemplation, Action and Mysticism' *(Contemplazione, Azione, Mistica)* by writing: 'We shall not commence, as all theologians do, from a systematic theological vision, which would be necessarily partial, and dependent on a particular philosophy and psychology, and which would presuppose a doctrine of the relations between nature and the supernatural, but from a general phenomenology.'[22] Nearly all of the writing by contemplatives about their life of prayer follows that same methodology, simply recording their personal experience of contemplation, and their reflection upon the experience, rather than attempting psychological, philosophical or theological syntheses.

William Johnston rejects the distinction between acquired and infused contemplation, along with a rejection of the terms ordinary and extraordinary, as applied to contemplation. 'Acquired and infused are not good terms. All prayer is infused; all prayer is a gift.'[23] This hardly does justice to the distinction. Those who used the terms were

---

21. de Guibert, *The Jesuits Their Spiritual Doctrine and Practice*, 72.
22. C Bernard, *Contemplazione, Azione, Mistica* (ad usum privatum) (Rome: Pontifical Gregorian University, 1980), 1-2: 'Non partiremo, come fanno tutti i teologi, da una visione teologica sistematica, che sarebbe necessariamente parziale e dipendente da una filosofia non che da una psicologia particolare, e che presupporrebbe una dottrina delle relazioni fra la natura e il soprannaturale, ma da una fenomenologia generale.'
23. W Johnston, *Being in Love*, 47.

well aware that all prayer is a gift. The words 'acquired' and 'infused' were used to point towards the difference between a kind of prayer resulting from the gradual development of a person's prayer life and a kind of prayer in which there was a crossing over into a new kind of passivity, so that God's activity not only initiated and supported the prayer, but became the prayer itself. For Ignatius all true consolation is a gift of the 'good spirit', that is, ultimately of God, but there is a kind of consolation 'without previous cause' which is a gift of God acting directly on the person.[24] Such a gift is totally out of proportion to all preparation, efforts, or acts of the praying person. Perhaps the words 'acquired' and 'infused' have unfortunate overtones, implying too strong a distinction between active and totally passive, but there seems to be a need for a terminology to distinguish these different divine gifts. St Teresa distinguished between the prayer of quiet and the prayer of union, between what she called prayer bordering on the supernatural, and supernatural prayer, or pure contemplation. William Johnston also rejects the distinction between ordinary and extraordinary ways of contemplative prayer: 'Again the terminology *ordinary* and *extraordinary* is not good. Mystical contemplation is not extraordinary, it is very ordinary. All Christians, I believe are called to it.'[25] Others would reject this same distinction on the grounds that the ability of a human person to enter into intimate relationship with God should always be regarded as extraordinary. Whichever of these two contrary rationales for rejecting the distinction is accepted, it is true that the distinction between ordinary and extraordinary has very little place in a modern understanding of contemplation.

Taking, with Gilles Cusson, contemplation to be 'presence in faith to mystery',[26] it is possible to avoid the dangers inherent in attempting to categorise prayer. Meditation is essentially ordained to contemplation, as to its proper end, something already commented upon by Master John Codure in the citation above (54–7) concerning meditation and contemplation. The same is in fact true of all prayer. The gift of contemplation is not something which is received only after passing through vocal prayer, meditation, discursive prayer and affective prayer, but is an essential dimension of all of these.

---

24. SE 330, 336
25. W Johnston, *Being in Love*, 48.
26. G Cusson, *The Spiritual Exercises Made in Every Day Life*, 72.

Normally, as growth in prayer life develops, the prayer becomes more contemplative. It is then quite legitimate to speak of a prayer which is simply identified as being contemplation. This truth was very nicely put by Jerome Nadal when he wrote: 'One arrives at that sublime contemplation and light through those illuminations which God grants from the meditations on the life of Christ, both his created, mortal life and his uncreated, immortal life. Meditation is the way, contemplation the truth and life. However, God also gives these two on the way, but as on the way.'[27] A highly developed gift of contemplation, characterised by great passivity before God and profound entry into mystery is what is meant by mystical prayer.

The attempt to categorise prayer led Joseph, de Guibert into some difficulty when reflecting on the interior life of a general of the Society of Jesus, John Roothaan. From Roothaan's personal spiritual notes, as well as from the many testimonies of other people, de Guibert finds in Fr Roothaan great holiness of life, but goes on to write: 'In these notes there is no trace of anything which could make one think of infused contemplation. But there is a deep and even baffling humility, a self-abnegation that is entire, a constant union with God whom he finds in everything, and a docility to grace which does not flag even in the most difficult moments.'[28] Clearly, de Guibert is describing here a man with a highly developed gift of contemplation, though not having the type of reflexive awareness of that gift that enabled him to write about it. This is evidently a matter of Roothaan's personality; but no particular personality types are excluded from God's gift of contemplation. It may be easier for some to be aware of the gift, to speak of it, and to write about it, but the reality is available to all. Roothaan helped countless people through his writing of the little book *De Ratione Meditandi*. In it he takes as his starting-point for meditation the Crucifixion of our Lord. There is no mention of the word contemplation, even in the presence of this most contemplative of all scenes.

---

27. MHSI 90A, 287, (938) in Orationis Observationes: 'Ad sublimem illam Dei contemplationem et lucem venitur per eas illustrationes quas gratificatur Deus ex meditationibus vitae Christi, tum creatae mortalis, tum increatae immortalis. Meditatio est via, contemplatio veritas et vita. Haec duo tamen in via etiam dat Deus, sed ut in via.'
28. de Guibert, *The Jesuits Their Spiritual Doctrine and Practice*, 495.

As we saw above (57ff) with Master John Codure's 'Annotation Two', where there is a movement from the intellect at prayer to the affectivity of the will, there is a movement 'from meditation to contemplation. Roothaan did not name this, nor probably did he even recognise it. It was his personality and temperament that prevented his doing so rather than the absence of a truly contemplative prayer life. Familiar as he was with the Spiritual Exercises, he gave far more than a notional assent to Ignatius' instruction: 'I will remain at rest on that point in which I find what I desire without any anxiety to go further till I am satisfied.'[29] So, Roothaan declared: 'If we feel some affection aroused in us, let us foster it at length, without anxiety to go on to other things which we planned to deal with in the same meditation, but let us continue in the same affection until we are satisfied.'[30] He had already established the principle that the exercise of the affections should continue throughout the whole meditation, 'so that the meditation becomes true prayer'. 'These affections should be spread throughout the whole meditation, certainly they should be as frequent as possible, since these give the strongest assurance that the meditation becomes genuine prayer.'[31] He then reinforced this instruction, emphasising that the affections should be present from the start, even in using the memory to recall the subject of prayer. 'Therefore, as we said, the affections should be spread throughout the whole meditation. And that is to be understood of the application of the memory as much as of the intellect. Anyone will easily understand, if he carefully considers what was said above about the application of each faculty; that some affections can be suitable, indeed should spontaneously arise, everywhere.'[32] When he comes to

---

29. SE 76.
30. Roothaan, *De Ratione Meditandi*, 50: 'Cum si affectum aliquem in nobis excitatum sentimus, eundem diutius foveamus, sine anxietate pergendi ad alia quae in eadem meditatione tractanda sunt, sed in eodem pergamus affectu donec nobis satisfaciamus.'
31. Roothaan, *De Ratione Meditandi*, 45: 'Hi affectus debent essere per totam meditationem sparsi, certe debent essere quam frequentissimi, cum hi potissimum faciunt ut meditatio vera oratio fiat.'
32. Roothaan, *De Ratione Meditandi*, 51: 'Affectus ergo, ut diximus, per totam meditationem sparsi debent. Idque intelligendum iam de memoriae quam de intellectus applicatione: ubique enim convenire posse, imo naturaliter quasi oriri debere aliquos affectus, quisque facile sentiet si attente consideret ea quae de utriusque potentiae applicatione supra ordine dicta sunt.'

deal with colloquy, the contemplative aspect of Roothaan's work is again strongly in focus: 'In this colloquy, first: Bear in mind what was said above about affections; namely, that it is not a matter of words but of feeling that comes from the heart. Don't worry in what way or what words you are to make this colloquy. Let the heart and the affections speak.'[33]

The kataphatic and apophatic ways

The distinction between the kataphatic (according to what can be spoken: otherwise known as *via positiva*) and apophatic (apart from what can be spoken; otherwise known as *via negativa*) ways of mystical contemplation has a long and revered history in Christianity, going right back to Origen, the theologian of light and Gregory of Nyssa, the theologian of darkness. Where Origen sees three degrees of light in the relationship of the contemplative person to God, Gregory sees three degrees of darkness. Given, in contradistinction to agnosticism, that it is possible to make valid affirmations about God, it still remains necessary to qualify such affirmations with the declaration that all of our knowledge about God is inadequate. In this regard the declaration of the fourth Lateran Council (1215) concerning the incomprehensibility and ineffability of God is often invoked: 'We firmly believe and simply confess that there is one true God, eternal, immense and incomprehensible, almighty and ineffable, Father, Son and Holy Spirit.'[34]

Often contemplatives and writers about contemplation are seen to fall into one or other of the categories kataphatic or apophatic. A contemplative like St Teresa of Avila or Bl Jan van Ruusbroec who combine both in balance are seen as exceptions. The leaders of

---

33. Roothaan, *De Ratione Meditandi*, 61: 'in hoc colloquio: Observa quod supra est de affectibus, non agi scilicet de verbis, sed de sensu cordis. Noli sollicitus esse quibus modis, aut quibus vocibus tuum hoc colloquium instituas. Loquatur cor, affectus.'
34. H Denzinger and A Schonmetzer, *Enchiridion Symbolorum, Definitionum, Declarationum* (Freiburg, 1967), 800, 259: 'Firmiter credimus et simpliciter confitemur, quod unus est Deus, aeternus, immensus et incommunicabilis, incomprehensibilis, omnipotens et ineffablis, Pater, et Filius et Spiritus Sanctus.' The word 'incomprehensible' is repeated by Vatican I (1870): *Enchiridion Symbolorum* 3001.

the apophatic tradition, Dionysius, the Pseudo-Areopagite, in his *Mystical Theology*, the author of the *Cloud of Unknowing*, in that work, and John of the Cross in *The Ascent of Mt Carmel* and *The Dark Night* insist that while praying apophatically any desire to pray kataphatically is to be treated as a temptation, but each of them also wrote positively at other times about kataphatic ways of prayer.

Bl Julian of Norwich and Ignatius of Loyola are silent about apophatic ways of prayer, but this does not mean that they were either ignorant of such ways, or did not practise them, or discouraged their followers from them, if this was God's gift to them. Nor does it mean that their kataphatic ways of Christian mysticism could be valid apart from the inclusion of the apophatic. The balance was well summed up by Harvey Egan when he wrote: 'Although authentic Christian mysticism may proceed apophatically or kataphatically, I propose to show that any genuine Christian mysticism must contain apophatic as well as kataphatic elements. I shall show the kataphatic basis of the *via negativa* and the apophatic basis of the *via affirmativa*.'[35]

In the tenth Annotation of the Spiritual Exercises Ignatius refers to the classic purgative and illuminative ways of prayer: 'For commonly the enemy of our human nature tempts more under the appearance of good when one is exercising himself in the illuminative way. This corresponds to the Exercises of the Second Week. He does not tempt so much under the appearance of good when he is exercising himself in the purgative way, which corresponds to the Exercises of the First Week.'[36] The 'three ways', purgative, illuminative and unitive, are abstractions from a unified reality, as was noted in our first chapter. They are not to be seen as mutually exclusive. Ignatius is well aware of this; hence the expressions he uses here: '... tempts *more* ... He does *not* tempt *so much* ...' There is movement in the Spiritual Exercises from an initially meditative way in the First Week to a very clearly contemplative mode in the Second Week.

In a letter to Francis Borgia, of 20 September, 1548, Ignatius wrote about an ascending order of degrees of contemplation: 'To seek more immediately the Lord of all, that is to say his most holy gifts, such as an infusion or drops of tears, whether this be: over one's own sins or the sins of others; in the mysteries of Christ our Lord in this life or in

---

35. H, Egan, 'Christian Mysticisms', in *Theological Studies*, 1978 (39): 405.
36. SE 10.

the other; in the consideration or love of the divine persons; and these are so much more valuable and precious in so far as the thoughts and consideration are more exalted: And although in itself the third is more perfect than the second, and the second more perfect than the first, that part is much better for a particular individual, where God our Lord communicates more of himself, displaying his most holy gifts and spiritual graces.[37] In his typically kataphatic way Ignatius directs the attention of Borgia to the thoughts and considerations connected with the three different 'degrees' of contemplation; but the fundamental principle remains that contemplation is always a divine gift, and the best gift for any person at any time is the one freely given to them by God.

Catechism of the Catholic Church

We are fortunate in having in the *Catechism* of *the Catholic Church*[38] an official commentary on contemplation, along with other aspects of prayer. The concluding part of the *Catechism* (Part Four: Christian Prayer) has been singled out for special praise by reviewers of the book.[39] What is relevant to our purpose here is Chapter Three: The Life of Prayer.

---

37. MHSI 26, 235–6: 'buscar mas immediatamente al Senor detodos, es a saber, sus sanctissimos dones, asi como na infusion o gotasde lagrimas, agora sea, 1.0, sobre los proprios pecados o ajenos, agora sea, 2.0, en los misterios de Xsto. N. S. en esta vida o en la otra, agora sea, 3.0, en consideracion o amor de las personas divinas; y tanto son de mayor valor y precio, quanto son en pensar y considerar mas alto. Y aunque en si el 3.0 sea mas perfecto que el 2.0, y el 2.0 mas que el primero, aquella parte es mucho mejor para qualquier indilliduo, donde Dios N. S. mas se cominica mostrando sus sanctissimos dones y gracias spirltuales.'
38. *Catechism* of *the Catholic Church* (New York: Catholic Book Publishing, 1994).
39. This was specially true of the review by Bernard Häring in *The Tablet* (28 May, 1994), 658, where he wrote: 'I suggest that the reader should begin with the last part: on prayer. I can think of hardly any book which treats this fundamental dimension of Christian life so profoundly and beautifully. I would like to see this section published separately in a handsome format, accessible to everyone. Christians of other Churches may well find it as useful for them as I do. It helps us to understand prayer as the integration of faith and life. It expounds how we listen to God with faith, hope and love and respond to him, firmly inclined to continue responding throughout our lives, so that our every thought, word and action culminates in thanksgiving and praise. Whereas in the other sections I made many notes with question-marks, here I hardly found a word to criticise.'

The *Catechism* follows the traditional division of personal prayer into three types: vocal prayer, meditation and contemplative prayer. Not that these three are mutually exclusive. On the contrary, in the treatment on vocal prayer, acknowledgment is made in paragraphs 2702 and 2703 of the essential unity of the human person. While the concern of the *Catechism* here is to provide a rationale for the bodily character of vocal prayer, the principle it elicits has a very important application for the appreciation of the fact that in all prayer it is the body-person who prays, so that any unhealthy dualism is avoided. In formally contemplative prayer the same essential unity applies to the union of the body and all the interior faculties: senses, memory, imagination, intellect and will.

Very relevant to our concern in this book is the remark of the catechism in paragraph 2704 that 'vocal prayer becomes an initial form of contemplative prayer.' This is intimately linked to the important principle that contemplation ought not to be understood so much as a separate division of prayer, but as a dimension of all authentic prayer. If we understand contemplation as a presence in faith to the divine, vocal prayer is simply one of many modes of being present. This is not to assert that all vocal prayer can be simply labelled 'contemplative'. It remains possible to 'say prayers' without that quality of presence in faith that authentic prayer or contemplation requires.

There is no limit that can be set a priori to the depth of contemplation that can be attained while praying vocally. Cuthbert Butler made this declaration, supporting it with a quotation from John Cassian: 'It has to be clearly asserted, in the first place, that vocal prayer may be contemplative, and this whether it be private vocal prayer or the public prayer of the Divine Office. Such is quite definitely the teaching of Cassian (see *Benedictine Monachism*, 70): 'A verse of a psalm may be the occasion of glowing prayer (contemplation) while we are singing.'[40] In a famous passage in *The Way* of *Perfection* Teresa Avila declares that while saying the 'Our Father' one can be raised to perfect contemplation:

> But since, as I say, I am dealing with vocal prayer, it may seem to anyone who doesn't know about the matter that vocal prayer doesn't go with contemplation; but I know that

---

40. Cuthbert Butler, *Western Mysticism*, 265–6.

> it does. Pardon me, but I want to say this: I know there are many persons who while praying vocally, as has already been mentioned, are raised by God to sublime contemplation (without their striving for anything or understanding how. It is because of this that I insist, daughters, upon your reciting your vocal prayer well.) I know a person who was never able to pray any way but vocally, and though she was tied to this form of prayer she experienced everything else. And if she didn't recite vocal prayer her mind wandered so much she couldn't bear it. Would that our mental prayer were as good! She spent several hours reciting a certain number of Our Fathers, in memory of the times our Lord shed his blood, as well as a few other vocal prayers. Once she came to me very afflicted because she didn't know how to practise mental prayer nor could she contemplate; she could only pray vocally . . . 'asked her how she was praying, I saw that though she was tied to the Our Father she experienced pure contemplation and the Lord was raising her up and joining her to himself in union. And from her deeds it seemed truly that she was receiving such great favours, for she was living a very good life. So I praised the Lord and envied her for her vocal prayer.'[41]

An advanced degree of contemplation while praying vocally is not the prerogative of monks chanting the Divine Office or of nuns. It is a common experience that numerous people who have never been formally taught to pray in any other way than by reciting vocal prayers, like the rosary, reach a stage of continual murmuring of the prayer, and show forth in their lives the fruits of intimate union with God through their transparent holiness, like the nun in Teresa's story.

In its four paragraphs on meditation the *Catechism of the Catholic Church* notes the advance from thinking about what we read: 'To meditate on what we read helps us to make it our own by confronting it with ourselves' (Paragraph 2706) to the threshold of contemplation: 'This form of prayerful reflection is of great value, but Christian prayer should go further: to the knowledge of the love of the Lord Jesus, to union with him' (Paragraph 2708). As with vocal prayer,

---

41. St Teresa of Avila, *The Way of Perfection*, chapter 30, in *The Collected Works of St Teresa of Avila*, volumr 2 (Washington DC: Institute of Carmelite Studies, 1980), 151–2.

meditation, a fortiori, is not divorced from contemplation, but is essentially ordered to it.

What, then, is contemplation? The *Catechism* answers this question in eleven paragraphs (2709–2719). Far from giving any one 'definition' of contemplation, the catechism commences nine of its paragraphs with different answers to the question: what is contemplative prayer? Furthermore, within paragraph 2712, and twice within paragraph 2713, it has sentences beginning: 'Contemplative prayer is . . .'. In none of these statements is there any reference to the old distinctions: apophatic and kataphatic, acquired and infused, ordinary and extraordinary. This approach is highlighted in the first statement, taken from St Teresa of Avila: 'Contemplative prayer *(oracion mental)* in my opinion is nothing else than a close sharing between friends; it means taking time frequently to be alone with him who we know loves us' (paragraph 2709). The citation from St Teresa is from her *Autobiography*.[42] The *Catechism* has quite legitimately translated Teresa's *'oracion mental'* as 'contemplative prayer'. In her use of the words *'oracion mental'* Teresa was concerned with contemplation rather than meditation.

This opening description of contemplative prayer by the *Catechism* is clearly paralleled in the *Spiritual Exercises,* where Ignatius writes of the colloquy: 'The colloquy is made by speaking exactly as one friend speaks to another, or as a servant speaks to a master, now asking him for a favour, now blaming himself for some misdeed, now making his affairs known to him and seeking his advice.'[43] In the Exercises colloquy belongs far more to contemplation than to meditation, even when it occurs within the framework of what Ignatius entitles a meditation. For him colloquy comes at the end of an exercise, not because it is a convenient, formal way to conclude a time of prayer, but because it gives expression to the proper development of meditation into contemplation, as the person at prayer is deeply moved or affected. Already in the late sixteenth and early seventeenth centuries Diego Alvarez de Paz and Bartolomeo Ricci taught a form of prayer which consisted entirely of colloquy. Referring to Alvarez de Paz, de Guibert wrote: 'This colloquy is employed continually in all the 'subjects for prayer' dealing with the life of Christ, of the Blessed Virgin, or the

---

42. St Teresa of Avila, *The Collected Works*, volume 1, 96.
43. SE 54.

divine perfections.'[44] The same de Guibert points out that Ricci in his use of 'colloquy or continual conversation with God our Lord, or the saints ... draws his inspiration continually from St Ignatius for the preludes, application of the senses, the contemplation of persons and their actions, and so on.'[45] This seems to be an attempt to justify the continual use of colloquy throughout the time of prayer as not really being a departure from the letter of the Exercises. Later de Guibert seems to draw attention to the daring of Ricci in proposing continual colloquy, when he writes: 'In a treatise such as that which Bartolomeo Ricci wrote right under Aquaviva's eyes for the novices of Sant' Andrea al Quirinale, we have found this. To these novices he taught a form of prayer of which explicit mention in the *Exercises* can only be sought in vain. It was that of a prayer made wholly in the form of a colloquy, that is of familiar conversation with our Lord or the Blessed Virgin Mary.[46]

In the second part of paragraph 2709, the one who is sought in contemplative prayer, he 'whom my heart loves' is declared to be 'Jesus, and in him, the Father.' Jesus, in other words, is here seen as the focus of contemplative prayer. The mystery of the person of the Jesus whom we contemplate is not simply a Christological mystery, but is always Trinitarian-Christological. To contemplate Jesus is to contemplate the life of the Trinity. This was eminently clear to Ignatius, for whom Jesus was 'God, our Lord', 'our Father', 'our Creator', 'the Eternal King', 'the Divine Majesty'. The blurring of clear verbal distinctions in consideration of the mystery of the Trinity in our prayer life is quite appropriate. It points to the error that would be involved in seeking an objectivity and a clarity that are impossible in the face of mystery. For Ignatius such a simple thing as a Christian Doctrine instruction on the sign of the cross was a way into the contemplation of Father, Son and Holy Spirit present in Jesus. He gave this instruction in Rome: 'To make the sign of the holy cross we place the hand on the head, which signifies God the Father, who proceeds from no-one; when we place the hand on the stomach it signifies his Son, our Lord, who proceeds from the Father, and came into the womb of the most holy Virgin Mary; when we place the hand on one shoulder and the other,

---

44. de Guibert, *The Jesuits Their Spiritual Doctrine and Practice*, 266.
45. de Guibert, *The Jesuits Their Spiritual Doctrine and Practice*, 272.
46. de Guibert, *The Jesuits Their Spiritual Doctrine and Practice*, 550.

it signifies the Holy Spirit, who proceeds from the Father and from the Son; when we place the hands together, it signifies that the three Persons are one true Essence; when we place the cross to our lips, it signifies that in Jesus our Saviour and Redeemer, there are the Father and the Son and the Holy Spirit, one only God our Creator and Lord, and that the divinity was never separated from the body of Christ in death.'[47]

The same truth of reaching beyond the person immediately contemplated applies to the contemplation of Mary, a contemplation that plays a very important part in the *Spiritual Exercises*. Harvey Egan, in describing the mysticism of Ignatius, uses among many other expressions, the term 'a Marian mysticism'.[48] To contemplate any of the saints, but Mary especially, is at the same time to contemplate Jesus, and Father, Son and Holy Spirit. The 'triple colloquy' of the Exercises is not the substitution by Ignatius of a new Trinity, Mary, Jesus, and the Father, for Father, Son and Holy Spirit. A full and open presence to Mary is a presence to her Son and through Him to the Father in the Holy Spirit. Jesus is the Eternal Word; wherever we find Him, in the Spirit we find the Father. Ignatius himself enjoyed a truly personal intimacy with each person of the Trinity, as we shall see in our next chapter. With a sure theological instinct he knew that there was no need to insist on a separate prayer to the Holy Spirit in a quadruple colloquy. All our praying is done in the Spirit. It is perfectly legitimate, and points to mystery, to speak as the *Catechism* does, of our relationship with the Lord (paragraph 2710), without declaring definitely whether it is the Father or Jesus, the Son, who is signified, though usually the expression 'the Lord' refers directly to the risen Lord, Jesus.

---

47. MHSI 42, 667: 'Per far il segno della santa croce ponemo la mano in capo, che significa Dio Padre, il quale non procede da nessuno; quando ponemo la man' al ventre significa il suo Figliuolo, nostro Signore, il quale procede dal Padre, et e venuto insino al ventre della sacratissima vergine Maria; quando ponemo la mana da na banda all' altra significa il Spirito Santo, il qual procede del Padre et del Figliuolo; quando ponemo le mani insieme signfica le tre persone esser vna vera essentia; quando ponemo la croce in boca significa in Jesu nostro saluator' et redentor, esser il Padre et il Figliuolo et il Spirito Santo, vno solo Dio nostro creator' et signor', et che la diuinita mai fu separata dal corpo di Christo nella morte.'

48. Egan, *Ignatius Loyola the Mystic*, 114–18

A distinction is made in paragraph 2710 between meditation and 'inner prayer' (i.e. contemplative prayer). This distinction comes in the context of perseverance in prayer 'no matter what trials and dryness one may encounter.' Though sometimes meditation is not possible, 'inner prayer' is always possible, since it may be simply an expression of one's poverty and faith. This ever-present faith is essential to the understanding of contemplative prayer. No matter what the experience of God's presence, even if the experience be one of absence, faith is, as St John of the Cross insists, the only immediate means for union with God—never vision, nor any psychological experience.

Rightly the *Catechism* insists in paragraphs 2710 and 2711 on the personal, ascetical effort that is needed for contemplative prayer. Perhaps the presentation would have been improved by putting first the gift aspect of contemplative prayer, which comes later in paragraph 2713. Whatever about that, contemplation requires determination of will, not in a voluntaristic sense, but as paragraph 2710 puts it, 'revealing the secrets of the heart'. This determination is needed to persevere in times of trial and dryness.

Paragraph 2711 continues the teaching on ascetical effort 'under the prompting of the Holy Spirit'. On our part we need to 'recollect our whole being, abide in the dwelling place of the Lord which we are, awaken our faith in order to enter into the presence of him who awaits us.' We must also 'let our masks fall and turn our hearts back to the Lord who loves us'. Here the *Catechism* draws attention to the purification which is effected through contemplative prayer, 'so as to hand ourselves over to him as an offering to be purified and transformed.' Contemplative prayer is not only illuminative and unitive, but purgative. This aspect of contemplation is present throughout the Spiritual Exercises. In the First Week conversion is effected through the intimacy of the very contemplative colloquies. The profound conversion of heart that is the proper fruit of the First Week is only possible through a unitive faith open to accepting the salvific grace of Christ crucified. This grace not only unites the praying person more radically to God in Christ, but is brought about and deepened through the gift of union. The following of Christ in the Second Week calls for continuing emptying of self or purification. In the Third Week one prays again for 'sorrow, compassion and shame because the Lord is going to His suffering for my sins.'[49] While the 'three ways' (purgative, illuminative and unitive) have a logical order and often a generalised temporal order, they are far from being mutually exclusive.

Paragraph 2712 of the *Catechism of the Catholic Church* corresponds to the transition in the Spiritual Exercises from the First Week to the Second Week. In its declaration that 'contemplative prayer is the prayer of the child of God, of the forgiven sinner' the *Catechism* is drawing attention to the fruit of genuine conversion, effected by Pauline faith in Christ as redeemer, leading to baptism and adoption as a child of God. Here we are touching upon the core of the thesis of this book. Entry into the Second Week of the Spiritual Exercises draws upon the grace of the First Week. This grace may be expressed as conversion of heart, acceptance of redemption as a free gift given in Christ, a profound sense or heartfelt knowledge of one's identity as a forgiven sinner and child of God.[50] It gives the person a new freedom to enter more fully into union with God in Christ through contemplating Christ in the mysteries of his life up to Palm Sunday (Second Week of the Spiritual Exercises). Contemplation will then continue into deeper levels in the contemplation of the Lord's death and resurrection. The appropriate, immediate response to an experience of the grace of conversion from sin is a total gift of self. The catechism draws attention in its footnote to the whole-hearted response to the gift of forgiveness of the sinful woman (Lk 7:36–50) and of Zacchaeus (Lk 19:1–10).

The *Catechism's* association of baptism with contemplative prayer, the prayer of the child of God, underlines the basic source of contemplation for a Christian. Through baptism into Father, Son and Holy Spirit, the Christian is brought into foundational, objective, ontological union with the triune God. Through contemplation this union will both be experienced and become a lived reality, showing its fruit in the exercise of the virtues. The importance of the link

---

49. SE 194.
50. The thirty second General Congregation of the Society of Jesus, in addressing the question, 'What it means to be a Jesuit today', for those formed by the Spiritual Exercises, very strikingly commenced with the idea of 'sinner': 'What does it mean to be a Jesuit? It is to know that one is a sinner, yet called to be a companion of Jesus as Ignatius was.' *Documents of the Thirty Second General Congregation of the Society of Jesus* (Washington, DC: The Jesuit Conference, 1975), 7.

between baptism and contemplation was already stressed by Joseph Cardinal Ratzinger in an earlier church document:

> '21. On the path of the Christian life, illumination follows on from purification, through the love which the Father bestows on us in the Son and the anointing we receive from Him in the Holy Spirit (cf 1 Jn 2:20). Ever since the early Christian period, writers have referred to the 'illumination' received in Baptism. After their initiation into the divine mysteries, this illumination brings the faithful to know Christ by means of the faith that works through love. Some ecclesiastical writers even speak explicitly of the illumination received in Baptism as the basis of that sublime knowledge of Christ Jesus (cf Phil 3: 8), which is defined as 'theoria' or contemplation. The faithful, with the grace of Baptism, are called to progress in the knowledge and mysteries of the faith by 'the intimate sense of spiritual realities they experience'. No light from God can render the truths of the faith redundant. Any subsequent graces of illumination God may grant rather help to make clearer the depth of the mysteries confessed and celebrated by the Church, as we wait for the day when the Christian can contemplate God as He is in glory (cf. 1 John 3: 2).
>
> 22. Finally, the Christian who prays can, if God so wishes, come to a particular sense of *union*. The Sacraments, especially Baptism and the Eucharist, are the objective beginning of the union of the Christian with God. Upon this foundation, the person who prays can be called, by a special grace of the Spirit, to that specific type of union with God, which in Christian terms is called *mystical*.'[51]

For the *Catechism* the status of a person engaged in contemplative prayer as a child of God is already implicitly trinitarian. Paragraph 2712 concludes by making this explicit: 'But he knows that the love he is returning is poured out by the Spirit in his heart, for everything is grace from God. Contemplative prayer is the poor and humble surrender to the loving will of the Father in ever deeper union with his beloved Son.' For Ignatius the 'surrender to the loving will of the Father in ever deeper union with his Son' is not a generalised

---

51. Congregation for the Doctrine of the Faith, *Letter to the Bishops of the Catholic Church on Some Aspects of Christian Meditation* (Vatican City: Libreria Editrice Vaticana, 1989), 18-19.

surrender, but through the election, the centre piece of the Spiritual Exercises, it is a surrender to the concrete will of the Father for the retreatant, which both takes place in the here and now and also will affect the whole of the rest of the person's life. It is precisely through the contemplative prayer of the Second Week of the Exercises that entry into the election takes place.

Paragraph 2713 of the *Catechism* draws attention to the essential simplicity of contemplative prayer: it is 'the simplest expression of the mystery of prayer.' This simplicity will often consist in the absence of any multiplicity of different acts on the part of the praying person, or, if such multiple acts should be present, an underlying simplicity of focus. The paragraph states the basic principle which must always be borne in mind regarding contemplative prayer, namely, that it is a gift. This gift 'can be accepted only in humility and poverty.' The deepening, through contemplation, of poverty and humility is at the heart of the Second Week of the Spiritual Exercises. What we are gifted with in contemplative prayer is 'a covenant relationship' and 'a communion'. Again the paragraph draws attention to the essentially Trinitarian character of contemplative prayer: 'Contemplative prayer is a *communion* in which the Holy Trinity conforms man, the image of God, 'to his likeness.' ' Here we have an echo of Romans 8, 29: 'For those whom he foreknew, he also predestined to be conformed to the image of his Son, in order that he might be the first of many brothers.' To be conformed to the 'likeness of God' and to be conformed to 'the image of his Son' are one and the same.

For the third consecutive paragraph the *Catechism*, in 2714, is explicitly trinitarian, when referring to contemplative prayer as 'the pre-eminently *intense time* of prayer'. The intensity is not to be found in any strenuous effort on the part of the praying person; rather the *Catechism* draws upon the powerful language of the letter to the Ephesians, in quoting 3, 16-17: 'The Father strengthens our inner being with power through his Spirit 'that Christ may dwell in (our) hearts through faith' and we may be 'grounded in love'.

In its paragraph 2715 the *Catechism* uses a change of language. Four times it has begun with the word: 'Contemplative prayer is . . .' (paragraphs 2709, 2712-2714), and it will resume with the same words four times again (2716-2719). But here, in this central paragraph, it changes to:

'Contemplation is...' Attention is drawn to the special importance of this particular description of contemplation, which will repeated in the summary of this Article in paragraph 2724. 'Contemplation is a gaze of faith fixed on Jesus'. Once again it is emphasised that the initiative always belongs to the Lord. We gaze in response to his gaze: 'His gaze purifies our heart; the light of the countenance of Jesus illumines the eyes of our heart and teaches us to see everything in the light of his truth and his compassion for all men.' One of the most basic understandings of the natural gift of contemplation is expressed by the word 'gaze' (22 above). When we come to treat of contemplation explicitly as prayer, the words 'of faith' are added. The expression 'a gaze of faith' is clearly something beyond the rational. We are in the realm of mystery here. We may attempt to promote our understanding by referring to a gaze of the supernatural understanding, or of the supernatural imagination, but again we are involved in mystery. Though the supernatural imagination operates in, with and through the natural imagination, it cannot be reduced simply to natural, sensory imagination.

The 'gaze of faith' may seem to the contemplating person like no gaze at all. As with St John of the Cross, it may take place in darkness. For John the darkness is a sure way of contemplation, and faith is the only immediate means of contemplative union with God. Christ is always the mediator of such union, so that a gaze of faith into the darkness remains truly a gaze of faith fixed on Jesus.

The *Catechism* clearly implies that the phrase 'a gaze of faith fixed on Jesus' is broader than the contemplation of the gospel mysteries, when it uses the word 'also' in its declaration: 'Contemplation also turns its gaze on the mysteries of the life of Christ.' The risen Lord Jesus is Lord of all that is, so that to gaze in faith upon anything is to exercise 'a gaze of faith fixed on Jesus'. Clearly, to gaze in imagination at the mysteries of the life of Christ is a direct way of exercising this gaze of faith; so the catechism rightly draws specific attention to this privileged mode of contemplation. It is the way of the Second Week of the Spiritual Exercises, and the *Catechism* here quotes St Ignatius: 'Thus it learns the 'interior knowledge of our Lord', the more to know and follow him.'[52]

---

52. SE 104.

Paragraph 2716 begins: 'Contemplative prayer is *hearing* the Word of God.' As with the 'gaze of faith', the Word of God is left open to its many meanings. Here again a privileged place must be accorded to that Word spoken in Scripture. We can legitimately see here a reference to the *lectio divina*. But the Word of God can be broadened to all the invitations and challenges received through all the events and persons encountered in one's life. The *Catechism* points out that the authentic understanding of 'hearing' implies response, the response of 'the obedience of faith, the unconditional acceptance of a servant, and the loving commitment of a child.' These are the characteristic attitudes of a religious person whenever they open their hearts to hearing the Scriptures read. So, once again the *Catechism's* explanation of contemplative prayer is essentially simple and available to all, through, for example, attentive participation in the Liturgy. This attentiveness 'participates in the 'Yes' of the Son become servant, and the *Fiat* of God's lowly handmaid.'

Paragraph 2717 draws attention to the quality of silence involved in contemplative prayer. Traditionally, at its highest level, this is described as the *silentium mysticum*. Two of the numerous possible citations are given: St Isaac of Nineveh: the 'symbol of the world to come', and St John of the Cross: 'silent love'. At the culmination of his writing on the mystical life John is reduced to silence at the end of *The Living Flame of Love*: 'I do not desire to speak of this spiration, filled for the soul with good and glory and delicate love of God, for I am aware of being incapable of doing so; and were I to try, it might seem less than it is.'[53] It is perhaps surprising that this is the only place in the article on Contemplative Prayer where the *Catechism* cites John of the Cross. The great preponderance of the article is explicitly kataphatic, and only implicitly apophatic. Even here after the reference to 'silent love', it returns to the kataphatic, writing about the function of words. Again, in paragraph 2719, after the reference to 'the paschal night of the Resurrection' and 'the night of the agony of the tomb', the response is to be the explicitly kataphatic one of staying in the presence of Jesus, 'being willing to "keep watch with (him) one hour"'.

---

53. St John of the Cross, *The Living Flame of Love*, 4, 17, in K Kavanaugh and O Rodriguez (translators), *The Collected Works of St John of the Cross* (Washington DC: Institute of Carmelite Studies, 1991), 715.

In treating of silence, the *Catechism* makes it clear that this is not to be understood as the absence of words, but rather a quality of the prayer which is quite compatible with the use of words. 'Words in this kind of prayer are not speeches; they are like kindling that feeds the fire of love.' Once again, the paragraph is explicitly trinitarian: 'In this silence, unbearable to the 'outer' man, the Father speaks to us his incarnate Word, who suffered, died and rose; in this silence the Spirit of adoption enables us to share in the prayer of Jesus.'

Paragraph 2718 commences: 'Contemplative prayer is a union with the prayer of Christ insofar as it makes us participate in his mystery.' We participate in the mystery of Christ through the adoptive sonship of Baptism, which is essentially ordered to, and receives its culmination in the Eucharist. The next sentence of the catechism draws attention to this Eucharistic dimension: 'The mystery of Christ is celebrated by the Church in the Eucharist'. But our baptism could remain a dead formality and our participation in the Eucharist could be merely perfunctory without that contemplation which makes the ontological presence of Christ in us, come alive through a living, personal relationship which will show itself in a virtuous life. One of the ways of contemplation which puts us in immediate contact with the grace of our baptism and the Eucharist is presence to Christ, the risen Lord, in the mysteries of his earthly life, which have constituted the present reality of the mystery of Christ. This is what is done through the contemplation of the life of Christ in the Second and subsequent Weeks of the Spiritual Exercises.

The *Catechism* affirms that it is the role of the Holy Spirit to make the mystery of Christ come alive through our contemplative prayer. The end or goal of this prayer is 'so that our charity will manifest it (the mystery of Christ) in our acts.' There can be no question of an authentic contemplative prayer which terminates in itself.

Much of the early controversies in the Society of Jesus about the style of Jesuit prayer, whether it could be contemplative or had to remain meditative, were be-devilled by an understanding, that contemplative prayer necessarily ended in 'repose', and so was contrary to the Society's apostolic end. Prior to the publication of the great letter of the General, Claudius Aquaviva, on Jesuit prayer in 1590, two of his assistants, Paulus Hoffaeus and Manuel Rodrigues took this position. As Joseph de Guibert recorded, they 'held that the true thought of St Ignatius was, in view of the Society's end, not to give much time either to the repose of contemplation or to severe penances. They further held that Jesuits ought to content themselves with the meditation that prepared them for apostolic action, and that the prayer which confined itself to contemplation alone was foreign to their vocation.'[54] This opinion was strongly rejected correctly, by Aquaviva. De Guibert cites (no 3) of his letter to the effect that 'the authority of the Fathers clearly guarantees to us that the true and perfect contemplation is more powerful than any other method of pious meditations for diminishing pride, promoting obedience, and enkindling zeal for souls.[55] And in number 4 of the same letter Aquaviva wrote: 'to claim that a member of the Society is never permitted in his prayer to pause on simply knowing and loving God, that he must always make a meditation which tends directly toward something practical, and that he is not free to meditate on what is not related to the practical—to say this is to be completely in error. It is not true to say: 'I love God in order to do what is pleasing to Him' instead the truth is: 'I do what pleases Him because of my love for Him.'[56]

The essentially apostolic end of contemplative prayer was very clear for St Teresa of Avila. In this she anticipated the understanding of St Therese of Lisieux on the apostolic nature of contemplation, and the teaching of the Second Vatican Council on the essentially apostolic character of all religious life. At the climax of *The Interior Castle*, in the seventh mansion Teresa advises her sisters: 'This is what I want you to strive for, my Sisters; and let us desire and be occupied in prayer not for the sake of our enjoyment but so as to have this strength to serve.'[57] Whereas, at the earlier stage of the spiritual journey, in the sixth mansion, a contemplative person desired to die to be with the Lord, the contrary is now true: 'What surprises me most of all now is that they have just as great a desire to serve Him and that through them He be praised and that they may benefit some souls if they can. For not only do they not desire to die but they desire to live very many years suffering the greatest trials if through these

---

54. de Guibert, *The Jesuits Their Spiritual Doctrine and Practice*, 239.
55. de Guibert, *The Jesuits Their Spiritual Doctrine and Practice*, 240.
56. de Guibert, *The Jesuits Their Spiritual Doctrine and Practice*, 241.
57. St Teresa of Avila, *The Interior Castle*, 7.4.12, in *The Collected Works*, volume 2, 448.

they can help that the Lord be praised, even though in something very small.'[58]

Joseph de Guibert draws attention to the unity and diversity of different spiritualities and mysticisms with regard to the notion of apostolic service:

> 'The mystics of union and transformation do not even in the slightest degree exclude the thought of service to Him who to them appears especially under the aspect of the Spouse of their souls. Similarly, St Ignatius does not in the slightest degree exclude the thought of our union with God in His Christ, or the transformation of our souls through grace and indwelling of the three Divine Persons in ourselves. . . To become fully aware of this difference in perspective, we need only to read side by side some passages in Ignatius and, to take one example, St John of the Cross. As we go through the equally strong expressions of an equal love of God, and through indications of an abnegation not less complete in one than in the other, we perceive at once that the fundamental thought which orientates everything is not the same. But must we ask which of the two points of view, union or service, is more traditional, more gospel-like or more perfect than the other? Obviously no. These are two different messages, equally willed by God. He entrusted them to two great saints for the benefit of their contemporaries in the sixteenth century, and also for future generations in the Church.'[59]

Paragraph 2718 of the *Catechism* continues the theme of the fruit of contemplative prayer with which 2717 concluded. Contemplation has the apostolic dimension of 'bearing Life for the multitude'. Surprisingly, this bearing of Life is linked to the apophatic dimension of contemplative prayer. It occurs 'to the extent that it (contemplative prayer) is content to abide in the night of faith.'

The *Catechism* fittingly concludes its article on contemplative prayer with the relationship of this prayer to the paschal mystery. Without quoting John of the Cross, it uses the theme of night here three times, an appropriate allusion to the importance of John as a sublime teacher of contemplation. The concluding words from the

---

58. St Teresa of Avila, *The Interior Castle*, 7.3.6, p 439.
59. de Guibert, *The Jesuits Their Spiritual Doctrine and Practice*, 179.

Gospel of Matthew capture the profundity as well as the simplicity and availability to all of contemplation: 'We must be willing to keep watch with (him) one hour.'

In its summary of contemplative prayer (paragraph 2724) the *Catechism* draws attention to aspects of contemplation that are particularly relevant to our purpose here. The second sentence is: 'It is a gaze of faith fixed on Jesus, an attentiveness to the Word of God, a silent love.' It would be difficult to offer a better summary of the contemplation of Christ in his mysteries to which St Ignatius invites a retreatant in the Second Week of the Spiritual Exercises.

Chapter Three

Ludolph of Saxony

It has been recounted numerous times, beginning from the *Reminiscences* of Ignatius himself, how the two principal influences that led to his conversion were the two books given to him at Loyola during his five to six months of convalescence: the *Life of Jesus Christ* by Ludolph, a Carthusian of Saxony, and the *Flos Sanctorum* of the Dominican bishop, Jacopo da Varazze, Another powerful influence was the *Imitation of Christ* of Thomas à Kempis (which was attributed at that time to John Gerson). During the Second Week of the Spiritual Exercises it is the *Imitation of Christ* and the *Lives* of *the Saints* that Ignatius recommends as supplementary reading for the retreatant. Of these three, the one that concerns us here because of its initial impact on Ignatius, its influence on his relationship to the Christ of the Gospels, and on his approach to praying with the gospel mysteries is *The Life* of *Christ* by Ludolph.

The work of Ludolph, entitled *The Life* of *Jesus Christ Gathered from the Four Gospels and from Orthodox Writers*,[1] is not simply an attempted harmony of the four gospels like books of the first half of the twentieth century with the title *The Life of Christ*. It is a profound theological reflection, as suggested by the phrase 'and from Orthodox Writers'; it is the fruit of the *lectio divina* of Ludolph's monastic tradition; it is dependent upon the *Meditaciones Vite Christi* of Pseudo-Bonaventure (Johannes de Caulibus); it is at the same

---

1. *Vita Jesu Christi e Quatuor Evangeliis* et *Scriptoribus Orthodoxis Concinnata* (Paris et Romae Victor Palme, MDCCCLXV).

time a consecutive expounding of the mysteries of the life of Christ and an invitation to prayer. The 'reader' is not just to read, but to pray over what is read, an exhortation that Ignatius took profoundly to heart. Ignatius remarked in his *Reminiscences* that he read the material many times and that it was during the long hours he spent in reflection when he had put the reading aside that really significant thoughts about penance and the service of God affected him.[2] This is precisely what Ludolph had encouraged his readers to do. 'Let them beware not to pass over the life cursorily by reading it, but let them take something from it in serial fashion each day . . . and wherever they should be, let them take care to return often to it, as to a certain and holy refuge against the wicked vacillations of human weakness that continually assault the servants of God.'[3]

Ludolph begins his introduction to *The Life of Christ* with the quotation from 1 Corinthians 3:11: 'For the foundation, nobody can lay any other than the one which has already been laid, that is Jesus Christ', so that the very first word is *Fundamentum*, suggestive of Ignatius' First Principle and Foundation. Far more significant than any exaggerated claim of literary dependence here is the fact that Ludolph sets out to propose to the reader in a folio volume of almost eight hundred pages that Christ Jesus is the foundation of the whole of one's living, the same understanding that dominates the Spiritual Exercises of Ignatius.

The first sentence of Ludolph's Introduction is about Christ as our foundation. The opening words of a monumental work such as this to which Ignatius gave such careful attention must be expected to have a very special influence upon him. The second sentence of Ludolph concerns sin and our need for conversion. Immediately, as will Ignatius in the Spiritual Exercises, Ludolph focuses on our need for conversion.

In line with our suggestion of the impact on Ignatius of the very first words of the Carthusian, Ludolph's third sentence draws attention to the words of Jesus: 'Come to me, you who labour and are

---

2. J Munitiz and P Endean, *Reminiscences*, (6)14.
3. Ludolph of Saxony, *Vita Jesu Christi*, 1: 'Caveat tamen provide, ne cursorie ipsam vitam legendo transeat: sed seriatim aliquid de ea per diem accipiat . . . et ad illud, ubicumque fuerit, velut ad certum et pium refugium, contra vitiosas humanae infirmitatis varietates, continue Dei famulos impugnantes, saepe recurrere.'

heavily burdened, and I will refresh you' (Matthew 11:28). In quoting these words, he refers to Jesus quite simply as God: 'Let him listen to God,'[4] something that becomes Ignatius's constant way of writing about Jesus. With all his attention to the humanity of Christ, Ignatius also refers to him repeatedly as the 'Divine Majesty', 'God our Lord', 'the Creator', 'our Father', 'the Eternal King'. He refers to Jesus also as simply 'Almighty God' in the formula of solemn profession: 'I, N, make profession, and I promise to Almighty God, in the presence of his Virgin Mother . . .'[5] This will be reinforced by Ludolph in his first chapter, a profound theological meditation on the prologue of the gospel of John, drawing on the Fathers of the Church, especially Augustine.

Already in his first page Ludolph draws attention to a grace that will be most precious for Ignatius in the Exercises, namely, the gift of tears. The life of Christ, available to the prayerful reader, is to be desired for many reasons. 'The third is because of grace of tears, very necessary for the sinner in this vale of misery, which Christ, who is the fountain of gardens and the well of living waters, is accustomed to give sinners who cling to him.'[6]

The conversion of the sinner then leads immediately, still on Ludolph's first page, to taking up the life of Christ: 'Let him make it his care to cling most diligently to his physician and acquire familiarity with him.'[7] As Ignatius will subsequently, Ludolph urges his reader to take up and indeed 'often have recourse to the principal mysteries *(memorialia)* of Christ, namely the incarnation, the nativity, the circumcision the epiphany, the presentation in the temple, the passion, the resurrection, the ascension, the outpouring of the Holy Spirit, the coming to judge.'[8] This is to be done for a specific end. 'Let

---

4. Ludolph of Saxony, *Vita Jesu Christi*, 1: '. . . audiat Deum . . . dicentem: Venite ad me omnes qui laboratis'.
5. Ignatius of Loyola, *The Constitutions*, (527) 238.
6. Ludolph of Saxony, *Vita Jesu Christi*, 1: 'Tertio, propter gratiam lacrymarum . . . quam Christus, qui est fons hortorum, et puteus aquarum viventium, consuevit peccatoribus sibi adhaerentibus dare.'
7. Ludolph of Saxony, *Vita Jesu Christi*, 1: 'Secundo peccator (sed jam in Christo fidelis effectus, tanquam ipsi per poenitentiam reconciliatus), studeat diligentissime medico suo adhaerere, et suam familiaritatem acquirere, ejus sanctam vitam recogitando omni qua poterit devotione.'
8. Ludolph of Saxony, *Vita Jesu Christi*, 1: 'Saepius recurrat ad principalia Christi memorialia; videlicet ad incarnationem, nativitatem, circumcisionem,

him read the life of Christ in such a way that he may strive to imitate, as far as possible, his way of life' (mores).[9] Ludolph cites Bernard and Chrysostom on the end of such reading; Bernard: 'Of what profit is it to read the holy name of the Saviour in books, unless you strive to have piety in your way of life?';[10] Chrysostom: 'Let the one reading about God, who wishes to find God, hasten to live worthily of God, and let good behaviour be a torch of light before the eyes of his heart, opening the way of truth.'[11] The ends of the *lectio divina* given here by the two saints go far beyond an external or moral imitation of Christ, suggesting the last stage of the *lectio*, a contemplative union. It is the *lectio divina* that Ludolph commends to his readers: 'It is clear that spiritual reading sanctifies, and awakens the grace of the spirit. Therefore, beloved, let us attend to the Scriptures: and if nothing else let the Gospels at least become our zealous study, and let us keep them at hand.'[12]

Clearly, Ludolph, and Ignatius after him, did not have available the critical tools or language of modern scripture scholarship; still, it would be naive to dismiss either of them as simply reflecting the historicity of all that appears in the gospel accounts. Ludolph writes: 'I do not however affirm this (the gospel order of what happened) is the true and certain and required order of what was done, because such is scarcely found expressed by anyone.'[13] He then goes on immediately to say that what the reader is to be concerned about is, equivalently, salvation history. 'However, what you find in the Gospel is the history of the Word incarnate, his commands and promises, in which you

---

apparitionem, presentationem in templo, passionem, resurrectionem, ascensionem, Spiritus sancti effusionem, adventum ad judicium.'
9. Ludolph of Saxony, *Vita Jesu Christi*, 1: 'Sic etiam ipsam vitam Christi legat, ut mores ejus pro posse imitari studeat.'
10. Ludolph of Saxony, *Vita Jesu Christi*, 1: 'Quid tibi prodest, pium Salvatoris nomen lectitare in libris, nisi habere studeas pietatem in moribus?'
11. Ludolph of Saxony, *Vita Jesu Christi*, 1: 'Qui legens de Deo, vult invenire Deum, festinet vivere digne Deo ...'
12. Ludolph of Saxony, *Vita Jesu Christi*, 6: '... manifestum est quod spiritualis lectio sanctificat, et spiritus evellit gratiam. Attendamus igitur, dilecti, Scripturis: et si nihilum aliud, Evangelia saltem circumstudiosa nobis fiant, et haec prae manibus habeamus.'
13. Ludolph of Saxony, *Vita Jesu Christi*, 6: 'Non tamen affirmo quod hic sit verus ac certus ac debitus rei gestae ordo descriptus, quia talis vix ab aliquo reperitur expressus.'

have the way, the truth and the life.'[14] Ludolph considers it quite legitimate to use one's imagination to expand upon the gospel texts, as long as there is nothing involved in this activity which is contrary to faith or morals. 'For we can in many ways meditate, understand and expound about divine Scripture, as we believe to be helpful, as long as it is not against the truth of life, or justice or doctrine, that is not against faith or good behaviour.'[15] But Ludolph is also loath to introduce fictional elements from apocryphal gospels into his account of *The Life of Jesus Christ*. So, he is praised by Edmund Colledge, for instance, who contrasts the restraint of Ludolph with respect to the hidden life of Jesus with the effusive style of Pseudo-Bonaventure (Johannes de Caulibus) in the *Meditaciones Vite Christi*.[16] As Colledge put it: 'When Ludolph has nothing to report, he can draw a moral from this, but with prudence and discretion.'[17]

While it is true to claim that Ludolph, and more especially Ignatius, had a grasp of what is now called salvation history, this is not to deny that as a late medieval and a renaissance man, each of them dealt with scripture in some ways no longer acceptable to the modern Christian. In the 1919 volume of the MHSI (57) on *The Spiritual Exercises* the parallels in the texts of Ludolph and the Exercises are treated from page 57 to page 94, along with some minor parallels from the *Flos Sanctorum*: The vast majority of these parallels consist of repetition of the words of the gospel. As Gilles Cusson observed: 'Though these similarities are not very profound, they nevertheless witness to the fact that Ignatius had a prolonged contact with Ludolph's text.'[18]

'Where Ludolph (and Jacopo) depart from the gospel text, Ignatius often echoes the pious accretions. In *The Spiritual Exercises* we have, as in Ludolph, the creation of Adam 'on the plain of Damascus (SE

---

14. Ludolph of Saxony, *Vita Jesu Christi*, 6: 'In ipso autem Evangelio, reperies Verbi incarnati historiam, mandata et promissa, in quibus habes viam, veritatem et vitam'.
15. Ludolph of Saxony, *Vita Jesu Christi*, 'Nam circa divinam Scripturam meditari, intellegere, et exponere multifarie possumus prout credimus expedire, dummodo non sit contra veritatem vitae, vel justitiae, aut doctrinae, id est, non sit contra fidem, vel bonos mores.'
16. E Colledge, 'When You Pray: The Prayer of Imitation' in *The Way* 13/1 (1973): 73–74.
17. Colledge, 'When You Pray', 73.
18. G Cusson, *Biblical Theology and the Spiritual Exercises* (St Loius: Institute of Jesuit Sources, 1988), 10.

51). Similarly Ignatius repeats Ludolph's and Jacopo's addition to the Gospel account that Mary and Joseph had with them an ox and ass(SE 111); but embellishes further with the addition from his own cultural milieu, of a maid. Cusson is right in passing over such additions as 'not very profound'. They do not interfere with the substance of the contemplation even though Ignatius gives a direction in the first point of the contemplation of the nativity to see the persons: 'our Lady, St Joseph, the maid and the Child Jesus after His birth' (SE 14). Perhaps the presence of the maid was a help to someone of Ignatius's culture to be present to the mystery of the birth of the Lord. She is hardly relevant today. A somewhat different case is the first resurrection contemplation: 'The apparition of Christ our Lord to our Lady' (SE 28) which is also common to both Ludolph and the *Flos Santorum*. Unlike the case of the maid, this really is the substance of the contemplation which often proves to be of very great importance for someone doing the Spiritual Exercises, while others may not find it helpful. To make such a contemplation in no way involves any judgment about the historicity of the event. Ludolph, Jacopo and Ignatius acknowledge its non-presence in scripture, and each argues for its historicity.[19] For them historicity was far more an issue than it is for us. What we are concerned with in this contemplation is our personal presence to the relationship that exists between the risen Lord and his mother. Another non-scriptural event common to Ludolph and Ignatius is Jesus' saying good-bye to Mary as he leaves home to go on his mission. Ludolph wrote: 'Jesus says to his mother that the time has come for him to leave . . . And reverently separating himself from her and his foster father, Joseph, he came from Nazareth in Galilee . . .'[20] and Ignatius: 'After Christ our Lord had bidden farewell to his blessed Mother, he went from Nazareth . . .'[21] The contemplation of this leave-taking does not come to us a part of the inspired Word of God; it cannot be the subject of *lectio divina:* yet, it is demanded by the sheer logic of the situation, and is a human event that very readily draws the person at prayer into the presence of Jesus and Mary, and

---

19. MHSI 57, 65.
20. Ludolph of Saxony, *Vita Jesu Christi*, 101–2: 'Dicit Jesus matri suae, quia tempus est ut vadat . . . Et reverenter se licentians ab ea, et nutritio suo Joseph venit a Nazareth Galilaeae.
21. SE 273.

perhaps Joseph too, and so into contemplation. Another addition to the gospel accounts which appears in the Spiritual Exercises and in Ludolph, and in the *Meditaciones Vite Christi*, (as do most of the other 'accretions' mentioned) is the apparition to Joseph of Arimathea after the resurrection. However, Ignatius is probably more influenced here by the *Flos Sanctorum*, where it also appears, as he notes that this apparition 'may be piously believed, as is read in the Lives of the Saints.'[22]

Three remarks of Gilles Cusson concerning the meditations of Ignatius on the work of Ludolph are particularly apposite: 'When we take everything into consideration, we see that Loyola remains the scene of a radical conversion which was genuine and lasting.'[23] Secondly: 'We can also deduce . . . the directly biblical character of the spiritual world into which Ignatius was introduced, with attention and delight.'[24] This 'world' was the world of the *lectio divina*. Thirdly: 'They (the meditations at Loyola) laid the basis for a spiritual life that was solidly structured around three principal realities: the Trinity, Christ, and our condition as creatures.'[25]

Ludolph not only proposed the virtues of Christ to his reader for imitation, but even endeavoured to sketch for the reader something of the external appearance of the Son of God. Not only his virtues, but his manners, his gestures and his appearance are subjects for our meditation or contemplation. 'For he was sweet in appearance, smooth in conversation, and benign in all his ways . . . And especially 'contemplate his face, if you can imagine it, which seems more difficult to do than anything, but perhaps more delightfully rewarding.'[26] Ludolph then goes on to give quite a description of the appearance of Jesus. 'It is read in annals that exist among the Romans that Jesus Christ, who was said by the Gentiles to be a Prophet of the truth, was of noble stature, of medium height and handsome.'[27] Ludolph continues

---

22. SE2 310.
23. Cusson, *Biblical Theology and the Spiritual Exercises*, 8.
24. Cusson, *Biblical Theology and the Spiritual Exercises*, 10.
25. Cusson, *Biblical Theology and the Spiritual Exercises*, 10.
26. Ludolph of Saxony, *Vita Jesu Christi*, 5: 'Erat enim aspectu dulcis, colloquio suavis, et omni conversatione benignus. Et maxime contemplare faciem ejus, si potes eam imaginari, quod supra omne videtur difficilius sed forte reficeret jucundius.'
27. Ludolph of Saxony, *Vita Jesu Christi*, 5: 'Legitur enim in libris annalibus apud

by fancifully describing the appearance of Jesus in great detail: his brow, his hair, his beard, his hands, his arms, with constant reference to his manners. 'He was cheerful, but kept his gravity. He sometimes wept, but never laughed.'[28] The only time Ignatius has anything like this in the Spiritual Exercises is in the first point of the meditation on Two Standards. 'Consider Christ our Lord, standing in a lowly place in a great plain about the region of Jerusalem, His appearance beautiful and attractive.'[29] But this is very different from Ludolph. Ignatius is here expressly presenting a highly imaginative construct in which Christ, his appearance and his way are put in stark contrast to Satan, his appearance and his way. Ignatius is not attempting to say anything objective about what Christ our Lord may have looked like, but to present him as the one who expresses in his person the message of eternal life in all its simplicity and attractiveness.

It is true that the language of Ludolph concerning the imitation of Christ sometimes points towards the moral and the external. 'In both your exterior and interior labour remember the labours and adversities of Christ'[30] sounds like 'good, pious advice', but hardly practical for most people. They will be far more sustained by a depth of relationship with Christ than by an effort to remember in the midst of life's difficulties. 'And universally in all your words and deeds, look to Jesus as your exemplar, walking and standing, sitting and lying, eating and drinking, speaking and silent, alone and in company . . .' But this is not external imitation for its own sake; it is directed towards the interior: '. . . for from this you will love him more, and you will acquire the grace of familiarity with him, and greater trust, and you will be more perfect in every virtue.'[31] Ludolph makes no distinction here: the exterior is intimately bound up with the spiritual and

---

Romanos existentibus, quod Jesus Christus, qui dictus fuit a gentibus Propheta veritatis, staturae fuit procerae, mediocris et spectabilis.'
28. Ludolph of Saxony, *Vita Jesu Christi* 5: '. . . hilaris, servata gravitate. Aliquando flevit, sed nunquam risit.'
29. SE 144.
30. Ludolph of Saxony, *Vita Jesu Christi*, 4: 'In labore etiam exteriori et interiori, recordare laborum et adversitatum Christi.'
31. Ludolph of Saxony, *Vita Jesu Christi*, 4: 'Et universaliter in omnibus dictis et factis tuis, quasi ad exemplar respicias in Jesum, incedens et stans, sedens et jacens, comedens et bibens, loquens et tacens, solus et cum aliis: ex hoc enim magis eum diliges, et familiaritatis ejus gratiam et fiduciam majorem assequeris, et in omni virtute perfectior eris.'

contemplative. Treating of the imitation of Christ, he quotes from the first letter of John: 'The one saying they abide in him ought to walk in the same way in which he walked.'[32] The 'abiding in' is the fruit of the contemplative phase of the *lectio divina*, as is 'walking in the way' understood on the deepest level. The appeal to change one's 'mores' in imitating Christ is an appeal to a *conversio morum*, the monastic phrase for a profound readjustment of one's values and whole interior life, not merely one's moral and exterior behaviour. On this text of John, Ludolph quotes the words of the Venerable Bede, that will be echoed many times in the Spiritual Exercises: 'The one who says that they remain in Christ ought also to walk as he walked: that is, not to be ambitious for earthly things, not to seek after passing money, to flee from honours, to embrace every contempt of this world for heavenly glory, willingly to be of service to all, to injure nobody, and to suffer patiently the injuries inflicted on oneself, but to ask of the Lord pardon for those who inflict them; never to seek one's own glory, but the Creator's.'[33]

Ludolph proposes to his reader the imitation of the virtues of Christ. 'In all virtues and good ways of living always put before yourself that totally clear mirror and exemplar of all holiness, namely the life and the ways of the Son of God, our Lord Jesus Christ, who for this reason was sent to us from heaven, that he should go before us on the way of the virtues, and should give us by his example the law of life and of discipline, and should educate us to be like him; so that, just as we were created naturally his image, so we should be reformed as far as possible after we have spoiled his image in us by sin, into the likeness of his way of life through the imitation of his virtues.'[34]

---

32. Ludolph of Saxony, *Vita Jesu Christi*, 4. The quotation is from 1 Jn 2:6.
33. Ludolph of Saxony, *Vita Jesu Christi*, 4: 'Qui dicit se in Christo manere, debet sicut ille ambulavit et ipse ambulare: quod est, non ambire terrena, non caduca lucra sectari, fugere honores, omnem mundi contemptum pro caelesti gloria amplecti, libenter cunctis prodesse, injurias nulli inferre, et sibi illatas patienter sufferre, sed et inferentibus a Domino veniam postulare; nunquam suam, sed Conditoris gloriam semper quaerere.'
34. Ludolph of Saxony, *Vita Jesu Christi*, 4: 'In omnibus itaque virtutibus et bonis moribus, semper praepone tibi illud clarissimum speculum et totius sanctitatis exemplar, scilicet vitam et mores filii Dei Domini nostri Jesu Christi, qui ad hoc de coelo nobis missus est, ut praeiret nos in via virtutum, et legem vitae ac disciplinae suo nobis daret exemplo, ut erudiret nos slcut semetipsum: ut sicut ad imaginem ejus naturaliter creati sumus, ita ad morum ejus similitudinem, per

'Consider every stage of Christ's life and his virtues in each one, and like a good disciple, try to imitate him as far as possible. In both exterior and interior labour remember the labours and adversities of Christ.'[35] Christ is for us, according to Ludolph, the model of every virtue: 'Nowhere will you find such examples of and teaching on the virtues such example and teaching on the virtues of poverty, humility, charity, good behaviour, obedience, patience and the other virtues.'[36] His imitation of Christ is clearly of supreme importance for Ludolph. He concludes each of his chapters with a beautifully crafted prayer *(oratio)*. At the end of his prologue he prays: 'Lord Jesus Christ, Son of the living God, grant to me a weak and wretched sinner always to have before the eyes of my heart your life and your ways, and, as far as possible for me, to imitate them.'[37]

There is no attempt on Ludolph's part to resolve the dilemma between the Christ of history and the Christ to whom the reader is invited to be present now. He frequently has recourse to the words 'as if' to describe the praying person's presence to the mysteries of Christ; 'If you wish to draw fruit from these things, leave aside all other cares and worries, and with the whole affection of your mind, diligently, delightfully, and for a long time, make yourself so present to what was said or done by the Lord Jesus, and what is narrated of his sayings and doings, as if *(ac si)* you heard with your ears and saw with your eyes, because these things are most delightful for one pondering them with desire, and much more for one tasting them. And therefore, though many of these many things are narrated as though *(tanquam)* they happened in the past, you however should meditate on all of them as though *(tanquam)* they were happening in the present. Put before

---

    imitationem virtutum, pro nostra possibilitate reformemur, qui ejus imaginem in nobis per peccatum foedavimus.'

35. Ludolph of Saxony, *Vita Jesu Christi*, 4: 'Percurrere ergo singulas quasque aetates Christi, virtutesque ejus per singulas, et sicut fidelis discipulus pro posse studeas imitari. In labore etiam exteriori et interiori, recordare laborum et adversitatum Christi.'

36. Ludolph of Saxony, *Vita Jesu Christi*, 3: 'Nam, paupertatis, humilitatis, charitatis, mansuetudinis, obedientiae, patientiae, caeterarumque virtutum exempla et doctrinam nusquam sic invenies, sicut in vita Domini virtutum.'

37. Ludolph of Saxony, *Vita Jesu Christi*, 6: 'Domine Jesu Christe Fili Dei vivi, concede mihi fragili et misero peccatori vitam et mores tuos prae oculis cordis semper habere, et pro mea possibilitate imitari.'

your eyes past events as if (*tanquam*) present, and so you will feel more savour and delight.'[38]

Elsewhere Ludolph invites his reader to be actually present at the gospel event that is being contemplated. 'Be present at his birth, and circumcision, like (the use of *quasi* here differs from the other cases of 'as if'; the presence we are exhorted to is real; it is just the role that is an imaginary one) a good foster-father, with Joseph. Go with the Magi to Bethlehem, and adore with them the infant king. Assist the parents to carry the boy, and to present him in the temple. With the Apostles, accompany the Good Shepherd, performing his glorious miracles. Be present at his dying, with his blessed mother and John, to suffer and to grieve with him, and caressing them with a kind of holy curiosity, touch each wound of your Saviour, who has died like this for you. With Mary Magdalene seek him as he rises, until you win the grace of finding him . . .' 'And if with a pious and devout and humble heart you so seek him for a short time on earth, he will raise you to himself, sitting at the right hand of God his Father in heaven according to his promise.'[39]

When he comes to the nativity, Ludolph emphasises the reality of the presence of the contemplating person with an even starker realism: 'You, too, go now to see the Word made flesh for you, and

---

38. Ludolph of Saxony, *Vita Jesu Christi*, 4: 'Tu autem si ex his fructum sumere cupis, totis mentis affectu, diligenter, delectabiliter, et morose, omnibus aliis curis et sollicitudinibus tunc omissis, ita praesentem te exhibeas, his quae per Dominum Jesum dicta vel facta sunt, et ex his quae narrantur ac si tuis auribus audires, et oculis videres, quia suavissima sunt ex desiderio cogitanti, et multo magis gustanti. Et ideo quamvis multa ex his tanquam in praeterito facta narrantur, tu tamen omnia tanquam in praesenti fierent mediteris: quia ex hoc majorem sine dubio suaviatem gustabis. Lege ergo quae facta sunt tanquam fiant. Pone ante oculos gesta praeterita tanquam praesentia, et sic magis sapida senties et jucunda.'
39. Ludolph of Saxony, *Vita Jesu Christi*, 2: 'Adesto ejus nativitati, et circumcisioni, quasi bonus nutritius, cum Joseph. Vade cum Magis in Bethleem, et adora cum eis parvulum regem, Adjuva cum parentibus portare puerum, et praesentare in templum. Comitare cum Apostolis pium pastorem, gloriosa miracula facientem. Adesto morienti, cum beato matre ejus, et Joanne, ad compatiendum et condolendum sibi: et quadam pia curiositate palpando, tracta singula vulnera Salvatoris tui, propter te sic mortui. Quaere resurgentem cum Maria Magdalena, donec merearis invenire. . . Et si pio ac humili et devote corde sit eum modico tempore fueris prosecutus in terris, ipse te sublevabit ad se sedentem in dextera Dei Patris in coelis, secundum quod promisit.'

kneeling adore the Lord your God and his mother, and reverently greet the holy old man Joseph. Then kiss the feet of the boy Jesus, lying in the manger, and ask our Lady to offer him to you or to allow you to receive him. Take him to yourself, then, and keep him in your arms. Look intently at his face and kiss him reverently, and your heart will delight in him. You can do all this confidently, because he came to sinners for their salvation, and dealt humbly with them, and finally left himself to be their food; so, the kind Lord will patiently allow himself to be touched according to your wishes, and will put it down not to presumption, but to love. However, do all this with reverence and fear, because he is the Holy of Holies.[40] For Ignatius this reverence was paramount, so that, with regard to the sense of touch, he restricted his instructions in applying the senses in the mysteries of the annunciation and nativity to touching or kissing the places where the person stood or sat, not the persons themselves. (SE 125) The explanation for this may lie in a cultural reserve on the part of Ignatius, or in the fact that the 'model' of the retreatant that he is presenting here is of one who is not yet ready for such intimacy. Whatever the reason, all this is to be discerningly dealt with in dialogue with the director, mindful of the fact that such cultural reservations are far rarer today, and mindful also of the need for true reverence.

Ludolph makes it abundantly clear that his preferred terminology, unlike Ignatius', is to write of 'meditation' rather than 'contemplation' of the life of Christ. At the same time, the substance of contemplation is present repeatedly. 'From frequent and assiduous meditation of his life, the soul is led into his love and confidence and familiarity.'[41]

---

40. Ludolph of Saxony, *Vita Jesu Christi,* 44: 'Vade nunc et tu ad videndum Verbum pro te carnem factum, et genibus flexis adora Dominum Deum tuum et ejus matrem, ac reverenter saluta Joseph sanctum senem, Delude osculate pedes pueri Jesu, jacentis in praesepio, et roga Dominam, ut eum tibi porrigat vel accipere permittat. Accipe ergo eum ad te, et inter brachia tua retine. Intuearis faciem ejus diligenter ac reverenter deosculare, et delecteris in eo ex corde, Confidenter haec facere potes, quia pro salute eorum venit ad peccatores, et cum eis humiliter conversatus est, et tandem se eis in cibum dimisit; unde benignus Dominus patienter permittet pro tuo velle se tangi, nec imputabit praesumptioni, sed amori. Semper tamen cum reverentia et timore hoc facias, quia ipse Sanctus Sanctorum est.'
41. Ludolph of Saxony, *Vita Jesu Christi,* 3: 'Ex frequenti enim et assidua meditatione vitae ipsius, adducitur anima in ejus amorem, ac confidentiam et familiaritatem.'

He cites St Bernard on the union with Christ to which devout meditation of his life leads: 'Hence, also it is that many confessors, and also others, are found to have been and to be in their labours and trials and weaknesses, not only patient, but happy; because from devout meditation of the life and passion of Christ, their souls seem to have been and to be not in their own bodies and entrails, but in those of Christ.'[42] It is not the specific meditation engaged in that is important, but a growing capacity to be present in contemplation to the Lord. He takes the classic example of contemplation, that of Mary of Bethany sitting at the feet of Jesus, to describe the one who is devoted to reading the life of Christ. 'This life is the 'best part', namely to sit at the feet of Christ and hear his word.'[43] 'And note as a general rule, that wherever in what follows you do not find the meditations remarkable, it is sufficient for you that you should place before the eyes of your mind what is said or done by the Lord Jesus, and that you should converse with him and become familiar with him. For in this there seems to be had greater sweetness, and more efficacious devotion, and the whole fruit of these meditations seems to be that everywhere and always you should gaze upon him in his action and his way of living.'[44]

Ludolph explicitly affirms that not only is the contemplation of the life of Christ the contemplation of the creator, but it is the necessary way to arrive at that contemplation. 'This is a clear and easy path to contemplating the creator; from which no one can excuse themselves; as from the contemplation of the highest majesty, which no one can speedily reach without going through the life of our Redeemer.'[45]

---

42. Ludolph of Saxony, *Vita Jesu Christi*, 3: 'Inde quoque est quod multi confessores, et etiam alii, in laboribus, et tribulationibus, et infirmitatibus suis, non solum patientes, sed et hilares fuisse et esse reperiuntur; quia ex devota meditatione vitae et passionis Christi, eorum animae non in eorum corporibus et visceribus, sed Christi fuisse et esse videntur.'
43. Ludolph of Saxony, *Vita Jesu Christi*, 2: 'Haec vita est optima pars, sciliciet sedere ac (misprint for ad?) pedes Christi, et audire verbum ejus.'
44. Ludolph of Saxony, *Vita Jesu Christi*, 5: 'Et nota pro regula generali, quod ubicumque in sequentibus meditationibus singulares non inveneris, sufficit tibi quod rem per Dominum Jesum dictam vel gestam, ante mentis oculos ponas, et cum eo converseris, ac familiaris ei fias. Nam in hoc videtur haberi major dulcedo, et devotio efficacior, et quasi totus fructus harum meditationum consistere, ut ubique et semper intuearis eum devote in actu suo et moribus.'
45. Ludolph of Saxony, *Vita Jesu Christi*, 2: 'Haec est vita plana et facilis ad

Contemplation of the life of Christ is the beginning of any higher contemplation. 'No tongue is sufficient to praise this life, so good is it, and holy, and most worthy above all lives, since it is the beginning of any higher contemplation whatsoever.'[46] This contemplation becomes habitual, not just at a fixed daily time of prayer, and it is accomplished through the most intimate sense of touch: 'Surely the blessed Virgin, mother of mercy, of filial devotion and of grace could not spurn you or turn her eyes away from you, although you are a sinner, when she sees not just once a day, but frequently her Son whom she loves above everything remaining in your arms and between your breasts.'[47] With reference to the sense of touch, Ludolph praises the practice of kissing the ground upon which Jesus stood. 'For who could sufficiently recount how many devout persons, visiting each place with powerful devotion, kiss the places in which they heard that Jesus stood or performed some action?'[48] In the only place in the contemplations of the Second Week where he encourages the use of the sense of touch, it is this kissing of the place that Ignatius recommends. 'This is to apply the sense of touch, by embracing and kissing the place where the persons stand or are seated, always taking care to draw some fruit from this.'[49] This kind of restraint is not always present in Ludolph. In fact, to the contrary, he wrote: 'However, not only when you are awake attend to the Lord Jesus, but also when you lay your body on the bed, and place your head upon the pillow, let it be for you as with the blessed John, reclining on the bosom of Jesus: and so reclining on

---

    contemplandum creatorem; de qua nullus excusare se potest; sicut de contemplatione summae majestatis, ad quam nemo potest raptim pertingere, nisi proficiendo per istam vitam nostri redemptoris.'

46. Ludolph of Saxony, *Vita Jesu Christi*, 2: 'Hanc vitam nulla lingua laudare sufficit, adeo bona est, et sancta, et super omnes vitas dignissima, cum sit initium cuiuslibet altioris contemplationis.'
47. Ludolph of Saxony, *Vita Jesu Christi*, 2: 'Numquid beata Virgo, mater misericordiae, pietatis et gratiae poterit te despicere, vel oculos suos a te avertere, quamvis sis peccator, quando non solum semel in die viderit, sed et frequenter Filium suum quem super omnia diligit, in brachiis tuis et inter ubera tua commorantem?'
48. Ludolph of Saxony, *Vita Jesu Christi*, 5: 'Quis enim enarrare sufficit, quot devoti, discurrentes per loca singula, in vehementi spiritu, osculantur terram, amplectuntur loca in quibus dulcem Jesum, vel stetisse, vel aliquid egisse audierunt?'
49. SE 125.

the bosom of Jesus, suck his breasts, and 'you will sleep and rest in peace (Ps 4:9).'[50] The silence of Ignatius about such intimacy cannot be interpreted as a desire on his part to exclude it; rather, in the brief notes he gives to the director in the book of *The Spiritual Exercises* he does not wish to encourage any flight of fancy, but always to leave room for the Creator to deal directly with the creature.[51]

Ignatius's reading and meditation of the text of Ludolph influenced not only his insertion into the world of *lectio divina* with its presence to the person of Christ in his mysteries, and presence to Mary and the other figures of the gospel, but led him into a profound relationship with the Trinity, which would be shortly manifest in his prayer life at Manresa. After the very dense prologue *(proemium)*, which is the main text we have looked, at above, the first chapter of *The Life of Christ* begins with a great flourish: 'The brilliant and outstanding work entitled *The Life of Christ*, most elaborately edited by Ludolph the Saxon, of the sacred order of Carthusians, a man of great learning and devotion: not indeed drawn from the apocrypha about the infancy of the Saviour, but entirely gathered from the sacred gospel, and the sacred Doctors of holy Church.'[52] The point about the hyperbole of this title is that it is the introduction to the very solemn 'foundation' of the whole work, the first chapter's meditation 'Concerning the divine and eternal generation of Christ'. The resounding splendour of its conclusion, so profound in its theology, could not fail to capture the mind and heart of Ignatius: 'Certainly, when you hear in what has gone before that the Son was begotten of God the Father; be careful that no weak carnal image comes to the eyes of your mind, but rather with the vision of the dove and the eagle simply believe, and profoundly contemplate that from that light, 'at the same time

---

50. Ludolph of Saxony, *Vita Jesu Christi*, 4: 'Non solum autem vigilans Domino Jesu intendas, sed et cum corpus strato recolligis, et caput reclinatorio imponis, sit tibi quasi cum beato Joanne apostolo super pectus Jesu recumbens: sicque recumbens super pectus Jesu suge ubera ejus, et in pace in idipsum dormies et requiesces. (Ps 4:9).'
51. SE 15, 16.
52. Ludolph of Saxony, *Vita Jesu Christi*, 7: 'Opus praeclarum atque insigne cujus titulus extat Vitae Christi a magnae litteraturae devotionisque viro Ludopho Saxone, sacri Carthusiensium Ordinis, elaboratissime editum: non quidem ab apocryphis de infantia Salvatoris extractum; sed ex serie sacri Evangelii, sacrorumque Doctorum sanctae Ecclesiae ex toto collectum.'

immense and totally simple, absolutely shining and most hidden, arises co-eternal, co-equal and consubstantial splendour, who is the highest virtue and wisdom, and in whom the Father disposed all things from eternity: *Through whom he created the world* (Heb1:2), and governs and orders that creation to his glory partly through nature; partly through grace, partly through justice, partly through mercy; in order that, in this way, there is nothing in this, world that remains unordered.'[53]

After his meditations upon this document and the contemplation of the life of Christ it inspired, Ignatius went on his way to Manresa with an image of the Christ of the gospels as God, as Creator, as the Divine Majesty, and with the beginnings of an involvement with the life of the Trinity that would lead to the content of his mystical experiences during his time at Manresa, and would flow over into the writing of the Spiritual Exercises.

What principally concerns our purpose here is the introduction that Ignatius had received from his many hours spent with Ludolph's work into the tradition of contemplation of the mysteries of the life of Christ coming from the *lectio divina*. We look now at the importance of the *lectio* for the understanding of contemplation in the Second Week of the Spiritual Exercises.

Lectio Divina

Of the many influences on the conversion of Ignatius of Loyola, the reading of Ludolph of Saxony's *Life of Christ* and Jacopo da Varazze's *Flos Sanctorum*, and the *Imitation of Christ* of Thomas à Kempis, there can be no doubt that the major one was the reading, pondering and praying over Ludolph's *Life of Christ*. Nor is there any doubt that Ludolph's work was an exposition of the fruit of the *lectio divina*, the

---

53. Ludolph of Saxony, *Vita Jesu Christi*, 9: 'Sane cum audis in praemissis Filium ex Deo Patre genitum, cave ne mentis tuae oculis infirmum aliquid carnalis cogitationis occurrat, quin potius columbino et aquilino intuitu simpliciter crede, ac perspicaciter contemplare quod ab illa luce simul immensa et simplicissima, fulgentissima et simul arcana, coaeternus, coaequalis, et consubstantialis splendor exoritur, qui est virtus summa et sapientia, et in quo omnia Pater disposuit ab aeterno: *Per quem fecit secula* (Hebr 1:2), factaque gubernat et ordinat ad gloriam suam, partim per naturam, partim per gratiam, partim per justitiam, partim per misericordiam; ut nihil ita in hoc mundo inordinatum relinquat.'

tradition to which he belonged and into which he invited his readers. The climax of the *lectio* was the contemplation expounded above from the 'Introduction' to *The Life of Christ*. It led the readers to be present to the mysteries of the gospel and the person of Christ. This contemplation was to be practised assiduously and continually. The Christ whom Ludolph's readers contemplated was the Word-made-flesh, the Christ of the great meditation in Ludolph's first chapter on the prologue of John's Gospel. Ignatius fell in love with the person of Christ, and with his mother, Mary, so much so that 'he set to writing a book with great industry *(this had about* three hundred *'leaves, all written in quarto)* for now he was beginning to get up a bit around the house. The words of Christ were in red ink, those of Our Lady in blue ink. The paper was glazed and ruled, and it was with very good lettering, because he was a good scribe.'[54] Since contemplation of the mysteries of the life of Christ, as Ignatius presents it in the Second Week of the Spiritual Exercises, is the fruit of the *lectio divina* of a text which was itself the outcome of *lectio divina*, a proper understanding of the contemplations of the Second Week of the Exercises clearly demands an appreciation of the link between those contemplations and the *lectio divina* on which they were based.

The link between *lectio divina* and the contemplations of the Second Week has been emphasised by several recent writers. In an article entitled 'Application of the Senses' in *The Way Supplement* 27 (Spring 1976) James Walsh was so occupied with commenting on Ludolph and the *lectio divina* that at the end of the article he confessed: 'I have chosen to treat in general, rather than specifically, of the use of the senses in Ignatian contemplation, and I am well aware of having said nothing at all directly of 'Application of the Senses' in its strict, Ignatian sense: the last exercise of every day during the second, third and fourth weeks, and the analogous 'Meditation on hell' which is the concluding exercise of each day of the first week.'[55] For Walsh *the lectio* leads to a presence to what is taking place between Christ and the praying person now: 'whereby, in faith-collaboration with the action of the holy Spirit, the devout Christian in his reading *(Lege . . . quae facta sunt)* and affective rumination *(cogitando ex desiderio)* of the word of scripture becomes present, in every fibre of his being, to what

---

54. J Munitiz and P Endean, *Reminiscences,* (11) 16.
55. J Walsh, 'Application of the Senses' in *The Way Supplement* 27, 68.

the Lord Jesus has said and done in history, but is saying and doing again and again in the graced contemplative memory *(praesentem te exhibeas—omnia tanquam in praesenti . . . Lege . . . quae facta sunt tanquam fiant . . . pone ante oculos gesta, praeterita tanquam praesentia).*[56] The beginnings of an answer to the question of the contemporaneity of the gospel mystery for the praying person have already been outlined in what was written above concerning 'natural contemplation' and will be examined later in greater depth. Writing of the contemplation of the gospel mysteries, Walsh refers to the part played by the imagination' in the whole contemplative process *(lectio divina).*[57] For him this contemplation and *lectio divina* are one and the same.

Another who saw the intimate link between *lectio divina* and contemplation in the Spiritual Exercises was David Stanley. He commenced an article in by declaring that it was precisely this link that led him to make a closer examination of the *lectio.*[58] Stanley goes on to quote the decree on Prayer of the Thirty-first General Congregation of the Society of Jesus (1966):

> In each of us, as the whole tradition of the Church attests; Holy Scripture becomes our saving word only when heard in prayer that leads to a submission of faith. *Lectio divina*, a practice dating back to the earliest days of religious life in the Church, supposes that the reader surrenders to God who is speaking and granting him a change of heart under the action of the two-edged sword of Scripture continually challenging to conversion. Truly we can expect from prayerful reading of' Scripture a renewal of our ministry of' the word and of the Spiritual Exercises, both of which derive their vigour from our familiarity with the Gospel.[59]

---

56. Walsh, 'Application of the Senses', 60; the bracketed Latin is the quotation from Ludolph of Saxony's *Vita Jesu Christi*, which Walsh was citing.
57. Walsh, 'Application of the Senses', 66.
58. 'A Suggested Approach to *Lectio Divina*' in *The American Benedictine Review* 23 (1972). This article was reprinted as an Appendix to *'I encountered God!' The Spiritual Exercises With the Gospel of St John* (St Loius: Institute of Jesuit Sources, 1986).
59. *Documents of the 31st and 32nd General Congregations of the Society of Jesus* (St Loius: Institute of Jesuit Sources, 1977), 139–140.

This was the first time a General Congregation had appealed to a monastic practice outside the traditional Jesuit patterns of prayer', and it was particularly timely in response to the call of *Verbum Domini* no 25, of the Second Vatican Council. The General Congregation encouraged the participation by Jesuits in the very fruitful practice of *lectio divina* common among religious of the second half of the twentieth century. In *A Modern Scriptural Approach to the Spiritual Exercises*, the same author, Stanley, like James Walsh, identifies *lectio divina* and Ignatius' contemplation of the gospel mysteries:

> By means of what St Benedict in the rule has *called lectio divina*, or Ignatius in the *Exercises* calls *contemplation*, I attempt to live my 'spiritual life' that is, existence under the divine domination of the Holy Spirit, by integrating myself into this conversation or dialogue. My purpose is to become involved personally, with the grace of God, in this sacred history, because I believe that I have a part to *play* in this history.[60]

Stanley parallels *lectio divina* and the contemplation of the mysteries of Christ in terms of their end. Arguing from the basic statement of the Dogmatic Constitution on Divine Revelation of Vatican II, *Verbum Domini*, No 11: 'Therefore, since everything asserted by the inspired authors or sacred writers must be held to be asserted by the Holy Spirit, it follows that the books of Scripture must be acknowledged as teaching firmly, faithfully, and without error that truth which God wanted put into the sacred writings for the sake of our salvation,'[61] he shows that the purpose of both the *lectio* and the contemplations is an opening to the truth present to us in the person of Christ. 'Why then was the Bible written? In order to make available to the man of faith that truth, which is not historical truth, nor scientific truth, nor philosophical truth, by the assimilation of which alone man can be saved.'[62] 'The goal of *lectio divina* is actually what St Ignatius has called

---

60. D Stanley, *A Modern Scriptural Approach* to *the Spiritual Exercises* (Chicago: Institute of Jesuit Sources, 1967), 85.
61. W Abbott (General Editor), *The Documents* of *Vatican II* (London: Geoffrey Chapman, 1972),119.
62. D Stanley, 'A Suggested Approach to *Lectio Divina*', in *The American Benedictine Review* 23 (1972): 445.

'an interior knowledge of our Lord, who has become man *for me,* that I may love him more and follow him more closely.'[63]

In an article entitled: 'Lectio Vere Divina: St Bernard and the Bible' in *Monastic Studies* 3 (1965), Peter Nober treated of the *lectio divina* in Bernard without specific reference to Ignatius. But, again, some of his remarks point to the intimate link between the *lectio* and contemplation of the mysteries of Christ for Ignatius: 'Further yet, the sacred text itself is a profound mystery of charity: after it united God with the sacred author, who together conceived it in living union, it now unites Bernard who reads it and God in a living union which is truly spiritual.'[64] Not that the literal meaning of scripture is unimportant for the practitioners of *lectio divina*. The first step in the process, the *lectio,* or reading, was often seen to involve careful study of the text.

> There were humanists among St Benedict's disciples, for example at the time of Charlemagne and his successors, to whom we owe the preservation of many ancient manuscripts. But already there was opposition between those who were in favour of a learned *lectio divine* and those, who practised a purely spiritual and 'claustral' form of it. The reformers of Citeaux only admitted a *lectio* which was truly sacred *(divina)* and spiritual, through which their piety could find its roots in living and mystical contemplation. The Victorines, on the other hand, wanted to be scholars and monks—and this certainly had a great influence on the history of exegesis.[65]

Naber appreciates that the literal meaning of scripture is important, but for Bernard it is not the primary effect of the inspiration of the sacred text: 'It follows from this point of view that 'inerrancy, (which, after all, is a quality shared by conciliar decrees as well) does not hold the first place among the effects of inspiration for Bernard. In so far as they are inspired, the words of Scripture are unique and incomparable instruments for bringing about a living union between God and Bernard, they are the atmosphere in which that generous and

---

63. D Stanley, 'A Suggested Approach to *Lectio Divina*', 455.
64. P Nober, 'Lectio Vere Divina: St Bernard and the Bible', in *Monastic Studies* 3 (1965): 169.
65. Nober, 'Lectio Vere Divina', 171.

intimate contact of each with the other can be obtained.'[66] Not that the *lectio divina* was used by Bernard in a way that was fundamentalist. He was both dependent on the Fathers of the Church, and original his use of Scripture:

> 'This dependence and originality can be seen most clearly in his use of Scripture, to which he goes constantly, just as they did. For none of the Fathers before him had of such set purpose and systematically sought in the Scriptures that mystical union with God, intimate and immediate, that Bernard sought. And so we are told in his *Life* that 'whatever glimpses of the truth and power of God he caught in them seemed to him to spring from a source within him rather than from the commentaries he read. Yet in his humility Bernard always goes back to the Fathers to sift the insights and glimpses received from his meditations on the sacred text, checking them against solid and universally accepted teaching.'[67]

In recent years Francesco Rossi de Gasperis has made a special study of of *lectio divina* in its connection with the Ignatian Exercises.[68] He declared that he himself experienced a real conversion from using the Bible in the Spiritual Exercises to inserting the Exercises into the Bible:

> Moving from this way of 'using the Bible in the Exercises' to another way of 'inserting the Exercises in the Bible' has been for me a real conversion, with a new horizon, involving an about-face, coming out of the old by repudiating the characteristic features, beginning a new sequence that can keep revealing ever greater depth and breadth and wealth.[69]

---

66. Nober, 'Lectio Vere Divina', 169.
67. Nober, 'Lectio Vere Divina', 178. The quotation from the Life of St Bernard is from JP Migne, *Patrologia Latina* (Paris, 1854), 185, 241 A.
68. Among the writings of Rossi de Gasperis on this subject are: *Bibbia ed Esercizi Spirituali: La Bibbia negli Esercizi Spirituali e gli Esercizi Spirituali nella Bibbia* (Rome: Pontifical Gregorian University, 1981/2); 'Lectio Divina in the Exercises', in *The Word of God in the Spiritual Exercises* (Centrum Ignatianum Spiritualitatis, Rome, 1979); 'The Spiritual Exercises as Profound Entry into the Journey of Faith', in *The Ministry of the Exercises in the Society Today* (Rome: Centrum Ignatianum Spiritualitatis, 1984); *Reading the Bible as a Spiritual Exercise* (Rome: Centrum Ignatianum Spiritualitatis, 1993).
69. de Gasperis, *Reading the Bible as a Spiritual Exercise*, 13.

This led him to declare: 'When we, as converted theologians and retreat-givers, carefully study both the Bible and the Ignatian Exercises, we discover that between them there is more than a certain relationship There is, indeed, an objective and dynamic, isomorphic parallelism which is commanded by their identical goal.'[70] Like Stanley and Nober, Rossi de Gasperis has both a profound respect for the literal and objective meaning of the scriptural text and for the spiritual and subjective meaning that is important for the praying person.

> 'Lectio Divina' is a way of reading the Scripture 'in the Spirit', i.e. *in the same Spirit in which it was written*. It does not ignore the historical, literary, archaeological, psychological, sociological, structural, cultural . . . interest of the Bible, but it explicitly looks for something else . . . 'Lectio Divina' goes beyond the 'scientific' objectivity of human sciences, in order to teach the much more real subjectivity of God's Word and Action, aiming at provoking the *subjectivity* of the reader, who is called to conversion by God's Word and Spirit.'[71]

Central to the thesis of Rossi de Gasperis of a permanent irreversible conversion of the praying person through exposure to the whole Word of God is the need to take up the reading of the whole of theScripture. '"Lectio Divina' supposes a *continuous, intense reading (lectio continua) of the whole Bible,* one book after another and each book read *in full.* Each book, each section of it, must be read, studied and meditated, understood and enjoyed, *appealing* to *the whole context* of *the biblical revelation, Old and New Testament.*'[72] This leads to the devising of creative ways of giving the Spiritual Exercises which allow for prolonged breaks in the making of the thirty-day retreat in order to assimilate the whole of the Bible through *lectio divina* and to achieve the insertion of the Exercises into the Bible, rather than to use the Bible in the Exercises. Praiseworthy though the motivation for such a scheme is, it is scarcely practicable, nor is it necessary in order to achieve the stated twofold end of Ignatius in writing *The Spiritual Exercises,* namely conversion of heart and seeking and finding the

---

70. de Gasperis, *Reading the Bible* as a *Spiritual Exercise,* 20.
71. de Gasperis, *Reading the Bible* as a *Spiritual Exercise,* 21–2.
72. de Gasperis, *Reading the Bible* as a *Spiritual Exercise,* 14.

will of God for the living of one's life. Rossi de Gasperis is not alone among scripture scholars since the Second Vatican Council calling for more respect for scripture in making use of it in the giving of the Spiritual Exercises. While this respect demands that a retreat giver make every effort to be as well informed as possible about the modern understanding of scripture, it does not require a reluctance to select for prayer particular texts which may be specially suited to the needs of a particular retreatant here and now. The practice of the Church itself in selecting the texts to be used in the Liturgy and grouping them thematically as well as to some extent continuously provides some justification for a prudent selectivity.

In the second Annotation of the *Spiritual Exercises* St Ignatius wrote: 'The person who gives to another the way and order of meditating or contemplating ought to relate faithfully the history of such contemplation or meditation, going over the points only with a brief or summary explanation, in order that the person who is contemplating may take the solid foundation of the history, and go over it and reflect on it for himself.'[73] The Annotation is clearly of great importance in the mind of Ignatius, given the prominent position he assigns to it in the text. The 'history' he is concerned with here has very little to do with our modern concept of history. Nor is Ignatius concerned with the historicity of the scripture when the matter of the contemplation is scriptural. He applies the same word 'history' to meditations based on purely mental constructs, those of the 'Two Standards' (SE 137) and 'Three Classes of Men' (SE 150). What Ignatius was concerned with, though not, of course, knowing the term, was 'salvation history' rather than history as understood in its modern sense. For him the history of the incarnation and of the nativity does not consist in the mere facts that occurred, but in the whole scope and plan of God's salvation in Christ for all of mankind, and specifically in the Spiritual Exercises for the individual involved in making them. He always directs attention to the concrete. God has acted in and throughout history, and continues to act in the life of the retreatant. Ignatius gives a 'history' for his great meditation of Two Standards: 'First Prelude. This is the history. Here it will be that Christ calls and wants all beneath His standard, and Lucifer, on the other hand, wants all under his' (SE 137). Michael

---

73. SE 2.

Ivens, reflecting on this 'history' wrote: '... history refers not to the past but to a faith-vision of the here-and-now world; "history" not in the sense of particular events but of an ongoing process.'[74]

The Spiritual Exercises are always concerned with the discernment of this action of God in the life of the individual retreatant, which is a particular application of the whole divine plan of creation and of redemption in Christ. The meditations on sin in the First Week are not concerned with sin in the abstract, but with the history of three particular personal sins (of the angels, of Adam, of one particular sinner who is damned) in order to throw light upon the personal history of the retreatant, and, more importantly, on the history of God's plan of salvation in Christ, which has been revealed and is now being revealed in the life of this particular retreatant here and now. As Pietro Schiavone put it:

> The Exercises do not have as their direct object defects, vices or virtues. They propose the history of salvation, totally founded on the incarnate Word, who, born of the Virgin Mary, after having shared our life in every way, in poverty, in justice, in care for the marginalised ... dies, rises and ascends to heaven to send, together with the Father, the Holy Spirit. Moreover, when there is no historical event, as in the meditation on sins, everything continues to focus on the figure of the Saviour, so that we have a 'concentration' of the history of salvation.[75]

From the beginnings of religious life in the Church those who practised it devoted themselves to the Word of God. The function of the scripture was to form the whole person. One's relationship with God, being seen as the key element in this formation, the occupation with the scripture was always designed to lead to prayer, and, if it was given, also to contemplation. But the importance of the study of

---

74. M Ivens, *Understanding the Spiritual Excercises*, 107.
75. P Schiavone, *S. Ignazio de Loyola Esercizi Spirituali*, 67: 'Gli EE non hanno per oggetto diretto difetti, vizi, virtu ... Propongono la storia della salvezza, tutta imperniata sul Verbo incarnate, che, nato della Vergine Madre, dopo avere condiviso la nostra vita in tutto, in poverta, giustizia, attenzione agli emarginat ... muore, risorge e ascende al cielo per inviare, insieme al Padre, lo Spirito Samto. Anche quando non si ha alcun evento storico, come nella meditazione dei peccati, tutto continua a gravitare sulla figura del Salvatore, si ha, anzi, una 'concentrazione' di storia di salvezza.'

the text was not neglected. Proper respect for the word of God has always demanded the making of every effort possible to determine the objective meaning of the text. Jean Leclercq put it this way: '*Lectio divina* is a precise reading which, in the first place, is connected to the literal sense of the Bible. Every allegorical interpretation presupposes the historical sense, at least in so far as the knowledge then available allowed it to be established. In this minute examination of the text use is made of all the resources of philology, especially through etymologies; passages are always elucidated by their context. Nothing must remain vague or imprecise'.[76]

The classic steps in the lectio divina: *lectio* (reading), *meditatio* (meditation), *oratio* (prayer) and *contemplatio* (contemplation) were sometimes enlarged to include after *lectio*, *cogitatio* (reflection) and *studium* (study). The role of the spoken word in the liturgy was also central to the life of the monk, so that one who had been truly formed by the *lectio divina* would speak 'divine words' from the heart. The formation effected by the *lectio* expressed itself in the manner of speaking of the one so formed. The abbot John of Saint-Arnulf wrote about Blessed John of Gorze: 'With hushed murmuring after the fashion of the bee, he would continuously repeat the psalms.'[77] This thought is often expressed through the other imagery so helpful for appreciating the *lectio divine,* that of food or nourishment. One formed in the school of *lectio divina* is like a ruminant, chewing its cud, continually giving expression through the lips to the nourishment that has been received. So, Peter the Venerable wrote of the holy brother Benedict that as he was dying 'without rest his lips ruminated the sacred words.'[78] St Caesarius of Arles (470–542) 'speaks already of *rumination.* Curiously, he attaches its purifying virtue to the fact

---

76. J Leclercq, 'La Lecture Divine', in *La Maison-Dieu* 5 (1946): 22: 'Lecture précise, d'abord, la *lectio divina* s'attache au sens literal de la Bible. Toute interpretation allegorique présuppose le sens historique, de moins tel que les connaissances dont on disposait alors permettaient de l'établir. Dans cet examen minitieux de la lettre, on fait appel à toutes les resources de la philologie, specialement sous les formes des etymologies: on éclaire toujours un passage par son context. Rien ne doit rester vague, imprécis.'
77. JP Migne, *Patrologia Latina* (Paris, 1853), 137, 280: 'in morem apis psalmos tacito murmure continue revolvendo'
78. JP Migne, *Patroloqie Latina* (Paris, 1854), 189, 887: 'os sine requie sacra verba ruminans'.

that 'pure' animals are ruminants. More profoundly rumination is the property characteristic of those who reflect on what they hear and so retain it in *ore cordis* (the mouth of the heart). Gregory (540–604) will also speak of *ruminatio*, of *masticatio*.[79] This notion of 'rumination' of the Word of the Lord goes right back to the Epistle of Barnabas, of the second century.[80]

The classical work on the *lectio divina* is the brief letter of Guigo II, the ninth prior of the Grande Chartreuse, who died in 1188. This short work, entitled '*A Letter on the Interior Life*', and also known as the *Scala Claustralium* (the Ladder of Monks) was addressed by Guigo to a brother religious, by the name of Gervase. The English translation of Edmund Colledge and James Walsh has been made available.[81] Already, in that year, 1965, the same journal had already published an extract from the writings of Guigo in which he dealt with the metaphor of eating as applied to the Word of God.[82]

Guigo sees 'The Ladder of Monks' as analogous to Jacob's ladder (Gen 28:12): 'These (the four stages of reading, meditation, prayer and contemplation) make a ladder for monks by which they rise from earth to heaven: its lower end rests upon earth, but its top pierces the clouds and touches heavenly secrets.'[83] The first rung, reading, is not for Guigo any kind of reading but is 'the careful study of the scriptures, concentrating all one's powers on it.'[84] Drawing on the very apposite imagery of eating, Guigo declares: 'Reading as it were puts food whole into the mouth, meditation chews it and breaks it up, prayer extracts its flavour, contemplation is the sweetness itself which gladdens and refreshes.'[85] Guigo presents to his brother, Gervase, an example of *lectio divina*, using the short text of scripture: 'Blessed are

---

79. The article 'Lecture Divine et Lecture Spirituelle' in *Dictionnaire de Spiritualité* Tome IX (Beauchesne, Paris, 1976), col 471: 'Cesaire d'Arles parle-t-il deja de rumination: curieusement, il en rattache la vertu purifiante au fait que les animaux 'purs' sont les ruminants (Sermons 88,6; 99, 3; 114,6; 117,6; 124,6; 161,2); plus profondement, la rumination est le propre de ceux qui réflechlssent sur ce qu'ils ont entendu et ainsi le retiennent in *ore cordis* (69,5; 99,3). Gregoire parlera lui aussi de *ruminatio*, de *masticatio*.'
80. F Ruppert, 'Meditatio–Ruminatio' in *Collectanea Cisterciana*, 39 (1977): 82.
81. *The Way*, 5/4 (October, 1965): 333–342.
82. *The Way* 5/2 (April 1965), pp 160-162.
83. Guigo II, 'A Letter on the Interior Life', in *The Way* 5/4 (October 1965), p 334.
84. Guigo II, 'A Letter on the Interior Life', 334.
85. Guigo II, 'A Letter on the Interior Life', 334.

the pure in heart, for they shall see God.' (Mtt 5:8). Though it is a small text, it is one that promises great sweetness, like a grape that is put into the mouth. This is the result of reading the text. Guigo then proposes the function of meditation, which is a further step along the way that leads to contemplation:

> When the soul is set alight by this kindling, and when its flames are fanned by these desires, it receives a first intimation of the sweetness, not yet by tasting but through its sense of smell, when the alabaster box is broken (cf Mk 14:3); and from this it deduces how sweet it would be to know by experience that purity which meditation has shown it to be so full of joy. But what is it to do? It is consumed with longing, yet it can find no means of its own to have what it longs for; the more it searches, the more it thirsts. As long as it is meditating, so long is it suffering, because it does not feel that sweetness which, as meditation shows, belongs to purity of heart, but which it does not give.[86]

What is a person to do, when they find themselves in this situation of being unable to attain what they suspect is still hidden from them? The answer is clearly to turn to the prayer of petition: 'So the soul, seeing that by itself it cannot attain to that sweetness of knowing and feeling for which it longs, and that the more the heart abases itself, the more God is exalted, humbles itself and betakes itself to prayer saying: Lord, you are not seen except by the pure of heart: I seek by reading and meditating what is true purity of heart and how it may be had, so that with its help I may know you, if only a little.'[87]

In answer to such prayer the gift of contemplation may well be received.

> So the soul by such burning words inflames its own desire, makes known its state, and by such spells it seeks to call its spouse. But the Lord, whose eyes are upon the just, and whose ears can catch not only the words (cf Ps 33:16; 1 Pet 3:12), but the very meaning of their prayers, does not wait until the longing soul has had its say, but breaks in upon the middle of its prayer, runs to meet it in all haste, sprinkled with sweet

---

86. Guigo II, 'A Letter on the Interior Life', 335.
87. Guigo II, 'A Letter on the Interior Life', 336.

heavenly dew, anointed with the most precious perfumes; and he restores the weary soul, he slakes its thirst, he feeds its hunger, he makes the soul forget all earthly things: by making it die to itself he gives it new life in a wonderful way, and making it drunk he brings it back to its true senses.[88]

This is the same language that Ignatius uses in the Spiritual Exercises when he writes about spiritual consolation: 'I call it consolation when an interior movement is aroused in the soul, by which it is inflamed with love of its Creator and Lord, and as a consequence, can love no creature on the face of the earth for its own sake, but only in the Creator of them all.'[89]

Ignatius concludes this paragraph on consolation with more words reminiscent of Guigo: 'Finally, I call consolation every increase of faith, hope and love, and all interior joy that invites and attracts to what is' heavenly and to the salvation of one's own soul by filling it with peace and quiet in its Creator and Lord.' There is for Ignatius a close link between consolation and contemplation. This is why he calls repetitions that are made after meditation no longer meditation, but contemplation. One returns in contemplation to the gift of consolation that has been received.[90] Ivens brings out the link between repetition and contemplation: 'The Ignatian prayer of repetition is to be understood in relation to two inseparable processes: the gradual assimilation of the given material, and the development of prayer towards the simple, receptive and personal quality of contemplation.'[91] The stuff of repetition, of course, is not only consolation or 'greater spiritual appreciation', but also desolation, in order to be freed from it, to grow through it, and to allow the Lord to be Lord of all one's interior movements, even those which in their initial impetus are leading away from Him.

Like Ignatius, Guigo is well aware that the effect of the fourth rung of the ladder, the contemplation he has just described is what is classically termed 'consolation'. William Peters: made this same point; 'So, contemplation is essentially and closely linked with consolation,

---

88. Guigo II, 'A Letter on the Interior Life', 336-337.
89. SE 316.
90. SE 62.
91. M Ivens, *Understanding the Spiritual Exercises*, 58.

for consolation is any interior movement in the soul by which it is inflamed with love or stirred by sorrow, or joy, in greater faith, hope and charity (SE 316). This link is so close that as soon as there is true consolation, meditation turns into contemplation, even though the subject matter remains the same.'[92] Like Ignatius, Guigo too is well aware that spiritual consolation does not always consist is pleasant feelings. Ignatius had written in the description of consolation quoted above: 'It is likewise consolation when one sheds tears that move to the love of God, whether it be because of sorrow for sins, or because of the sufferings of Christ our Lord, or for any other reason that is immediately directed to the praise and service of God.' Guigo confronts the problem presented by this consolation which involves 'negative' feelings: 'Can it be that the heralds and witnesses of this consolation and joy are sighs and tears? If it is so, then the word consolation is being used in a completely new sense, the reverse of its ordinary connotation. What has consolation in common with sighs, joy with tears, if indeed these are to be called tears and not rather an abundance of spiritual dew, poured out from above and overflowing, an outward purification as a sign of inward cleansing?'[93]

For Guigo there is an ineffability about the gift of contemplation: 'But why do we give this public utterance to what should be said in secret? Why do we try to express in everyday language affections which no language can describe? Those who have not known such things do not understand them, for they could learn more clearly of them only from the book of experience where God's grace is itself the teacher (cf 1 Jn 2:27). Otherwise it is of no use for the reader to search in earthly books: there is little sweetness in the study of the literal sense, unless there be a commentary, which is found in the heart, to reveal the inward sense.'[94]

Guigo strongly identifies contemplation and consolation, and uses the passing nature of the experience of contemplation to give the classical teaching about the fleeting nature of consolation. But, though the experience may be passing, the reality of what is given in contemplation remains: 'He goes, it is true, for the visitation ends, and with it the sweetness of contemplation; but yet he stays, for he

---

92. W Peters, *The Spiritual Exercises*, 38.
93. Guigo II, 'A Letter on the Interior Life', 337.
94. Guigo II, 'A Letter on the Interior Life', 337.

guides us, he gives us his grace, he joins us to himself.'[95] As a true contemplative, Guigo is well aware of the futility of attempting to capture the reality of contemplation in words, so he is self-critical, and repeats the criticism, that he is going on too long about the gift of contemplation: 'I am afraid that I have talked too long of this to you, but I have been compelled to it by the abundance and the sweetness of my material: I have not deliberately drawn it out, but its very sweetness has drawn it out of me against my will.'[96] So, Guigo recapitulates: 'Reading comes first, and is as it were the foundation; it provides the subject matter which we must use for meditation. Meditation considers more carefully what is to be sought after; it digs (cf Prov 2:4), as it were, for treasure which it finds (cf Mt 13:44) and reveals, but since it is not in meditation's power to seize upon the treasure, it directs us to prayer. Prayer lifts itself up to God with all its strength, and begs for the treasure which it longs for, which is the sweetness of contemplation. Contemplation when it comes rewards the labours of the other three: it inebriates the thirsting soul with the dew of heavenly sweetness. Reading is an exercise of the outward senses, meditation is concerned with the inward understanding, prayer is concerned with desire, contemplation outstrips every faculty.'[97] The four rungs of the *lectio* lead Guigo to add a fourth to the classical division according to 'the three ways' of beginners, proficients and the perfect. Contemplation, he declares, belongs to the blessed.

The link between reading, meditation, prayer and contemplation must always be respected: '... the first degrees are of little use without the last, whilst the last can never or hardly ever be won without the first.'[98] '... reading without meditation is sterile, meditation without reading is liable to error, prayer without meditation is lukewarm, meditation without prayer is unfruitful: prayer when it is fervent wins contemplation, but to obtain it without prayer would be rare, even miraculous.'[99] But Guigo does go on to declare that God acts like a prodigal father, 'when he enters where he has not been

---

95. Guigo II, 'A Letter on the Interior Life', 338.
96. Guigo II, 'A Letter on the Interior Life', 339.
97. Guigo II, 'A Letter on the Interior Life', 339.
98. Guigo II, 'A Letter on the Interior Life', 339.
99. Guigo II, 'A Letter on the Interior Life', 340.

invited, when he dwells in the soul which has not sought him.'[100] The gift of contemplation is not something to be possessed, once for all, but needs to be carefully nurtured:

> But let such a man beware lest after this contemplation, in which he was lifted up to the very heavens, he plunge violently into the depths, and after such great graces turn again to the sinful pleasures of the world and the delights of the flesh. Since however the soul has not the power to bear for long the shining of the true light, let it descend gently and in due order to one or other of the three degrees by means of which it made its ascent: let it rest now in one, now in another, as the circumstances of time and place suggest to its free choice, even though, as it seems to me, the soul is the nearer to God the further it climbs from the first degree. Such, alas, is the frailty and wretchedness of human nature.[101]

Very realistically Guigo declares that despite the promise that the *lectio divina* holds out, there are few who reach the goal: 'In this way, then, we see clearly by reason and the testimony of the scriptures that the perfection of the blessed life is contained in these four degrees, and that the spiritual man ought to occupy himself in them continually. But is there anyone who holds to this way of life? 'Tell us who he is and we will praise him' (Sir 31:9). There are many who desire it, but few who achieve it. Would that we were among these few!'[102]

The practice of *lectio divina* was strongly recommended to all who are engaged in the ministry of the Word by the Dogmatic Constitution on Divine Revelation of Vatican Council:

> All clerics, particularly priests of Christ and others who, as deacons or catechists, are officially engaged in the ministry of the Word, should immerse themselves in the Scriptures by constant sacred, reading and diligent study. For it must not happen that anybody becomes an empty preacher of the Word of God to others, not being a hearer of the Word in his own heart (St Augustine), when he ought to be sharing the boundless riches of the divine Word with the faithful committed to his

---

100. Guigo II, 'A Letter on the Interior Life', 341.
101. Guigo II, 'A Letter on the Interior Life', 341.
102. Guigo II, 'A Letter on the Interior Life', 341.

care, especially in the sacred liturgy. Likewise, the sacred synod forcefully and specifically exhorts all the Christian faithful, especially those who live the religious life, to learn 'the surpassing knowledge of Jesus Christ' (Philippians 3:8) by frequent reading of the divine Scriptures. 'For ignorance of the Scriptures is ignorance of Christ' (St Jerome). Therefore let them go gladly to the sacred text itself, whether in the sacred liturgy which is full of the divine words, or in devout reading, or in such suitable exercises and various other helps, which, with the approval and guidance of the pastors of the church, are happily spreading everywhere in our day. Let them remember, however, that prayer should accompany the reading of sacred Scripture, so that a dialogue takes place between God and the person. 'For we speak to God when we pray; we listen to God when we read the divine oracles.' (St Ambrose).[103]

This exhortation of the Council was remarkable in its timeliness and actuality. It was at the very time when modern translations of Sacred Scripture were becoming available, and one group among those mentioned in the above quotation, 'especially those who live the religious life', and more especially women, really set about putting the exhortation into practice by taking up *lectio divina* as their regular form of daily prayer. This *lectio* was combined often with the fruit of having made the contemplations of the mysteries of Christ in the Spiritual Exercises. The result in terms of the gifts of contemplation that have been developed is well summed up by Mary Sharon Riley in an article entitled 'Women and Contemplation'. The following are the opening three and concluding two paragraphs of that article:

'Formed by and through the Ignatian Exercises and/or other spiritualities such as Benedictine or Franciscan, these women pray the Gospels over and over, imaging the scene, seeing the people in it, hearing what they say, noticing what they do, speaking with the Lord about all they experience. These women live as 'one there' in the Gospel passage they pray. Sometimes they are there as one of the persons in the story. At other times they are themselves with those the evangelist named. Because they have a place to sit or stand and a voice with which to speak they know they are 'in the scene'. They talk

---

103. W Abbott, The Documents of Vatican II, 127.

about their lives, feelings and concerns and beg for what is needed for themselves and those they love.

They make time to pray because in the prayer experience they meet Jesus Christ and the God who sent him. Being with him has become important, even vital to their well-being. Speaking their minds and hearts, talking about their lives in the give and take which is the stuff of real communication keeps them alive.

Loved, liked, considered worth spending time with by Jesus Christ, these women change. Nothing in their lives, their relationships to self, world and others nor in their activities, work or role, remains unaffected.'[104]

'Slowly she learns to see the world from Christ's perspective. Viewing herself more clearly because she looks through his lenses, she sees something of what he sees, that is, someone limited, broken and sinful, someone also infinitely important. Drawn by this vision, she moves towards it, grounded ever more truly from within herself. She claims her personal authority more while needing to prove it less. She speaks therefore, as one with a voice.

Freed to recognise and respond to God's presence and so to choose freely to live her life in communion with God, she prays. When active, quiet or consoled, when hurting, restless or tempted, she can 'be with'. She can contemplate. Whatever means and methods she uses, this time in her spiritual life, she has formed a genuinely contemplative attitude within her. She realises the invitation to contemplation offered by 'Nothing'—the invitation to tranquil abiding in the presence of God with Jesus Christ.'[105]

Use of the Gospels according to modern exegesis

As a result of the rapid advance in Catholic Scripture studies after *Divino Afflante Spiritu* (1943) and leading up to *Dei Verbum* (1965) and beyond, exegetes were concerned about the way in which scripture was used in the giving of the Spiritual Exercises. It no longer seemed legitimate for retreat givers simply to follow Ignatius, without reference to the weight of scholarship which required a

---

104. MS Riley, 'Women and *Contemplation*', in *The Way Supplement* 82 (Spring 1995): 35.
105. Riley, 'Women and *Contemplation*', 43.

whole new approach to dealing with the Word of God. Gilles Cusson rightly observed that 'Ignatius, a man of his own time, certainly knew nothing of these preoccupations of contemporary exegetes, legitimate and fruitful as they are.'[106] The main concern of the exegetes was that modern givers of the Spiritual Exercises should not continue to accept the historicity of the Gospels in the way it had been accepted in the past. Frank McCool has raised the question for preachers.[107] The same question was then addressed with specific reference to the Spiritual Exercises by Joseph Fitzmyer.[108]

Fitzmyer is concerned not just with the role of a preacher in a 'preached retreat' based on the Spiritual Exercises, but with the whole use that Ignatius makes of the Gospels in presenting the mysteries of Christ. 'For Ignatius was a child of his time and did not view the Scriptures as a modern man would. He looks on the Gospel accounts as a literal and exact reproduction of what actually took place, and does not even suspect a problem of literary dependence or redactional embellishment or transmissional modification. When faced with an obvious problem, he harmonises the text like the rest of his generation.'[109] This mentality occasionally led Ignatius into error, as in his acceptance, following the *Flos Sanctorum* and the *Vita Jesu Christi*, of the harmonisation of three separate incidents from the four Gospels on the call of the apostles (SE 275). In order to do justice to the text of the Gospels in the light of modern scholarship a retreat master, if preaching on the Gospels, must take into account the three *Sitz im Leben* of the text that is being addressed: the *Sitz im Leben Jesu*, the *Sitz im Leben der Kirche* and the *Sitz im Evangelium*. But, Fitzmyer argues, it is not helpful for the purpose of Ignatius in the Exercises to go through the very difficult process of trying to establish the *Sitz im Leben Jesu*, and the *Sitz im Leben der Kirche* is hardly relevant to the purposes of a retreatant in making the Spiritual Exercises. While it is necessary for a retreat giver to have a good understanding of modern exegesis, so as to avoid the kind of mistake

---

106. Cusson, *Biblical Theology and the Spiritual Exercises*, 221.
107. 'The Preacher and the Historical Witness of the Gospels' in *Theological Studies* 21 (1960).
108. 'The Spiritual Exercises and Recent Gospel Study' in *Woodstock Letters* 91 (1962).
109. Fitzmyer, 'The Spiritual Exercises and Recent Gospel Study', 257.

coming from a harmonising mentality, there is something further at stake here, namely, the retreatant's personal response in the here and now to the Christ whom they meet in the contemplation of the gospel mysteries. Fitzmyer is very clear that Ignatius was concerned, like Ludolph of Saxony before him, with salvation history, rather than with historicity.[110]

At the conference on 'The Spiritual Exercises in the light of Vatican II', held in Loyola, Spain, in 1966, there were two presentations touching closely upon our theme: that of Donatien Mollat, entitled 'The Use of Sacred Scripture in the Exercises According to Modern Exegesis' *(Uso de la Sagrada Escritura en los Ejercicios Segun la Exegesis Moderna),*[111] and that of David Stanley, entitled 'Sacred Scripture and the Spiritual Exercises' *(Sagrada Escritura y Ejercicios Espirituales).* The work of Stanley will be dealt with later in chapter 4.

Mollat commences by declaring that 'St Ignatius asks the retreatant to contemplate the events of the Gospel story.'[112] The word 'event', in this context, was used constantly in *The Jesuits, Their Spiritual Doctrine and Practice* in mistranslation of Joseph de Guibert's phrase 'mysteries of the life of Christ'.[113] The distinction was rightly important to William Peters, who declared that 'the subject matter of the contemplations, with the exception of the repetition and resumption of the first week, are mysteries of Christ's life: mysteries, not events.'[114] The word 'mystery' is the one repeatedly used by Ignatius. For Mollat the purpose of this contemplation of the 'events' is for the retreatant 'to make them present to himself and to make himself present to them, so as to draw spiritual fruit from them and thus to actualise their

---

110. Fitzmyer, 'The Spiritual Exercises and Recent Gospel Study', 59.
111. D Mollat, 'Uso de la Sagrada Escritura en los Ejercicios Segun la Exegesis Moderna', in C Espinosa (ed), *Los Ejercicios di S. Ignacio a la Luz del Vaticano II* (Madrid: Biblioteca de Autores Cristianos, 1968). This paper appeared in English translation as 'The Use of Scripture in the Exercises According to Modern Exegesis' in *The Word of God and the Spiritual Exercises* (Rome: Centrum Ignatianum Spiritualitatis, 1979).
112. D Mollat, 'The Use of Scripture in the Exercises', 25.
113. See, for example, de Guibert, *The Jesuits Their Spiritual Doctrine and Practice*, 129, 133, 206, where 'contemplation of the events of the life of Jesus (or of Christ) occurs as the translation of 'contemplation des mysteres de la vie de Jesus (or du Christ) in J de Guibert, *La Spiritualite de la Compagnie de Jesus* (Rome: Archivum Historicum Societatis Iesu, 1953), 117, 121, 194.
114. W Peters, *The Spiritual Exercises of St Ignatius*, 38.

power.'[115] This hardly brings out the full import of the preoccupation of Ignatius with 'what I want, namely, here, to ask for an intimate knowledge of our Lord, who has become man for me, that I may love Him more and follow Him more closely' (SE 104). Mollat declared: 'In the thought of St Ignatius, this method evidently supposes that we receive the Gospel narrative as the pure transcription of the words and deeds, perhaps harmonising among themselves the accounts that report the words and deeds and completing them with each other wherever there are several parallel versions of the same event.'[116] While it is true, as Fitzmyer wrote, that Ignatius was a man of his time, with a knowledge of Scripture limited to that time, it is not true that 'this method evidently supposes' any such limitation. The limitation belongs accidentally to the lack of scriptural insight of the times, not to the mode of contemplation Ignatius proposed. That way of contemplation, as is asserted by many modern exegetes, like Fitzmyer, Cusson, and Mollat himself later in the same article, is open-ended, and able to be adapted without difficulty to the progressively clearer insights of scriptural scholarship

Rightly Mollat declares that in giving the Spiritual Exercises one must respect those persons receiving them who have the benefit of modern training in scripture. At the same time, the end of the Exercises, conversion of heart and seeking and finding the will of God, or here in the Second Week, growing in heart knowledge of the Lord, must always be borne in mind, and it is not the role of the retreat master to get into technical, intellectual discussions with the retreatant. The exclamation of the religious after a day of meditation on the infancy of Christ: 'I can only meditate on the truth.'[117] is certainly valid, but one hopes that the truth envisaged was the truth of salvation history, revealed in the personal movement of God's Spirit within the retreatant in question, rather than simply an intellectual grasp of the teachings of an exegete about some aspect of the infancy of Christ.

Very pointedly Mollat asks the question how can 'a taste for Scripture read, explained and meditated according to the rigor of the text' be reconciled with 'the freedom Ignatius leaves to the play of

---

115. D Mollat, 'The Use of Scripture in the Exercises', 25.
116. Mollat, 'The Use of Scripture in the Exercises', 25.
117. Mollat, 'The Use of Scripture in the Exercises', 27.

the imagination, the spiritual faculties and creativity of the retreatant under the motion of grace.'[118] In giving a positive answer to this difficulty Mollat goes as far as suggesting that 'Ignatian contemplation, in its spirit and profound intention, anticipated the results of modern exegesis.'[119] It would be better perhaps to draw attention to the open-endedness of the Ignatian Exercises. Ignatius presents the contemplation of Christ in the gospel, as he does with his other exercises, with a very marked restraint, dictated by his fundamental principle that it is God who must be allowed to lead the retreatant as God wills. Neither the retreat director, nor the author of the book of the Exercises is to say too much (SE 2) and so run the danger of obstructing the work of God's Spirit. In this regard Ignatius differs markedly from so many of his followers, who produced large volume of carefully planned and worked out meditations. This movement had begun as early as Borgia,[120] Canisius and Nadal, and really proliferated in later centuries.[121] Hermann Cladder in the late nineteenth century is a typical example among a host of others. De Guibert recorded that he 'utilised his great competence in exegesis in composing his seven volumes of meditations on the Gospel.'[122] Apropos of the work of Borgia, de Guibert remarked: 'They are clearly according to the Ignatian formula. They have preludes, a Gospel text as the basis, short considerations, practical applications and a colloquy at the end. This is the contemplation of the gospel mysteries as Ignatius had taught that contemplation in the second week of the *Exercises*, but it has a movement which is a little less imaginative.'[123] Fundamental to the thesis of this book is that there is far more to understanding contemplation of the gospel mysteries according to the mind of St Ignatius than simply providing a formal structure that looks like that proposed in the Second Week of the Spiritual Exercises. The same sort of problem arose after the restoration of the Society of Jesus in the attempt to be faithful to St Ignatius by making a 'condensed version' of the whole Spiritual Exercises in the annual eight-day retreat. The

---

118. Mollat, 'The Use of Scripture in the Exercises', 27–28.
119. Mollat, 'The Use of Scripture in the Exercises', 28.
120. de Guibert, *The Jesuits Their Spiritual Doctrine and Practice*, 196.
121. de Guibert, *The Jesuits Their Spiritual Doctrine and Practice*, 32–72.
122. de Guibert, *The Jesuits Their Spiritual Doctrine and Practice*, 521.
123. de Guibert, *The Jesuits Their Spiritual Doctrine and Practice*, 196–97.

error was made of promoting the content over the process, so that as long as one 'did' exercises with the names of those in the book of *The Spiritual Exercises* and followed the 'mechanics' of each exercise, one was thought to be following Ignatius. This led de Guibert to ask: 'As a result of this impetus which Roothaan gave, has there not been in some an excessive literalism, going so far as to reduce the manner of giving the Exercises to merely a verbose dilution of Ignatius' text? The danger is all the greater since he himself throughout the twenty-four years of his generalate made all his annual retreats by following this original text.'[124]

Mollat notes the restraint of Ignatius: 'One need only go through the series of "mysteries". There one realises very quickly that ordinarily the text of Scripture is found, briefly evoked, without any of the oftenimaginative developments that less discreet commentators have sometimes added on.'[125]

And very significantly he adds: 'St Ignatius presents the text, it is true, according to the rudimentary synoptic principles of his time, but without binding the text to these principles in a constraining way.' Cusson had underlined this sobriety of Ignatius. He pointed out the futility of lengthy discourses on the mysteries of the gospel: 'Here we are talking about that way of proposing the points for contemplation which gives a long account of the facts of the mystery to be considered, explains in detail all the applications, lessons and conclusions, and lengthily exploits the sentiments associated with the event contemplated. This method is very negative, in the sense that it exhausts, in concepts strictly human, what God desires to make understood through an inexhaustible mystery. As far as possible it deprives the mystery of its transcendence.'[126] The only appropriate approach to mystery is, of course, contemplation, not lengthy discourse Ignatius, by contrast, Cusson wrote, 'carefully avoids this first danger by soberly and faithfully proposing the 'historical foundation' of the mysteries or events to be contemplated. In the Second Week he presents a choice of eighty-two points to be contemplated (from SE 101 to 164, and 262 to 268). Of these, forty-eight consist virtually of quotations from Scripture, thirty-one consider deeds as they are

---

124. de Guibert, *The Jesuits Their Spiritual Doctrine and Practice*, 468.
125. Mollat, 'The Use of Scripture in the Exercises', 28.
126. Cusson, *Biblical Theology and the Spiritual Exercises*, 223.

narrated in the Gospels, and three treat of matters not found in Scripture.'[127] As Mollat put it: 'St Ignatius imposes no decor. He does not describe. He recalls briefly the data on the Gospel.'[128]

Mollat sees the Gospels and *The Spiritual Exercises* as coinciding in leading to the very same end.

> They (the Gospels) are the work of the Holy Spirit, sustaining and infallibly guiding the memory of the sacred authors (Jn 14:26) and fixing it on the essential events, introducing the generation of the first witnesses to 'all the truth' (Jn16:13), and unfolding the mystery of Christ in all its glory (Jn16: 14). But this is what the contemplations in the Exercises essentially tend toward. If they aim at putting the retreatant in immediate contact with the saving events, and in a concrete and living way, it is not through curiosity or estheticism or sentimentalism; it is in view of 'intimate knowledge' of the mystery of Christ, that is to say, an intimate knowledge of the mystery of divine love that is realised in his life, death and resurrection; and that so as to be inflamed and drawn to that following after Christ which alone leads men to life (SE 139; cf Jn 8:12; 12:26.[129]

Again, Gilles Cusson had made the same point. In addressing the often expressed concern about subordinating the scripture to the Spiritual Exercises and so using it in a way not respectful of the purpose for which it was written, Cusson wrote:

> 'In general, some will reprovingly accuse the author of the *Exercises*—or the director—of subordinating the Scriptures to the explicit purpose which he is seeking in preparing his retreatant for the Election; and this sometimes seems to go beyond or even contradict the objective interpretation of the revealed message. However, because many have never really understood the profound meaning of the Ignatian Election, they do not even think of asking whether this subordination might not have precisely the same objectives as the proclamation of the divine word and the transmission of the Gospel message. Furthermore, because many have

---

127. Cusson, *Biblical Theology and the Spiritual Exercises*, 223.
128. Mollat, 'The Use of Scripture in the Exercises', 28.
129. Mollat, 'The Use of Scripture in the Exercises', 31.

> not understood the genuine dialectical interactions of the Exercises, they fail to notice that, in truth, this subordination does indeed coincide with the very same purpose which the Evangelists had in proclaiming the Gospel events; and that in fact the Election does evolve in total dependence on the revealed message.'[130]

Mollat uncovers something of the essence of the contemplations of the Second Week when he declares that 'it is a welcome to the word of God, hearing, dialoguing with him, noticing his presence and discovering his love.'[131] In support of this understanding he cites Jerome Nadal: 'The Exercises have that efficacy because they teach the way of preparing oneself for the word of God and the Gospel.'[132] This understanding led Mollat somewhat surprisingly to declare: 'Ignatian contemplation is not an exercise of the imagination.'[133] The word 'imagination' was very sparingly used by Ignatius. Yet, he certainly presented the use of the imagination as the way into contemplation. But Mollat is quite right in appreciating that the reality of contemplation goes far beyond the use of merely the interior sense faculty of imagination. There is always a 'beyond' involved in contemplation. Mollat makes this an apt conclusion to his presentation: 'The role of exegesis is normative in the sense that it indicates the first meaning, the original direction; it makes the sense of the deeds and words precise at their source. But, in service of the word of God, it stops at the threshold of the dialogue that God inaugurates with his own in the very intimacy of that word which expresses his unspeakable love.'[134]

The depth of Ignatius's Trinitarian and Christological conversion

When Ignatius left his home in Loyola after his initial experience of conversion, he had already made a rudimentary decision to follow the way of a pilgrim, rather than the other way that had attracted

---

130. Cusson, *Biblical Theology and the Spiritual Exercises*, 221.
131. Mollat, 'The Use of Scripture in the Exercises', 33.
132. MHSI 90, 988: 'Efficaciam illam habent (Exercitia), quia docent modum preparandi se ad suscipiendum verbum Dei et Evangelium.'
133. Mollat, 'The Use of Scripture in the Exercises', 33.
134. Mollat, 'The Use of Scripture in the Exercises', 34.

him, namely, the Carthusian life of his mentor, Ludolph, his character being one of strength of will and absolute commitment. He had undergone a radical conversion within which many elements were inextricably linked. As Gilles Cusson remarked, he had been introduced into a biblical world, which fascinated him. He had fallen in love with Jesus, through his pondering of Ludolph's *Life of Christ*, and with Mary. He was determined to emulate and excel saints like Dominic and Francis, and would commit himself to the imitation of the long-haired St Onuphrius. So he set out with great desires and an unshakeable commitment, but very little knowledge of spiritual things. His following of the Christ whom he loved so much was oriented towards the external, especially through the practice of extreme penances. The often told story of the Moor and the donkey is Ignatius' way of reporting, thirty years after the event, how spiritually naive he was at that time.[135]

Yet, from the very beginnings of Ignatius' dwelling on the things that he read in Ludolph's *Life of Christ* and in the *Flos Sanctorum*, and his daydreams of the princess, God seemed to lead him on a very clear path through stage after stage of spiritual growth, culminating in the extraordinary mysticism of the *Spiritual Diary*. The story of this development has been often repeated; from the *Reminiscences* of Ignatius, to the witness of his first companions, right through to the writing of Pedro Arrupe in 1980 on 'The Trinitarian Inspiration of the Ignatian Charism'.[136] Our purpose here is to show the relevance of the contemplative experience of Ignatius for the understanding of his presentation of the contemplation of the mysteries of Christ in the Second Week of the Spiritual Exercises. Relevant to this are some of his personal reminiscences, as told to his companions in Rome in the last three years of his life, the testimony of many of his early companions, and the witness of Ignatius's developed mysticism that is available in his Spiritual Diary.

---

135. J Munitiz and P Endean, *Reminiscences*, (15)19.
136. P Arrupe, 'The Trinitarian Inspiration of the Ignatian Charism' in *Five Recent Documents from Fr General Pedro Arrupe on Spirituality for Today's Jesuits* (New Orleans: Southern Printing,1980).

Personal reminiscences

In the last three years before his death Ignatius yielded to the constant requests of his companions and narrated the story of his conversion and early 'pilgrim years'. A testimony to the accuracy of an account such as this is given by Luis Gonçalves da Câmara in his *Memoriale:* 'And he has such a good memory for events, and even for important words, that he recounts ten, fifteen or more times something that happened, exactly as it happened, so that his hearers can actually see it; and lengthy statements about things of importance he recounts word for word.'[137]

A most significant part of the story Ignatius told in response to the repeated requests of his companions in Rome is that of the eleven months he spent at Manresa, in prayer for seven hours each day, in reflection, participation in the liturgy and service in the hospitals.[138] He experienced an initial period of about four months in which, very happily and with great resolution and application he began to carry out his initial plan of prayer and outstanding penance. 'He was resolved, as has been said, to do great penances, with an eye at this point not so much to making satisfaction for his sins as to pleasing and being agreeable to God. And so, when he would make up his mind to do some penance that the saints did, his aim was to do the same, and more besides. And in these thoughts he had all his consolation, not considering anything within himself, nor knowing what humility was, or charity, or patience, or discernment in regulating and balancing these virtues. Rather, his whole purpose was to do these great exterior deeds because the saints had done them for the glory of God, without considering any other more individual circumstances.'[139]

But then the initial period of happiness gave way to a time of testing, especially through scruples, which left Ignatius desperate, even contemplating suicide.[140] His release from this time of torment came in what Ignatius saw as a clear divine intervention: 'and with

---

137. MHSI 66, 586: 'Y tiene tanta memoria de las casas, y aun de las palabras importantes, que cuenta una cosa que paso, diez, 15 y mas vece, omnino como paso, que la pone delante de los ojos; y platica larga sobre casas de impartancia la cuenta palabra por palabra.'
138. J Munitiz and P Endean, *Reminiscences,* (26) 24.
139. J Munitiz and P Endean, *Reminiscences,* (14), 18–19.
140. J Munitiz and P Endean, *Reminiscences,* (24), 23.

this the Lord willed that he woke up as if from sleep'[141] This was accompanied by the gift of discernment and a very firm conviction that 'God was dealing with him in the same way as a school teacher deals with a child, teaching him… were he to doubt this, he would think he was offending his Divine Majesty.'[142]

At this point in his *Reminiscences* Ignatius reports five great mystical experiences: concerning the Most Holy Trinity, the way in which God created the world, how Jesus is present in the Blessed Sacrament, the humanity of Christ, and finally the great mystical experience beside the river Cardoner. There is no evidence that Ignatius was relating these events chronologically.[143] The context of his recording them was to show how God was dealing with him in the same way as a schoolteacher with a child.

Ignatius reports his way of praying to the Trinity, 'each day to the three persons separately; and to the Most Holy Trinity as such'. He then tells of 'seeing the Most Holy Trinity in the form of three keys on a keyboard, and this with so many sobs that he could not control himself.'[144] Of some relevance to the thesis of this book is the fact that Ignatius was granted this mystical vision of the Trinity while praying the office of Our Lady. His contemplative presence to Mary during this prayer became the occasion of God's granting him what fits his later description of a 'consolation without preceding cause' in the form of a personal presence to the Trinity. The Trinitarian character of the prayer of Ignatius was from this time firmly established, and he remarked that 'the impression has remained with him the whole of his life, and he feels great devotion when praying to the Most Holy Trinity.'[145]

Each of the other four mystical experiences of this period is reflected in his later life and in his writing of *The Spiritual Exercises*. The way in which God created the world is clearly reflected in

---

141. J Munitiz and P Endean, *Reminiscences*, (25), 24.
142. J Munitiz and P Endean, *Reminiscences*, (27), 25.
143. See J de Guibert, *The Jesuits Their Spiritual Doctrine and Practice*, 28, footnote 18, for a discussion of whether the vision beside the river Cardoner came at the beginning or as the climax of the series of mystical experiences. Qualitatively, it was certainly the climax. Chronologically, there is no evidence about the order of the five experiences Ignatius reported.
144. J Munitiz and P Endean, *Reminiscences*, (28) 25–26.
145. J Munitiz and P Endean, *Reminiscences*, (28) 26.

his ever-present sense of seeing all of creation as coming from on high *(de arriba)*, and being led back to the Creator. The experience of the presence of Christ in the blessed sacrament influenced his extraordinary devotion to te Eucharist, shown in his taking a full year of preparation after ordination for the celebration of his first Mass, and shown especially in the accounts in his *Spiritual Diary* of the ongoing great mystical experiences that took place in the context of his celebration of Mass.

The fourth experience Ignatius recorded was his vision of the humanity of Christ and of our Lady. 'Often and for a long time, as he was at prayer, he used to see with his interior eyes the humanity of Christ. As for the form that used to appear to him, it was like a white body, not very big, nor very small, but he did not see any distinction of limbs. . . Our Lady too he has seen in similar form without distinguishing the parts.'[146] Not only did he have these experiences 'often and for along time' at Manresa, but they were repeated over and over throughout his life. In his *Reminiscences* Ignatius mentions them from time to time: 'In that time when he was in Vicenza (1537) he had many spiritual visions and many consolations, as if they were a matter of course (the opposite to when he was in Paris) and most of all when he began to prepare himself to be a priest in Venice and when he was preparing himself to say Mass. Throughout all these journeys he had great supernatural visitations of the kind he was accustomed to have at Manresa.'[147] In the *Reminiscences* he had earlier recorded seeing Christ in his travels by ship (1523): 'Throughout this time Our Lord often appeared to him, which gave him great consolation and energy. Moreover, it seemed to him he repeatedly saw a large round object, apparently of gold;'[148] when being led away in Jerusalem(l 523): 'And as he went along the path in this fashion, grabbed by the Christian of the cincture, he had great consolation from Our Lord, in that it seemed to him he was seeing Christ always over him;'[149] and traveling from Ferrara to Genoa (1524): 'On this journey the pilgrim had, as it were, a representation of when they took Christ, althoughthis

---

146. J Munitiz and P Endean, *Reminiscences*, (29) 26.
147. J Munitiz and P Endean, *Reminiscences*, (95) 60.
148. J Munitiz and P Endean, *Reminiscences*, (44) 33.
149. J Munitiz and P Endean, *Reminiscences*, (48) 35.

was not a vision like the others.'[150] On the subject of visions, we can add the testimony of Gonçalves da Câmara from his Epilogue to the *Reminiscences:* 'And that now too he (Ignatius) had visions often, especially those which have been talked about above, when he saw Christ like a sun.'[151]

It would seem incontrovertible that the visions of which Ignatius wrote belonged in some way to the imagination. He uses the verb 'see' and describes a white body, a round object of gold, a sun. The description of the 'white body' is one which rings true for the imagination: corporeal, but not clear, with no distinction of limbs. Moreover, Ignatius is careful to distinguish these visions of the imagination from others, which sometimes he declared to be intellectual, or, as in that of the journey from Ferrara to Genoa, explicitly declared not to be a vision like the others. These kinds of vision are what retreatants are invited to in the Second Week of the Spiritual Exercises: a use of the interior faculty of imagination that will not provide the clarity of sight, but a powerful sense of presence, in so far as granted by God's grace.

As de Guibert remarks, all these experiences of Ignatius were more than 'simple imaginative visions'. At the same time, the imagery is not without its significance, and the conclusion that de Guibert draws seems quite illegitimate: 'the graces which Ignatius received were in reality eminent intellectual lights, directly infused by God into his faculty of understanding . . . the images which he recorded were simply the reaction from these lights in his soul—his soul which was by nature imaginative but still very poor in symbolic images adaptable to this order of understanding.'[152] The 'vision' by the Cardoner was of the kind that de Guibert proposed, but to attempt to bypass the imagination by calling all five of Ignatius's Manresa experiences 'eminent intellectual lights, directly infused by God into the faculty of understanding', with the images recorded by Ignatius 'simply the reaction to these lights' appears quite at variance with the data that Ignatius himself provided, and seems to emerge from a wish to downplay the imagination, for the sake of the 'higher' faculty of intellect. Ignatius' account of his experiences is a description of

---

150. J Munitiz and P Endean, *Reminiscences* (52) 37.
151. J Munitiz and P Endean, *Reminiscences* (99) 63.
152. de Guibert, *The Jesuits Their Spiritual Doctrine and Practice*, p 31.

the effect of the divine gifting upon his whole person, and he was careful to distinguish the various levels of that gifting, which de Guibert attempted to include under the one preconceived category of 'understanding'.

In the Second Week of the Spiritual Exercises a person is invited to endeavour through the use of the imagination to be present to the person of Christ, in order to enter more deeply into relationship and to be available to receive the grace of knowing and loving him more intimately, so as to follow him more closely. The type of image will vary greatly from person to person, but generally some image will be involved in presence to the persons and mysteries being contemplated.

Finally, the great synthesising experience beside the river Cardoner will become for Ignatius his main point of reference for the discernment of God's action in the rest of his life, especially with regard to the Society of Jesus and its apostolate. 'One cannot set out the particular things he understood then, though they were many: only that he received a great clarity in his understanding, such that in the whole course of his life, right up to the sixty-two years he has completed, he does not think, gathering together all the helps he has had from God and all the things he has come to know (even if he joins them all into one) that he has ever attained so much, as on that single occasion. And this left him with the understanding so enlightened in so great a way that it seemed to him as if he were a different person, and had another mind, different from that which he had before.'[153]

Testimony of Ignatius's companions

The early companions of Ignatius referred often to the evident signs of his ongoing mystical life as well as to his accounts of the experiences he had had at Manresa and later. Juan de Polanco mentioned the ineffability of the Cardoner mystical experience, so that Ignatius kept silent about the content of it: 'However Father Ignatius explained to nobody the secret content of this vision, since it was so difficult to communicate his experiences; nevertheless, he did speak of the fact of its happening.'[154] His companions knew, however, that this

---

153. J Munitiz and P Endean, *Reminiscences*, (30) 27.
154. MHSI 73, 527: 'Nulli autem P Ignatius huius visionis secretum quid sibi vellet explicavit, ut erat in suis rebus communicandis difficilis; factum tamen ipsum

like so many of Ignatius' mystical experiences could be accurately translated by him into practical outcomes. Both Jerome Nadal and Luis Gonçalvez da Câmara report that Ignatius's explanation of decisions he made about practical matters in the Society of Jesus was simply that he came to these decisions 'because of something that happened to me at Manresa.' Gonçalvez recorded that Ignatius was asked his motives for the absence of religious habit, the absence of choir and for including pilgrimages. 'And to all these things he replied with something that happened to me in Manresa.'[155] Similarly Nadal reported:

> He went from the chapel of St Paul to the river, where he was raised above himself, so that all the principles of things were opened up to him. In this rapture he seems to have received a knowledge of the whole Society, because, when he was asked why he instituted this or that, he used to say: 'I refer it all to Manresa.'[156]

Munitiz and Endean point out that the 'knowledge of the whole Society' received at the Cardoner was in principle rather than in detail: 'Some commentators have held that Ignatius at this point received a kind of detailed revelation of the Society's future constitution. Ignatius's own account underplays any sense that God revealed particular information, and stresses the total transformation of the understanding, the change of identity wrought by conversion. Interpreters do well to respect his reticence.'[157]

Nadal gives another brief account of the Cardoner experience in which he reflects on the profound influence that it had on the whole life of Ignatius:

> 'After he had set out through the grace of devotion for the church of St Paul outside the city, he was suddenly seized by

---

retulit.'
155. MHSI 66, 609–610: 'Y a estas cosa todas se responders con un negocio que paso por mi en Manresa.'
156. MHSI 73, 406: 'Hic de sacello D. Pauli ad flumen, ubi fuit supra se levatus, ita ut aperirentur sibi omnia rerum principia. In quo raptu videtur totius Societatis cognitionem accepisse, quia solebat dicere: - Ego me refero ad Manresam - quando querebatur quare hoc aut illud ita institueret.'
157. J Munitiz and P Endean, *St Ignatius of Loyola Personal Writings*, 363–65.

> an ecstasy of mind, or rather a rapture; the eyes of his inner understanding were opened with such a vastness and richness of light, that in that light he understood and contemplated the mysteries of faith and spiritual things and matters of scientific knowledge; and a new truth concerning all of reality seemed to come to him, together with most wonderful understanding. Ignatius always esteemed this gift greatly; concerning it he developed a powerful modesty and humility of spirit; from it there began to shine on his face an indescribable spiritual enthusiasm and light. He used to refer to the light of that grace if at any time he was asked either about the rationale of the Society's Institute, if anything needed defining, or about other serious matters; as if he had seen there the reasons or causes of all things. From it he received a wonderful experience of spiritual realities and the discernment of spirits; from it, too, came a rather frequent familiarity with God, with Christ, with the Blessed Virgin and with the saints.'[158]

Finally, Nadal gives his personal testimony to the life of prayer of Ignatius flowing from the great mystical event that happened by the river Cardoner. Not only was it a continuing relationship with each person of the Trinity, but it graced Ignatius with the ability to contemplate the life of the triune God in the midst of all his activities:

> 'However, it is certain that prayer is a major and especially necessary part of a religious institute; I am referring to that prayer about which Paul wrote: 'I will pray with the spirit; I will also pray with the mind' (1 Cor. 14: 15). This includes

---

158. MHSI 73, 239–40: 'Quum enim devotionis gratia ad aedem D. Pauli extra urbem profisceretur, subita mentis extasi vel potius raptu correptus est; aperti vero illi oculi fuerunt mentis internae tanta lucis amplitudine atque ubertate, ut in illa luce mysteria fidei et res spirituales quaeque ad scientias pertinent intellegeret ac contemplaretur; novaque sibi repraesentari rerum omnium veritas videretur, atque illustrissima intelligentia. Hoc donum semper magnifecit Ignatius, de hoc vehementem animi modestiam atque humilitatem concoepit, ex hoc in eius vultu relucere coepit nescio quid spiritualis alacritatis ac lucis. Ad illam gratiam ac lucem referre solebat, si quando interrogaretur vel de aliis rebus seriis, vel de ratione Instituti Societatis, si quid esset definiendum, quasi rerum omnium ibi sive rationes sive causas vidisset. Hinc eximiam rerum spiritualium experientiam atque spirituum discretionem adeptus est; hinc frequentiorem cum Deo, cum Christo, cum Beata Virgine ac Sanctis familiaritatem.'

all the divisions of spirituality: the purgative, the illuminative and the unitive. The Society, therefore, embraces all of these diligently and with great eagerness in the joy of the spirit in Christ Jesus; for none of its members fails to undertake first those exercises which lead to repentance, and the stripping away of the old man, and next the contemplation of all of the mysteries of Christ, in which we desire to aspire to attain an appreciation of the way, the truth and the life; finally we rest in love, so that we find our goal in that from which all prayer ought to begin; that is to say, in charity, the highest theological virtue, so that we go out to our ministries animated by the fervour and zeal of that charity. We then go forth courageously in a happy spirit, and in the humility of our hearts in Christ Jesus, we get all this from the Exercises. But here is one thing I will not omit (even if this is not the right place to speak of prayer, but elsewhere): We know that our father, Ignatius, received a special grace from God that he could exercise himself freely and come to rest in the contemplation of the most Holy Trinity. At one time he would be led by the grace of contemplating the whole Trinity; he would be drawn into It, he would be united to It with his whole heart, with a great sense of devotion and spiritual consolation; at another time he would contemplate the Father; at another time the Son, at another time the Holy Spirit. While he received the gift of this contemplation frequently at other times, he received it specially, you could say uniquely, in the last years of his life. Father Ignatius received this kind of prayer as a great privilege, through a most special gift; in addition to this, in everything, his actions, his conversations he experienced and contemplated the presence of God and the consolation of spiritual realities, simultaneously in action and contemplative. He used to explain this by saying that God must be found in all things. This grace and light of his soul we have seen shine out in a kind of splendour of countenance and in the clarity and certainty of his actions in Christ, to the great wonder of us all and the great consolation of our hearts; and we felt something of that grace to be shared with us. We believe that the same privilege that we understand to be given to FatherIgnatius has been granted to the whole Society. We trust that the grace of that prayer and contemplation has been prepared in the Society for all of us, and profess that it is linked to our vocation.'[159]

Besides giving his testimony to the contemplative and mystical life of Ignatius, Nadal was ahead of his time in understanding how the charism of a founder is shared by the members of the religious order. 'Since this is so, let us also place the perfection of our prayer in the contemplation of the Trinity, and in the love and union of charity, extended certainly to our neighbour through the ministries of our vocation; which indeed we easily give preference to the taste and

---

159. MHSI 27, 651–2: '... orationem autem magnam esse religiosi instituti partem certum et, eamque inprimis necessarium, orationem eam dico, de qua Paulus: 'Orabo (inquit) spiritu, orabo et mente' (1 Cor XIV, 15), quae omnes complectitur spiritualis exercitii partes, purgativam, illuminatiuam atque unituam. Diligenter igitur haec et magna auiditate complectitur Societas in dulcedine spiritus in X.o. Jesu; nullum enim e suis non exercet primum illis meditationibus, quae ad poenitentiam attinent, ueterisque hominis expoliationem, dein contemplationibus omnium mysteriorum Christi, in quibus ad sensum uiae, ueritatis ac uitae aspirare desideramus; demum in amore conquiescimus, ut inde proficisci debet oratio, in eo finem collocemus, in charitate, scilicet, summa ac diuina uirtute, ut ex hac eiusque feruore ac zelo ad nostra ministeria egrediamur in hilaritate spiritus atque humilitate cordis nostri ac suauitate fortiter in X.o. Jesu. Haec ex libro exercitiorum nostrorum colligimus. Illud uero non omittam (etiamsi proprius hic locus non est, ut de oratione dicam, sed alius): Patrem Ignatium scimus singularem gratiam accepisse a Deo vt in contemplatione S.mae Trinitatis exerceretur libere ac conquiesceret: Nunc quidem gratia contemplandae totius Trinitatis ducebatur, in illam ferebatur, in illam uniebatur toto corde magno sensu deuotionis atque spiritualis gustus; nunc Patrem contemplabatur, nunc Filium, nunc Spiritum sanctum; et hujus quidem contemplationem accepit, cum alias frequenter, tum uero (quasi si unice dicas) ad annos suae peregrinationis ultimos; hanc rationem orationis concepit Pater Ignatius, magno priuilegio, selectissime; tum illud praeterea in omnibus rebus, actionibus, colloquiis, ut Dei praesentiam rerumque spiritualium affectum sentiret atque contemplaretur, simul in actione contemplatiuus (quod ita solebat explicare: Deum esse in omnibus rebus inueniendum); hanc uero gratiam ac lucem animae suae, quodam quasi splendore uultus, claritate ac certitudine actionum suarum in X.o explicari vidimus, magna nostra omnium admiratione et magna cordis nostri consolatione, et quasi deriuatam in nos nescio quid illius gratiae sensimus. Quod igitur priuilegium Patri Ignatio factum intelligimus, idem toti Societati concessum esse credimus, et gratiam orationis illius et contemplationis in Societate omnibus nobis paratam esse confidimus, eamque cum uocatione nostra coniunctam esse confitemur...'

sweetness of prayer.'[160] The members of the order are formed in the school of the Spiritual Exercises. While it is evident that the charism of Ignatius does not extend to all those who make the Exercises, it is precisely through the contemplations that they contain that the gift of contemplation is developed in those who make them.

3. The Spiritual Diary

The greatest insight into the sublimity of the mystical life of Ignatius is provided by the few pages of his Spiritual Diary that have survived. There are two note books, the first of fourteen folios, from February 2nd, 1544 to March 12th, 1544, the second of eleven folios, from March 13th, 1544 to February 27th, 1545. These are thought to be part of a 'large bundle of written notes' seen by Luis Gonçalves da Câmara,[161] the rest of which Ignatius managed to destroy. The section of the diary that we have begins twenty-one and a half years after Ignatius's profound experiences of the Trinity at Manresa, and eleven and a half years before his death, so that it provides only a glimpse of that ongoing relationship of his with the persons of the Trinity, about which Nadal wrote.

Adolf Haas divides the diary chronologically into four stages of mystical focus:

1. February 2nd, to 21st: From the Divine Persons to the Unity of Their Mutual Indwelling (Perichoresis)
2. February 22nd to 28th: From Jesus as Man to Jesus as God.
3. February 29th to March 6th: From the Perichoretic Unity of Persons to the Divine Essence.
4. March 7th, 1544 to February 27th, 1545: A Mysticism of Reverential Love.[162]

---

160. MHSI 90, J Nadal, *Annotationes in Examen*, c. IV, (83) 163: 'Haec cum ita sint, perfectionem nostrae orationis constituamus in contemplatione Trinitatis, in charitatis amore atque unione, extensa quidem in proximum per nostrae vocationis ministeria; quae quidem gustui ac suavitati orationis facile praeferimus.'
161. J Munitiz and P Endean, *Reminiscences*, (99) Epilogue, 63.
162. A Haas, 'The Mysticism of St Ignatius According to His Spiritual Diary', Study 6, in Friedrich Wulf (ed), *Ignatius of Loyola His Personality and Spiritual*

Throughout, Ignatius is unashamedly kataphatic in writing of his relationships with Mary, with Jesus, with each of the Divine Persons, and with the Divine Essence, and about his own interior states in these relationships. What he records is nearly always what happens before, during and immediately after the daily celebration of Mass. He repeats most often the experience of tears, but also repeats words like: sobbing, devotion, deep affection, confidence, much peace of mind, interior movement, interior peace and quiet of soul, clearness and light, elevation of mind, tranquility. In other words, his mystical experiences put him in touch with his own inner movements that can be clearly expressed. The persons of Mary, of Jesus, of Father, Son and Holy Spirit can also be clearly identified, though it is also clear that there is something quite apophatic which cannot be expressed in the words of the journal. With admirable clarity Ignatius conveys the element of mystery in the Incarnation when writing about the Son, who is both Son of Mary and eternal Son of the Father: 'wishing to present this to the Father through the mediation and prayers of the Mother and the Son, I prayed first to her to help me with her Son and the Father, and then' prayed to the Son to help me with His Father in company with the Mother . . .'[163] He is lucidly clear about Jesus as the Son of Mary, the Son of the Father and the Second Person of the Trinity.

What Nadal wrote about Ignatius's personal communion with each person of the Trinity and with the whole Trinity is constantly, borne out in his writing in the journal: 'Eternal Father, confirm me; Eternal Son, confirm me; Eternal Spirit, confirm me; Holy Trinity, confirm me; my only God, confirm me!'[164] Ignatius goes beyond what Nadal had written about him in adding a fifth prayer to God, as God.

The Spiritual Diary reads like an account of the Spiritual Exercises in practice at their highest level. Aspects of the Exercises that are brought into sharp focus throughout are: a) reflection and attention to detail, b) writing a journal, c) indifference, d) self-examination

---

Heritage 1556–1956, 170-172.

163. WJ Young (translator), 'Spiritual Diary of Ignatius Loyola', in S Decloux, *The Spiritual Diary of St Ignatius Loyola Text and Commentary* (Rome: Centrum Ignatianum Spiritualitatis, 1990), (8) 20. The bracketed numbers are from the numbering of the paragraphs in *Obras Completas de San Ignacio de Loyola* (Madrid: Biblioteca de Autores Cristianos, 1963), 318-386.

164. S Decloux, *The Spiritual Diary*, (48) 30.

and purification, e) the important role of intercessors in prayer, f) the constant use of colloquy, g) contemplation and familiarity with God, h) the election, and especially its confirmation, i) discernment of spirits, j) the role of the imagination.

a) The whole of the Spiritual Diary is an exercise in that reflection which Ignatius valued so highly from the time of his conversion. In this reflection no detail is unimportant. Ignatius is constantly giving a testimony to the fact that God is indeed at work in all things, no matter how externally trivial. So, he goes to great pains to record the circumstances in which each event occurs: 'going to bed', 'on rising', 'after dressing', 'while vesting', 'in preparing for the altar', 'walking through the town', 'at table', 'by the fire', even: 'I got up and dressed, with nothing remarkable either one way or the other'. 'Later, as I considered whether I should go out or not, I decided with great peace to go out', and so on. He carefully records parts of his experience that may seem of very little significance: 'But I made the customary prayer without any or very little relish until about halfway through';[165] 'There was much devotion and from the middle on, devotion was much increased, although I felt in it, especially in the first part, physical weakness or indispositlon.'[166] 'Later, going out of my room because of the noise, and also on my return, I was somewhat confused, either struggling with the thoughts about the noise, or being annoyed to such a point that even after vesting for Mass, the thought came not to say it.'[167]

b) From the earliest days of his conversion, keeping a journal to note down and reflect later on God's dealings with him was very important to Ignatius. After his all-night vigil at Montserrat on the eve of the Annunciation 1522, he narrated that he 'took a detour to a town called Manresa, where he was set on staying a few days in an almshouse, and also to note down some things in his book. He was carrying this with much care, and thanks to it he was travelling along in great consolation.'[168] He constantly committed to writing the results of his reflection, and in the diary from paragraph (52) to paragraph (88) he boxed in with lines on fourteen occasions more significant

---

165. Decloux, *The Spiritual Diary*, (43) 29.
166. Decloux, *The Spiritual Diary*, (79) 36.
167. Decloux, *The Spiritual Diary*, (93) 39.
168. J Munitiz and P Endean, *Reminiscences*, (18) 20.

things he had recorded, so as to rewrite them and ponder them again. In the Spiritual Exercises he recommends that there should always be up to a quarter of an hour of reflection after each period of prayer,[169] and, though he does not explicitly recommend writing, that is what is consistent with his whole approach, and has in fact been followed in practice.

The fruit of constant reflection and the keeping of the journal is to keep in touch with the continuity of God's action within one's life, and so enable the ongoing appropriation of one's personal history as part of God's great plan of salvation history. It is not surprising, then, that Ignatius recalls at different times the two most profoundly formative experiences of his life, the one at the river Cardoner, and the Father's election of him at La Storta. On 19 February 1544, he wrote: 'with very many lights and spiritual memories concerning the Most Holy Trinity which served as a great illumination to my mind, so much so that I thought I could never learn so much by hard study, and later, as I examined the matter more closely, I felt and understood, I thought, more than if I had studied all my life.'[170] And on 23 February: 'and thinking that the appearance of Jesus was in some way from Most Holy Trinity, I recalled the day when the Father placed me with the Son.'[171]

c) Ignatius models the 'indifference' about which he wrote in the First Principle and Foundation. The struggle he went through right through the time of the journal was his effort to be totally open to the will of God, whatever it should be. As Decloux put it: '. . . even if one has followed all the movements of his soul, so eager to strip itself of everything before its God . . .'[172] In Ignatius's own words: 'I offered myself to be guided and led, etc, He being above me in these steps, wherever He would take me.'[173] Again he wrote: 'I think in some parts of those of the past, thoughts and reflections as to what the Most Blessed Trinity wished to do with me . . .'[174]

---

169. SE 77.
170. Decloux, *The Spiritual Diary*, (52) 31. Significantly, this is the first of Ignatius's 'boxed in' sections.
171. Decloux, *The Spiritual Diary*, (67) 34. Again these words are one of the 'boxed in' sections.
172. Decloux, *The Spiritual Diary*, 102.
173. Decloux, *The Spiritual Diary*, (114) 43.
174. Decloux, *The Spiritual Diary*, (119) 45.

d) The time of the *Spiritual Diary*, like all times in human life, is for Ignatius a time of exposure to his own weakness, doubts and fears. The struggle is constant. Decloux wrote: 'Faced with the greatness and wisdom of God, how can a man who knows and feels that he is finite, be without doubts and fears of being mistaken? In a sense, these feelings will always be present; we find them even three weeks later on the very day, 12 March 1544, when St Ignatius finally decided to terminate his election process.'[175] On that day Ignatius wrote: 'Finishing Mass, and afterwards in my room, I found myself alone and without help of any kind, without power to relish any of my mediators, or any of the Divine Persons, but so remote and separated, as if I had never felt anything of Them, or would ever feel anything again. Rather, thoughts came to me sometimes against Jesus, sometimes against another, being so confused with different thoughts, such as to quit the house and hire a room to get away from the noise, or to go without eating, or to begin the Masses over again, or to put the altar on a higher floor. Nowhere finding peace, I had a desire to finish up at a time when my soul was consoled and completely at rest.'[176] This desolation and these temptations were quickly resolved for Ignatius, and he was soon able to write in peace: 'Finished.'

Two earlier 'faults' had led Ignatius to much more need for reconciliation. The first occurred on 12 February when he rose from thanksgiving 'to see whether I could stop the racket in the room.'[177] This led him on the next day to resolve not to say the Mass of the Trinity 'for the whole week, doing penance by thus absenting myself from Them.'[178] But on that same day he reported that 'I saw my mediators regain what I had lost'. Yet, two days later his sensitive conscience was at work: 'Later, on going out to say Mass, when beginning the prayer, I saw a likeness of our Lady, and realised how serious had been my fault of the other day, not without some interior movement and tears, thinking that the Blessed Virgin felt ashamed at asking for me so often after my many failings, so much so, that our Lady hid herself from me, and I found no devotion either in her or fromon high.'[179] In the

---

175. Decloux, *The Spiritual Diary* 97.
176. Decloux, *The Spiritual Diary*, (145) 50–51.
177. Decloux, *The Spiritual Diary*, (22) 23.
178. Decloux, *The Spiritual Diary*, (23) 24.
179. Decloux, *The Spiritual Diary*, (29) 25.

context of his faults and need for reconciliation he wrote: 'comparing my own dignity with the greatness and wisdom of God,'[180] and again later: 'I never got through saying to myself: "Who are you? Where do you come from? etc. How did you deserve this? or whence did it come?" and so on.'[181]

This clearly recalls the fourth point of the second exercise of the First Week of the Exercises: 'I will consider who God is against whom I have sinned, going through all His attributes and comparing them with their contraries in me: His wisdom with my ignorance, His power with my weakness, His justice with my iniquity, His goodness with my wickedness.'[182] Twice in his Spiritual Diary Ignatius mentions his examination of conscience: 'I examined first my conscience, covering the entire day, and asked pardon . . .';[183] and then later: 'On awakening in the morning and beginning my examination of conscience and prayer'.[184] The latter reference is to the morning of 19 February 1544, the day after Ignatius found himself 'becoming impatient with the Trinity'. From this time till the end of the election, reconciliation will play a large part in the prayer of Ignatius as he struggles for liberation from doubts and fears.

e) Though Ignatius was gifted with a remarkable immediate access to the Persons of the Trinity, he continued throughout his election process to approach his intercessors, especially our Lady and Jesus. He mentions the presence of our Lady from day one to the second last day of the election[185] and Jesus, or the Son, from the fourth day to the fourth last.[186] His prayer through them is often the way for him into union with the Trinity, as in one of his 'boxed in' passages: 'I felt or rather saw beyond my natural strength the Most Holy Trinity and Jesus, presenting me, or placing me, or simply being the means of union in the midst of the Most Holy Trinity in order that this intellectual vision be communicated to me.'[187] In the diary the threefold colloquy of the Spiritual Exercises is spelt out more clearly

---

180. Decloux, *The Spiritual Diary*, (50) 30.
181. Decloux, *The Spiritual Diary*, (60) 33.
182. SE 59.
183. Decloux, *The Spiritual Diary*, (35) 26
184. Decloux, *The Spiritual Diary*, (51) 31.
185. Decloux, *The Spiritual Diary*, (1)19 and (39) 50.
186. Decloux, *The Spiritual Diary* (4) 19, and (137), (140) 49.
187. Decloux, *The Spiritual Diary*, (83) 37.

by Ignatius than it was in the text of the Exercises. 'Soon after Mass, with devotion and not without tears, going through the elections for an hour and a half or more and making an offering of what seemed to be better supported by reason, and by a stronger inclination of will, that is, to have no revenue, wishing to present this to the Father through the mediation *(medio)* and prayers of the Mother and the Son, prayed first to her to help me with her Son and the Father, and then prayed to the Son to help me with His Father in company with the Mother, I felt an impulse to go and betake myself to the Father, and in doing so my hair stood on end with a most remarkable warmth in my whole body.'[188]

The intercessors for Ignatius are not only Jesus and Mary, but the angels and the saints, and on two key occasions in the diary he mentions the image of 'the whole heavenly court', that was so important at three key points of the Exercises: the offering of the Kingdom, the meditation on the Three Classes of Persons and the Contemplation to Attain the Love of God:[189] 'I felt that the very veins and members of my body made themselves sensibly felt, and I made the final commendation to the Most Holy Trinity, in the presence of the whole heavenly court, giving thanks with great affection, first to the Divine Persons, then to our Lady and to her Son, then to the angels, the holy fathers, the apostles and disciples, and to all persons for the help they had given me in this matter.'[190] As in the Exercises, the image of the whole heavenly court comes at key moments. Ignatius had written this on 18 February 1544, the day on which he thought there was an end to his election process. It would reappear on 12 March, the day the process was truly finished: 'To keep on seeking, or to wait for the evening, would still be wishing to seek, there being no reason to, and so I proposed in the presence of God our Lord, and all His court, etc, putting an end to this point, not to proceed any further in this matter.'[191]

f) Obviously, in the prayers of intercession, Ignatius was involved constantly in colloquy, and, as mentioned above, spelt out in detail how he understood the practice of the threefold colloquy of the

---

188. Decloux, *The Spiritual Diary*, (8) 20.
189. SE 98, 151, 232.
190. Decloux, *The Spiritual Diary*, (47) 29–30.
191. Decloux, *The Spiritual Diary*, (149) 51–52.

Spiritual Exercises. Twice in the course of the diary he writes about making a colloquy, the first time being colloquy with the Holy Spirit: 'later, making a colloquy with the Holy Spirit before saying His Mass, with the same devotion and tears, I thought I saw Him, or felt Him, in a dense brightness, or in the color of a flame of fire.'[192] Coming towards the end of his process of election, Ignatius wrote: 'many movements came upon me and tears, and from moment to moment over some space of time, great movements, sobs and floods of tears, drawing me entirely to the love of the Most Holy Trinity with many colloquies.'[193]

g) There is no commentator who doubts that in the Spiritual Diary of St Ignatius we have one of the greatest testimonials of contemplative prayer and mysticism in practice. Ignatius, as always, is quite kataphatic, and he writes with great clarity and precision about both his own experiences and his relationships with each of the persons involved, both human and divine; These relationships are extremely intimate; and we see in practice the kind of 'familiarity with God', which he wrote of in his *Constitutions* as being one of the main means for the preservation and development of the Society of Jesus.[194] This 'familiarity with God' was one of the characteristics that Nadal named in him.

While the contemplation for Ignatius enables him to focus on each of the Persons of the Trinity, the triune God and the divine Essence, the contemplation of our Lady and his other intercessors; and especially of Jesus is an essential part of the whole process. It was a thought that reminded him of his focus of the Second Week of the Exercises, namely the Third Degree of Humility that led him into what Haas called the second stage of the diary: From Jesus as Man to Jesus as God. 'While preparing the altar, the thought of Jesus occurring to me, I felt a movement to follow Him, it seemed to me interiorly, since He was the head of the Society, a greater argument to proceed in complete poverty than all the other human reasons, although I thought that all the reasons of the past election tended towards the same decision.'[195] The contemplation of Jesus that follows over the next six days, 23 to 28 February, contains no fewer than eight

---

192. Decloux, *The Spiritual Diary*, (14) 22.
193. Decloux, *The Spiritual Diary*, (130) 47.
194. St Ignatius of Loyola, *The Constitutions*, (813) 332
195. Decloux, *The Spiritual Diary*, (66) 33–4.

of Ignatius's fourteen 'boxed in' sections. It includes 'Jesus, presenting me, or placing me, or simply being the means of union in the midst of the Most Holy Trinity',[196] and terminates in the vision of 'Jesus at the feet of the Most Holy Trinity'.[197]

h) The occasion for Ignatius' providing this insight into his contemplative life is the same as in the culmination of the Second Week of the Spiritual Exercises, namely the election. Though the subject here is an issue in the *Constitutions* of the Order, rather than choice of state of life, the principles and process are the same. Rational factors had an important role to play in this election, as well as the affective ones described in the diary, and Decloux appends to the text of the diary Ignatius's rational analysis of the disadvantages and advantages to be found in the different possible decisions. When Ignatius did start recording the process of the election in his diary, within a very short time, on the seventh day (8 February), he was able to write: 'I found myself with a certain elevation of soul and a deep peace, without the contradictory thought of possessing anything, and was relieved of the desire of proceeding any further with the election, as I had thought of doing a few days earlier.'[198]

For no fewer than thirty-four more days Ignatius will be involved in the process of confirmation of this election. This length of time is a clear sign of the fact that the essential of election is not so much the human choice, however clear, well thought through and affectively satisfying, but God's choice to which the person is responding. In the Exercises Ignatius gives two ways of making a choice of a way of life in the 'third time', a time of tranquillity. He concludes the first way with the following 'sixth point': 'After such a choice or decision, the one who has made it must turn with great diligence to prayer in the presence of God our Lord, and offer Him his choice that the Divine Majesty may deign to accept and confirm it for His greater service and praise.'[199] After presenting the 'second way for making a correct and good choice of a way of life', Ignatius repeats the instruction on the need for confirmation: 'Guided by the rules given above for my eternal salvation and peace, I

---

196. Decloux, *The Spiritual Diary*, (83) 37.
197. Decloux, *The Spiritual Diary*, (88) 38
198. Decloux, *The Spiritual Diary*, (10) 21
199. SE 183.

will make my decision, and will offer it to God our Lord as directed in the sixth point of the First Way of Making a Choice of a Way of Life.[200] The fact that Ignatius spent thirty four days seeking confirmation of his decision does not mean that an election made in a shorter time is not valid. It is not just a question of a right or wrong decision, but of a quality of personal presence to God to allow God to communicate God's choice in God's own way and time. Such a factor as the length of time involved must depend upon the quality of the unique relationship that God has with each unique person.

In the process of election as detailed by Ignatius, it is clearly passivity that dominates rather than his personal activity. The same is true of any authentic election: the principal element is the contemplative reception from God of God's election of the person in the matter being decided. As Decloux put it in the case of Ignatius, 'as he gives up waiting for more signs, Ignatius discovers the need to be taken over, in a purely gratuitous way, by the God of all goodness and consolation.'[201] One of the principal signs of the passivity of Ignatius is his constant reception of the gift of tears. These are present throughout the diary, but really dominate in its second part. During this second part he also receives over a period of eighteen days (11 to 28 May) the gift of divine *loquela* (mystical speech, discourse mentioned by John of the Cross).

i) During the forty days of the first part of his diary Ignatius experienced an abundance of consolation, expressed in such words as devotion, warmth, confidence, tears and sobs, rejoicing, clearness, peace, tranquillity, elevation, light, and many similar positive expressions. At the same time he was not free of what he was clearly able to distinguish as attacks of the evil spirit in the form of impatience, hesitance, doubts, fears, thoughts against Jesus, darkness, looking for further proof. He is able to name these as coming from the evil spirit or tempter.[202] Identifying the source of these movements, he even addresses 'the tempter' directly: 'for a good space the tempter did nothing, but he sought to have me make some sign of hesitating, and answering at once, without any disturbance, rather as in the event of victory, 'Down, where you belong!''[203] This direct addressing of the evil

---

200. SE 188.
201. Decloux, *The Spiritual Diary*, 102.
202. Decloux, *The Spiritual Diary*, (57) 32, (148) 51, (151) 52.
203. Decloux, *The Spiritual Diary*, (151) 52.

spirit is a valuable addition to the Rules for Discernment of Spirits in the Exercises, where it was not included. The evil spirit disguises itself as an angel of light, but is still recognised: 'And when the thought of saying three Masses of the Holy Trinity in thanksgiving came to me, I thought it came from the evil spirit, and deciding that I would say none, I grew much in divine love.'[204]

The main attacks of the evil spirit were experienced by Ignatius on those days (18 February and 12 March) when first he thought to end, and second did in fact finish his process of election. Because he recognised their source, they were on both occasions transient in nature, and did not at all detract from the grace God had given. It took only a quarter of an hour for Ignatius to come to a clear understanding of how 'the tempter' had been trying to undermine him on the final day, and arrive at 'every firmness and confirmation of the matter and this with a feeling of spiritual relish, and my eyes filled with tears with great security of soul.'[205]

j) It cannot be denied that throughout the process of Ignatius' election his imagination was very active. Over and over again he declared: 'I felt or saw', with various nuances and modifications of the two verbs *sentir y ver*. It is impossible to capture in the English translations 'felt' and 'saw' the richness of meanings in what Ignatius was expressing, but at the same time, they are the nearest translations available and cannot be simply dismissed as inadequate. They do convey something of the meaning.

Alexandre Brou wrote of the difficulty of translating into French the meaning of the Ignatian *sentir*, which was for Ignatius often clearly intellectual, and at other times was more concerned with deeper realities touched upon through contemplation. One is then involved with far more than a speculative knowledge of the truth; it is a matter of 'realising' it. Moreover, Brou goes on to say Ignatius is concerned with the realm of faith, and of grace, so that in the kind of heart knowledge involved in *sentir* the gifts of the Holy Spirit are at work.'[206] The second word Ignatius uses repeatedly, 'to see' *(ver)* does not have as much difficulty as *sentir*, but once again is open to a wide range of meanings. This is true of the English as well as the Spanish.

---

204. Decloux, *The Spiritual Diary*, (148) 51.
205. Decloux, *The Spiritual Diary*, (152) 52.
206. See A Brou: *Saint Ignace, Maître D'Oraison*, 140-41.

But in trying to grasp Ignatius' meaning in the use of both verbs, we have the advantage that he was very careful to spell out as precisely and clearly as he could many of his different shades of meaning.

When looking for the role of the imagination, we must also bear in mind the common teaching about mystical experience, that a greater integration of the faculties often occurs, so that it can become very difficult for the person describing, and much more for the person reading what is described, to make an accurate analysis. Over and above that, there remains the radical ineffability of the experience itself. Ignatius pointed to this ineffability when he wrote in one of his important 'boxed in' sections: 'But in the Mass I recognised, felt or saw, the Lord knows, that in speaking to the Father, in seeing that He was a Person of the Most Holy Trinity, I was moved to love the Trinity all the more that the other Persons were present in It essentially. I felt the same in the prayer to the Son, and the same in the prayer to the Holy Spirit, rejoicing in any One of Them and feeling consolations, attributing it to and rejoicing in the Being of all Three.'[207] In another of the 'boxed in' sections he wrote: 'I felt and saw this in a way that I cannot explain.'[208] When using the word 'imagination' here, we are clearly concerned not just with the natural, interior sense faculty, but in some way with the 'spiritual imagination'.

At times Ignatius distinguished quite clearly what is an intellectual vision, as in writing: 'a sight of the heavenly fatherland, or of its Lord, after the manner of an intellectual vision of the Three Persons, and in the Father the Second and the Third.'[209] He was equally clear about an intellectual seeing of Jesus: 'Later in the day, as often as I thought of Jesus, or remembered Him, I had a certain feeling, or saw with my understanding, with a continuous and confirming devotion.'[210] He also used a strongly visual expression ('rather saw') for what he declared to be in fact an intellectual vision: 'In this I received some light and strength, and going into the chapel and praying, I felt or rather saw beyond my natural strength the Most Holy Trinity and Jesus, presenting me, or placing me, or simply being the means of union in the midst of the Most Holy Trinity in order that this intellectual vision

---

207. Decloux, *The Spiritual Diary*, (63) 32–3
208. Decloux, *The Spiritual Diary*, (77) 36.
209. Decloux, *The Spiritual Diary*, (88) 38–9.
210. Decloux, *The Spiritual Diary*, (70) 34.

be communicated to me."[211] When using the striking verbal image of 'Jesus at the feet of the Trinity', Ignatius described it as a 'revelation or a seeing' *(un descubrirseme o viendo)*, and declared that it was not as clear as the vision just described.[212]

There are times when the language used by Ignatius would not make sense apart from the imagination, as: 'it would be pleasing to Him to be asked through our Lady, whom I could not see', followed by 'the clear view of our Lady'.[213] A strong argument for imagination is the distinction made between 'I saw', and 'I felt it in another way': 'I thought in spirit I saw just Jesus, that is, the humanity, and at this other time I felt it in my soul in another way.'[214] 'I saw a representation of the name of Jesus'[215] clearly belongs to the imagination, as does the phrase 'Jesus, when he showed himself to me',[216] and: 'Later, at the fire, there was a fresh representation of Jesus with great devotion and movement to tears. Later, as I walked through the street, I had a vivid representation of Jesus with interior movements and tears.'[217]

When Ignatius speaks of seeing the Trinity or the Holy Spirit, there is obviously need for caution in interpreting his words. For instance, he writes in one of his 'boxed in' passages: 'Likewise all of a sudden, I clearly saw the same vision of the Most Holy Trinity as before, with an ever-increasing love for His Divine Majesty, and several times losing the power of speech.'[218] Even though he used the words 'clearly saw', when we look back to 'before', we find that he was writing of an intellectual vision. But, in another 'boxed in' section he wrote: '(when one) deals with the operations *ad extra* of the Divine Persons, or their procession more by feeling and seeing than by understanding.'[219]

Of the Holy Spirit he wrote: 'I felt intense devotion and tears at realising *(sentir)* or beholding *(ver)* in a certain manner the Holy Spirit',[220] This is evidently not necessarily a visual 'beholding', but

---

211. Decloux, *The Spiritual Diary*, (83) 37
212. Decloux, *The Spiritual Diary*, (88) 38.
213. Decloux, *The Spiritual Diary*, (30) and (31) 25.
214. Decloux, *The Spiritual Diary*, (86) p 38.
215. Decloux, *The Spiritual Diary*, (71) 34–5.
216. Decloux, *The Spiritual Diary*, (73) 35.
217. Decloux, *The Spiritual Diary*, (74) 35.
218. Decloux, *The Spiritual Diary*, (85) 37.
219. Decloux, *The Spiritual Diary*, (55) 31.
220. Decloux, *The Spiritual Diary*, (18) 22.

earlier he had written: 'making a colloquy with the Holy Spirit before saying His Mass, with the same devotion and tears, I thought I saw him or felt Him, in a dense brightness, or in the color of a flame of fire.'[221] It is impossible to interpret these as other than visual images. But he did not say that he saw the Holy Spirit.

Finally, there is the vision of the Essence of God in the form of a sphere. On 6 March 1544 Ignatius wrote: 'I felt and saw, not obscurely, but clearly and very clearly the very Being or Essence of God, under the figure of a sphere, slightly larger than the appearance of the sun, and from this Essence the Father seemed to go forth or derive, in such a way that on saying 'Te', that is 'Pater', the Divine Essence was represented to me before the Father, and in this vision, I saw represented the Being of the Most Holy Trinity without distinction or sight of the other Persons . . .'[222] There is visual imagery involved here in Ignatius's presence to the Divine Essence. He certainly saw a sphere that was like the sun, and this seeing filled his whole being with the presence of God, so that the experience was one of 'feeling or seeing very clearly the very Being or Essence of God'. In other words, Ignatius had an imaginative vision intimately bound up with an intellectual vision of the Divine Essence. This is not the same as the simple objective fact: 'He saw God'. The words of John's Gospel remain: 'No one has ever seen God; it is the only Son who is close to the Father's heart, who has made him known.' (John 1:18). The same is true of what Ignatius wrote later that same day: 'After unvesting, in the prayer at the altar, the same spherical vision presented itself to my sight, and in some way I saw the Three Divine Persons, in the manner that the First, that is the Father on the one hand, the Son on the other, and the Holy Spirit on the other, proceeded from the Divine Essence, without leaving the outlines of the sphere.'[223] Ignatius's final two accounts of this vision contain the strongly visual elements of 'lucid color' and 'a fairly large spark': 'Later . . . the same Divine Being presented Itself to me in the same lucid color, so that I could not help seeing it;'[224] and 'Later at night, several times, while I was writing this, I saw the same representation, with some understanding of the

---

221. Decloux, *The Spiritual Diary*, (14) 22.
222. Decloux, *The Spiritual Diary*, (120) 45.
223. Decloux, *The Spiritual Diary*, (123) 46.
224. Decloux, *The Spiritual Diary*, (124) 26.

intellect, although to a great extent it was not so clear or so distinct, nor of such great size, but like a fairly large spark, appearing to the understanding, or drawing it to itself, and showing itself to be the same.'[225]

In the light of these experiences, it is hardly surprising that in the Spiritual Exercises Ignatius presents the use of the imagination as the way into authentic contemplation.

Has the extraordinary mystical life of contemplation led by Ignatius a close relationship to what he wrote in *The Spiritual Exercises;* or did he somehow manage to ignore the relevance of his own personal experience, and, as some have claimed, write a book of asceticism, or of discursive prayer, or of meditation, or certainly nothing higher than affective prayer? A priori this would seem impossible to believe.

It is worth mentioning three further pieces of evidence. First, Polanco recorded that after his first great mystical experience of the Trinity at Manresa, Ignatius set himself, though quite uneducated, to write a treatise on the Most Holy Trinity: 'After these struggles he received from the Lord during the time he was at Manresa enlightenments concerning the mystery of the Most Holy Trinity and the creation of the world and other mysteries of faith; but as far as the mystery of the Trinity is concerned, as a man who otherwise had no knowledge of these things, but had been instructed in this way, he then began to write a treatise on the Most Holy Trinity. Not only did he receive the knowledge of this mystery with extraordinary spiritual consolation in the very many hours he was as it were absorbed in the abyss of divine goodness on that day, but, as long as he lived, he received a special devotion and a sense of divine visitation in his prayers and his Masses of the Holy Trinity.'[226] Ignatius in fact abandoned the project of the treatise on the Trinity, but he applied

---

225. Decloux, *The Spiritual Diary*, (125) 46.
226. MHSI 73, 528-29: Juan de Polanco: 'Miras etiam, post haec certamina, a Domino illustrationes circa mysterium Sanctissimae Trinitatis et mundi creationem et alia fidei mysteria, eo tempore quo Manresae versatus est, a Domino accepit; sed, quod attinet ad mysterium Trinitatis, vir alioqui harum expers, sic fuit edoctus, ut eo tempore tractatum de Sanctissima Trinitate scribere sit aggressus. Nec solum cum spirituali consolatione singulari, quam multis horis quasi absorptus in abysso divinae bonitatis eo die huius mysterii cognitionem accepit, sed quamdiu vixit, in orationibus et missis de Sancta Trinitate peculiarem devotionis et divinae visitationis sensum accepit.'

himself to incorporating into his Spiritual Exercises what he had received at Manresa, and continued to receive as he progressively refined what he had first written.

Any sense of Ignatius' pulling back in the Exercises from his own intimate experience of mystical relationship, with Father, Son and Holy Spirit, with Mary and her Son is clearly denied in his writing to Fr Manuel Miona. On 16 November 1536, trying to persuade Fr Miona to do the Exercises, Ignatius wrote: 'The Spiritual Exercises are all the best that I have been able to think out, experience and understand in this life, both for helping somebody to make the most of themselves, as also for being able to bring advantage, help and profit to many others.'[227]

Hugo Rahner understood the endeavour of Ignatius to share his mystical experience with those who would make the Spiritual Exercises:

> If then, in the contemplation on the Incarnation, we look on the 'whole expanse or circuit of all the earth' before the three divine Persons (N 102, n. 103, n. 106), if in the meditation on the Two Standards, Christ is considered as the 'Lord of all the world' (N 145), if the soul in prayer is ever 'in the presence of his divine Majesty and the whole heavenly court' (N 71, N 98, N 151, N232)—then it is the continual effort of the mystic to communicate as best he may his own interior prayer and contemplation to the prayer of those whom, through the Exercises, he wants to show the way he himself went at Manresa. And yet it is all done in such a simple and unaffected style that, at first glance, we would never judge these plain statements and directions could come from such deep mystical sources.[228]

---

227. J Munitiz (ed), *Inigo: Letters Personal and Spiritual* (Inigo Enterprises, Hurstpierpoint, 1995), 31.
228. J Munitiz (ed), *Inigo: Letters Personal and Spiritual* (Inigo Enterprises, Hurstpierpoint, 1995), 31.

Chapter Four

a) The conversion-discipleship dynamic.

St Ignatius stated the aim of his Spiritual Exercises in the first Annotation as 'preparing and disposing the soul to rid itself of all inordinate attachments, and, after their removal, of seeking and finding the will of God in the disposition of our life for the salvation of our souls.'[1] Again, in the title of the book, he gives the twofold end as 'the conquest of self and the regulation of one's life in such a way that no decision is made under the influence of any inordinate attachment.'[2] It is impossible to draw a hard and fast line between the two aspects of the goal: conversion, and seeking and finding the will of God. At the same time, it is quite clear that the First Week of the Exercises focuses primarily on the first part of the goal, and the Second Week on the second part. It is *after* the removal of inordinate attachments that one is to seek and find the will of God for one's life. However, conversion of heart is certainly not left behind at the end of the First Week. It will be taken up again explicitly in the Third Week, when one prays for 'sorrow, compassion and shame because the Lord is going to his suffering for my sins.'[3] Moreover, the Christ who is contemplated in the Second Week is the one who has come specifically as Saviour, and the exposure to his person involved in the contemplations is a powerful means of meeting him in his mission of healing and forgiveness. It remains true that the dynamic of the kind of personal involvement with Christ that the Exercises propose

---

1. SE 1.
2. SE 21.
3. SE 192.

requires initially an opening up to the redemptive aspect of Christ's mission, before venturing on the project of committing one's life to Christ more fully in discipleship

It could be reasonably argued that a 'week' of around five to eight days seems hardly long enough to guarantee that a person will be able to come to terms with sin and forgiveness in such a way that basic Christian conversion is really arrived at in such a short time. The counterbalance to this is the fact that it is of capital importance to enter upon the Spiritual Exercises with the dispositions of the fifth Annotation, wanting to make a total response to the total love of God. To this must be added the need for appropriate preparation. Ignatius himself, in dealing with his first companions, like Xavier and Favre, gave them the full Spiritual Exercises only after a very careful time of preparation, when he judged that they were ready to benefit from them to the full. In modern times people are very aware that they are making a great personal investment in terms of generosity when they undertake to do the full Exercises, and very often report that they come to make them at a time in their life when they feel ready to respond to God's call in the kind of radical way that the Exercises require.

An appropriate entry into the making of the Spiritual Exercises certainly demands that a person come to awareness, as far as possible, of the significance of the history of their own lives; and of God's constant love and involvement at every moment of their journey up to the present time. This is the climate in which an openness to the gift of radical Christian conversion becomes possible.

The exercises of the First Week are not geared simply to 'making a good confession' and being satisfied with a sense of being truly forgiven. The author of *The Cloud of Unknowing* rightly declared that if a person is conscious of particular sins, they should approach the sacrament of confession and receive forgiveness, but if they want to address the roots of their sin, they must take themselves to contemplative prayer.[4] Both these aspects of conversion are clearly in the mind of Ignatius. He gives careful attention to the 'general

---

4. See J Walsh (ed), *The Cloud of Unknowing* (New York: Paulist Press, 1981), XXVIII, 176–77: 'In this exercise the whole root and the ground of sin which always remains in the soul after confession, no matter how earnest it has been, all withers away.'

confession' and its preparation during the First Week of the Exercises. But there is more to it than that. The goal of the First Week is freedom from inordinate attachments, an ordering of a person's profound affectivity in such a way that no decision will be made in the future through an attachment that is disordered. In modern psychological terms, this implies coming to a greatest degree of freedom from compulsions, obsessions and addictions. This freedom has a prominent place in the First Week of the Spiritual Exercises. When Ignatius invites the retreatant to pray for the grace of conversion insistently through the, often repeated threefold colloquy to Mary, to Jesus and to the Father, he does not stop at asking for the grace of 'an interior knowledge of one's sins and a detestation of them', but proceeds to ask for 'a knowledge of the disorder of one's actions', what is called today one's sinfulness, and thirdly a 'knowledge of the world', so as to guard against it.[5]

This knowledge of the world points to the fact that the sin that is being grappled with in the First Week of the Exercises is by no means a private, personal affair. Already in these meditations and contemplations there is being opened up the whole mystery of the global conflict between good and evil that runs right through the heart of each person, and which will be highlighted by Ignatius in his great meditation on Two Standards. The person who receives the grace of the First Week of the Exercises does not receive a merely personal and private forgiveness, but is converted to Christ in such a way as to enter with him into the universal struggle against evil in all its dimensions. Mark, in his Gospel, presents four great confrontations of Jesus with cases of demonic possession: 1) at the start of his ministry, the demoniac of Capernaum (1:21-28); 2) the Gerasene demoniac (5:1-20); 3) the daughter of the Syro-Phoenician woman (7:24-30); 4) the epileptic boy (9:14-29). Matthew retells the second, third and fourth of these incidents, and Luke the first, second and fourth. Jesus comes to confront the whole mystery of sin and evil that holds people in bondage, and the retreatant, in facing up to the mystery of sin in all its dimensions in the First Week, accepts a place with Jesus in commitment to the liberation of all persons from whatever holds them in bondage. Already, in the First Week, the Spiritual Exercises have an apostolic dimension.

---

5. SE 63.

The basic essentials of the dynamic of the first stages of the Spiritual Exercises are: 1) that a person enters upon the Exercises with a spirit of desire to respond totally to God's initiative. (Annotation 5); 2) that from the start they become aware of the overall plan of God's loving initiative in creating, their need to be liberated from lack of freedom in their attitudes to creatures, and the possibility of making a free, total and effective response to God. (First Principle and Foundation).

With a firm grounding in these dispositions, the retreatant enters upon the confrontation with evil, both global and personal, in order to be open to the gift of a radical and far-reaching conversion of heart. The initial pedagogy of Ignatius in the first exercise parallels that of Paul in Romans 1:18–2:1. The interiorisation of the sense of sin seems to require looking out to see sin in so far as it is observable in its effects 'out there', leading to the deeply felt conviction that I, too, am guilty of what I find so abhorrent in its effects in other people. So, Paul proposes for consideration the sins of both the Gentile and the Jewish world, bringing out in powerful terms the horrendous nature of the sin involved in their behaviour. He then brings home to his readers their share in the same abomination: 'Therefore you have no excuse, whoever you are, when you judge others; for in passing judgment on another you condemn yourself, because you, the judge, are doing the very same things.'[6] This pedagogy of Paul has the twofold effect of bringing home to each one their involvement in global sin, and of helping them to interiorise their sense of personal sin. Ignatius does the same in the first exercise of the First Week through the use he makes of the meditation on the sin of the angels, the sin of Adam and the sin of one who went to hell for one mortal sin. 'Here it will be to ask for shame and confusion, because I see how many have been lost on account of a single mortal sin, and how many times I have deserved eternal damnation, because of the many grievous sins that I have committed.'[7]

After showing that salvation does not come through the law, nor through circumcision, nor through a presumptuous appeal to God's fidelity, Paul opens the way to the only means of salvation: 'But how, apart from I am, the righteousness of God has been disclosed, and is attested by the law and the prophets; the righteousness of God

---

6. Rom 2:1.
7. SE 48.

through faith in Jesus Christ for all who believe.'[8] Again: 'they are now justified by his grace as a gift, through the redemption that is in Christ Jesus whom God put forward as a sacrifice of atonement by his blood, effective through faith.'[9] And a third time: 'Therefore his (Abraham's) faith "was reckoned to him as righteousness". Now the words, "it was reckoned to him", were written not for his sake alone', but for ours also, 'it was reckoned to him who believe in him who raised Jesus our Lord from the dead, who was handed over to death for our trespasses and was raised for our justification.'[10]

It is in the spirit of these Pauline texts that Ignatius invites the retreatant to come to the foot of the Cross in the colloquy of the first exercise. As was remarked above, when dealing with paragraph 2709 of the *Catechism of the Catholic Church*, colloquy belongs more to contemplation than to meditation. Michael Ivens draws attention to the fact that here Ignatius introduces the kind of presence via the imagination that belongs to the contemplation of the second and subsequent Weeks. Commenting on paragraph 53 in the text of the Exercises, 'Colloquy. Imagining Christ our Lord present before me and nailed to the Cross . . .', Ivens wrote: 'The mode of prayer changes and in the colloquy the exercitant enters on what will be later understood as "imaginative contemplation".'[11] Using the imagination, perhaps in combination with the tactile symbol involved in holding the crucifix, the person at prayer is present to Christ crucified, and enters contemplatively into the mystery of redemption. They opened up at the depth at which the gift is given and received to that faith in Christ 'who was handed over to death our trespasses and was raised for our justification which brings about true, profound and lasting conversion of heart.

In the third exercise Ignatius invites the retreatant to return in 'repetition' to the points in which they have experienced greater consolation or desolation or greater spiritual appreciation *(mayor sentimiento spiritual)*[12] in the previous exercises; the consolations in

---

8. Rom 3:21-22.
9. Rom 3:24-25.
10. Rom 4:22-25.
11. M Ivens, *Understanding the Spiritual Exercises* (Leominster: Gracewing, 1998), 53.
12. SE 62.

order to deepen them, the desolations in order to allow them to be changed into consolations. Dwelling on consolation is a contemplative rather than a meditative exercise. In his Rules for the Discernment of Spirits Ignatius defines consolation:

> 'I call it consolation when an interior movement is aroused in the soul, by which it is inflamed with love of its Creator and Lord, and as a consequence, can love no creature on the face of the earth for its own sake, but only in the Creator of them all. It is likewise consolation when one sheds tears that move to the love of God, whether it be because of sorrow for sins, or because of the sufferings of Christ our Lord, or for any other reason that is immediately directed to the praise and service of God. Finally, I call consolation every increase of faith, hope and love, and all interior joy that invites and attracts to what is heavenly and to the salvation of one's soul by filling it with peace and quiet in its Creator and Lord.'[13]

The appropriation of the kind of gifts outlined here by Ignatius clearly belongs to contemplation. They are not gifts to be received once and for all, but to be progressively deepened by deliberately focusing on them in contemplative prayer. That deepening occurs not through thinking about the gifts, but through experiencing them, through the kind of 'intimate understanding and relish' that Ignatius wrote about in the second Annotation.

It is in the third exercise of the First Week that Ignatius introduces the threefold colloquy with Mary, with Jesus and with the Father; and colloquy, as mentioned above, is a form of contemplation. Really to be present to Mary, to Jesus or to the Father is to be engaged in contemplation in the strict sense. Presence in faith to anyone of the three is presence to the triune God carrying out the work of redemption. The fourth exercise, the 'resume', is explicitly contemplative: 'I have said "resuming" because the intellect without any digression assiduously ranges over, through the memory, the matters contemplated in the preceding exercises; the same three colloquies are to be made.'[14] The recommendation in the Exercises, as structured by Ignatius, to make the threefold colloquy twice on each

---

13. SE 316.
14. SE 64.

day of this First Week is a clear emphasis on the character of sheer gift of the grace that is being sought. Conversion must be deliberately and sincerely prayed for in repeated petitionary prayer.

The key concepts in the process of justification are repentance, conversion, faith, baptism. At Pentecost the hearers of Peter's sermon 'were cut to the heart and said to Peter and to the other apostles, "Brothers, what should we do?" Peter said to them, "Repent, and be baptized everyone of you in the name of Jesus Christ so that your sins may be forgiven; and you will receive the gift of the Holy Spirit."'[15] For those who came to faith in Jesus Christ as Lord and Saviour, as in the case of Saul of Tarsus (Acts 9:1-19) and of the eunuch whom Philip evangelised (Acts 8:27-38), the immediate response was the reception of baptism. The same link between 'first' conversion and baptism is later made eminently clear in cases of striking; radical conversion, like the classic case of Augustine.

The correlative of salvific, Pauline faith is baptism, in which sacramentally, formally and officially through the grace of the risen Lord Jesus present in the Church the Holy Spirit takes possession of the person baptised, conferring: on them adoption in the Son, enabling them to cry 'Abba! Father!', to pray the Lord's Prayer in communion with all the baptised and to participate in the' Eucharist.

In the making of the Spiritual Exercises the conversion experience of the First Week would rarely, if ever, lead to baptism. The vast majority of those who have made the Exercises, from the time of Ignatius to the present, were already baptised. The sacrament is unrepeatable. But the radical character of the fruit to be expected in the First Week leads to an ecclesial celebration of reconciliation, the general confession. It is often remarked that the celebration of the sacrament of penance without genuine conversion is an anomaly. The principal reason for the existence of this anomaly is the inadequacy of the preparation. The prayer of the First Week, involving the sincere and prolonged facing up to sin, forgiveness and redemption provides the ideal preparation for the celebration of the sacrament. While the repetition of baptism is not possible, a radical experience of the fruit of the First Week of the Spiritual Exercises involves, perhaps for the first time in the retreatant's life, a truly radical appropriation

---

15. Acts 2:37-8.

of baptismal grace. The importance of baptism in the process of the Exercises was well expressed by David Stanley:

> I must throughout my life be assimilated gradually more and more to Jesus Christ, in whom the paschal mystery is now completely realized. This means that the Christian life is a gradual process in which, over and over again, I am 'elected' by God in Christ with my own free cooperation. It is this basic truth which St Ignatius understood so deeply, a truth which governed, more than mere logic or psychology, the structuring of *The Spiritual Exercises*. This little book is most basically a precious recipe for advancing step by step in the 'imitation of Christ', ie the gradual realization, in a most personal manner of the grace of baptism.[16]

The salvific effect of faith is not a uniquely Pauline concept. It belongs also to each of the synoptic gospels. As Jesus exercises his healing and saving mission, it is the faith of people that enables them to be saved.[17] That faith involves a personal relationship with him, in surrender to his saving power. This kind of personal relationship is developed in the First Week through the colloquy with Christ on the Cross, made in the first exercise, though, of course, not limited to this one exercise, but repeatable whenever there is more fruit to be gained from entering into this colloquy. In the case of Bartimaeus, the blind beggar of Jericho, when Jesus first passed by, he was sitting at the side of the way (verse 46). Then he experienced the saving power of Jesus—'Jesus said to him, "Go, your faith has made you well." Immediately he regained his sight and followed him on the way.'[18] A person who has received the grace of the First Week of the Spiritual Exercises has had a profound experience of the love of the crucified and risen Lord as being *the way* to the Father. Such a person cannot walk away from the crucified Jesus, but is compelled by the dynamic of what is happening to follow him on the way. More than that, in the gospel of John, Jesus proclaims that he is the way. 'Thomas said to him, "Lord, we do not know where you are going. How can we know

---

16. D Stanley, 'Contemplation of the Gospels, Ignatius Loyola, and the Contemporary Christian' in *Theological Studies* 29/3 (September, 1968): 433.
17. See Mtt 9:22; 15:28; Mk 2:5; 5:34; 10:52; Lk 7:50; 8:48; 17:19; 18:42.
18. Mk 10:52.

the way?' Jesus said to him, 'I am the way, the truth and the life. No one comes to the Father except through me.'[19]

The language of union with Jesus and the Father and the Holy Spirit that, in John's gospel, runs through the discourse and prayer of Jesus at the Last Supper is appropriate for understanding the real situation of the redeemed Christian, who is not only a follower *on* the way, but is *in* the risen Lord, who is the way. The discipleship of the Christian has a distinctive character in that the disciple is in union with the Master. Other teachers had disciples who, when they had mastered the Scriptures, became teachers themselves, and moved off to find other disciples. The Christian disciple enters a community of disciples who are in the most intimate union with their Lord, and live with the life of the Lord, sharing his mission. The community of the disciples truly constitutes the body of Christ.

This is clearly involved in the understanding of Christian baptism, through which the baptised becomes a temple of the Holy Spirit, and an adoptive son or daughter in union with Jesus, *the* Son. The grace of actualising one's baptism, the gift of redeeming faith, the grace of forgiveness and conversion of heart, and entry into discipleship of the risen Lord are all fruits of the First Week of the Spiritual Exercises. As was remarked above, in most cases this will not be the first occasion of receiving these graces, but they are received in a new and radical way. The Spiritual Exercises are a dynamic process. The dispositions of the fifth Annotation are of paramount importance as a foundation upon which all that will follow in the course of the Exercises must be built. The quality and depth of the 'grace of the First Week', presently under consideration, is *the* turning point upon which all the rest will depend. It must profoundly influence each step of the journey that is to follow.

In the schematic structure that Ignatius presents in the Spiritual Exercises the retreatant 'emerges from the First Week' with a new sense of being totally loved by God and by Christ. This love reaches even to the depths of sinfulness. Together with the evident response of gratitude, there is a desire to follow Christ in discipleship. This desire will be developed and fulfilled through the consideration of 'the call of the King' and all the exercises of the Second Week. The Christ whom one follows is not just the historical Jesus of 2000 years

---

19. Jn 14:5–6.

ago; but the risen Cord of today. The following is not from afar, but from within an already existing union.

The person making the Spiritual Exercises comes, through the prolonged prayer of the First Week, to a deeper appropriation of the gift of redemptive faith in Christ crucified. There is a new and more radical conversion of heart. There is a sense of being totally loved and forgiven, leading to a profound gratitude. Such a person is ready to draw on the grace of their baptism to commit themselves as fully as possible to the following of Christ in discipleship This following is an activation of the gifts of the Holy Spirit, the Spirit of the risen Lord, who dwells within the baptised. The following of Christ, therefore, will be no merely external or moral imitation. The disciple will enter the Second Week ready to hear the constantly repeated call to become 'another Christ' *(alter Christus)*. Writing of the contemplation of Christ in the Second Week of the Exercises, George Aschenbrenner entitled his article 'Becoming Whom We Contemplate'. He opened and concluded that article with these sentences: 'Contemplation is a radically transforming process. Through contemplation we truly become whom we contemplate and whom we are all meant to be.[20]

For Karl Rahner identification with Christ is not merely something moral, but requires ontological foundation:

> We should not reduce this participation in the life of Jesus to some sort of a moral relationship Moral influence coming from Jesus must be made possible by and based on an ontological influence. By reason of the Incarnation of the Word and the whole history of the life and death of Jesus, each one of us is already personally involved in the life of Jesus. In fact, the whole world including the life of every human being is really affected and determined by His human existence. In a narrower and historically more perceptible sense, after being affected by Him we were incorporated by Baptism into that community which is His Body, and by this sacramental-ontological determination of our historical existence, we were drawn even further into His life . . . Still, our entrance into the blessedness of the inner Trinitarian life of God really only

---

20. G Aschenbrenner, 'Becoming Whom We Contemplate', in *The Way Supplement* 52 (Spring, 1985): 30, 42.

takes place when we are drawn into the concrete life of Jesus as it is present to us now.[21]

The same union with Christ was already present in the writings on prayer of Jerome Nadal:

> Receive and diligently exercise that union with Christ Jesus and his faculties with which the Spirit of the Lord graciously gifts you, so that you sense in your spirit that you understand with his intellect, that you desire with his will, you recollect with his memory, and your whole person exists and lives and operates, not in yourself, but in Christ; this is the highest perfection of this life, its divine virtue, its wonderful sweetness.[22]

Ignatius, in his characteristic style, gives a summary overview of what will be involved in discipleship through the preliminary consideration of the 'call of the King'. He had done the same with regard to the whole of the Exercises in the First Principle and Foundation. Though the consideration of the Kingdom (as it is called in the Vulgate translation) is preliminary, and to be made just once or twice on the day intervening between the Weeks, it is of capital importance in the structure of the whole Exercises, and ranks with the later Two Standards meditation as a most powerful means of inviting the retreatant into a truly efficacious following of Christ as totally as possible.

The consideration of the Call of the King concludes with the suggestion of an offering of oneself to the following of Christ in the most radical commitment. The setting for this offering is 'in the presence of Thy infinite goodness, and of Thy glorious mother, and of all the saints of Thy heavenly court'.[23] This setting is used by Ignatius twice more in the Spiritual Exercises, at moments of the greatest

---

21. K Rahner, *Spiritual Exercises* (New York: Herder and Herder, 1965), 115–16.
22. MHSI 27, (Orationis Observationes -70, 163) 697: 'Accipe et exerce diligenter vnionem, quam tibi gratificatur spiritus Domini ad Christi Jesum, atque eius potentias, vt sentias in spiritu te per eius intellectum intellegere, per voluntatem velle, per memoriam recordari, totumque te et esse et viuere et operari, non in te, sed in Xpo.; haec est huius temporis perfectio summa, virtus diuina, admirabilis suauitas.'
23. SE 98.

solemnity in the meditation of the Three Classes of Persons,[24] and in the final Contemplation to Attain the Love of God.[25] As with the First Principle and Foundation, the mature fruit of the Kingdom consideration is not to be expected immediately, but will develop through the contemplations of the mysteries of the life of Christ upon which the retreatant is about to enter. Though Ignatius did not give a clear instruction on the matter, the offering of the Kingdom ought to be used frequently throughout the ensuing contemplations, as a 'touchstone' to remind the retreatant of the kind of response to which the dynamic of these contemplations is ordered.

The person making the Spiritual Exercises comes, through the prolonged prayer of the First Week, to a deeper appropriation of the gift of redemptive faith in Christ crucified. There is a new and more radical conversion of heart. There is a sense of being totally loved and forgiven, leading to a profound gratitude. Such a person is ready to draw on the grace of their baptism to commit themselves as fully as possible to the following of Christ. This following is an activation of the gifts of the Holy Spirit, the Spirit of the risen Lord, who dwells within the baptised. Through the continual contemplation of the life of the risen Lord, revealed in the gospels, the retreatant will grow in the gift of faith already developed through the Exercises of the First Week. That faith is a personal relationship with Christ, which is the immediate means to union with' Father, Son and Holy Spirit.

Contemplation of the mysteries of the life of Christ

What is involved in the contemplation of the mysteries of the life of Christ, revealed for us in the four gospels?

What is not involved
Looking at the text of the Spiritual Exercises from the perspective of modern psychology, one could draw parallels between the use of the imagination in the Second Week Exercises and the Jungian technique of 'active imagination', or the methods of Gestalt therapy or Psychosynthesis. These do not concern us here. This is not to deny the operation of natural psychological processes during the life of prayer,

---

24. SE 131.
25. SE 232.

nor to deny that one making the Spiritual Exercises may come to a greater integration and harmony of their psychic life through exercise of the imagination. Such psychological considerations are secondary to the spirituality of what is involved in the use of the imagination to enter the mystery of God's self-communication in Jesus Christ.

Use of the imagination
When Ignatius invites a retreatant to exercise the senses of the imagination in the presence of a gospel mystery, he instructs them to see the persons, to hear what they are saying, and to see what they are doing. Because this exercise is 'imaginative', it does not involve getting to know about the person of Christ or other persons involved in the mysteries, but rather getting to know them. This is quite different from taking the instructions about using the senses so literally that we think that the important thing here is to be able to reproduce clear, imaginative representations of the persons, their words and their actions. The contemplation is not dependent on the quality of the retreatant's imagination, whether it be well-developed or not. It remains true that God uses all our natural faculties in our life of prayer, and a well developed imagination may prove helpful. A great contemplative like Jerome Nadal produced his books of 'Pictures of the Gospel History' and 'Annotations and Meditations on the Gospels.'[26] He made it his practice to start out on the contemplation of a gospel mystery with the use of pictures or engravings. Beginning with Borgia, Nadal and Canisius, Jesuits continued to produce books of meditation on the gospels, often illustrated with symbols or with engravings depicting the gospel scenes. Writing of Jesuit history in the seventeenth century, de Guibert commented: 'The tradition of illustrations also continued in books of meditation on the life of Christ. In these the engravings were no longer symbolic, but represented scenes and parables of the Gospels in order to aid the imagination of those contemplating them.'[27] However, the quality of the fruit of a vivid or strong imagination is incidental to the essential presence to the person of Christ contemplated in the gospel.

---

26. M Nicolau, *Jerome Nadal, SI (1507–1580) Sus obras y doctrinas espirituales* (Madrid: Urania, 1949), 114–132.
27. de Guibert, *The Jesuits Their Spiritual Doctrine and Practice*, 345.

Nadal, on one occasion, gave a lengthy account of a personal meditation on the nativity of Jesus. It is a piece of preaching that is very discursive, filled with images, ideas and feelings:

> On the day of the Nativity of Christ Jesus. Prayer. The reading of the gospel and looking at the picture gives the history, along with the simple consideration of the facts. Contemplate Nazareth in the tribe of Zebulun, near Mt Tabor, a city situated on a mountain to the north, the road through Issachar, Manasseh, Ephraim and Samaria, through the tribe of Benjamin and Jerusalem and the tribe of Judah, right to Bethlehem Ephrathah, situated on a small hill. Consider the house and in it the shack, and the manger hollowed out in the cave; the road, at one part flat, at another hilly; these places, this road will arouse a pious affection in you, as the road along which the virgin mother of God made her journey, having in her womb Christ Jesus, the word of God; the road along which Joseph drove the ox and led the ass on which the virgin mother was sitting. Join this most holy and divine company; kiss their footprints; contemplate the angels in the air, preceding and following. What could be or could be said to be more sublime than this company? more divine? what by contrast, more poor or simple?[28]

Nadal continued at great length in the same effusive, discursive style. Commenting upon Nadal's writing, Alexandre Brou remarked: 'There we have a good example of what the Exercises call a contemplation—a series of affectionate considerations on the deeds, the persons, the

---

28. MHSI 27, 723-24: 'In Die Natalis Xpi. Jesu. Oratio—Historiam dabit lectio euangelii et imaginis conspectus, simplici item cum rerum consideratione locum contemplare Nazareth, in tribu Zabulon, iuxta montem Thabor, in monte sitam vrbem ad septentrionem, viam per Isachar, Manasse, Ephraim, et Samariam, per tribum Beniamin et Hierusalem et Juda tribum, vsque ad Bethlehem Ephrata in monticulo positam. Considera domum et in ea tugurium, et excisum in antro presepe, viam modo planam, modo montosam; haec loca, haec via, pium in te mouebit affectum, vt per quam iter habebat virgo Dei mater, per quam in eius vtero Dei verbum Xpus. Jesus, per quam Joseph agens bouem, ducens vero asinum, cui virgo mater insedebat. Junge te illi comitatui sacerrimo ac diuino, deosculare vestigia, contemplare angelos in aere et praecedentes et sequentes: quid dici vel esse potest hoc comitatu augustius? Quid divinius? quid contra pauperius ac simplicius?

words of the gospels.'[29] Nadal's preaching, helpful though it could be, is not a good example of contemplation. For authentic contemplation in the spirit of the Second Week of the Spiritual Exercises there is far more involved than 'a series of affectionate considerations on the deeds, the persons, the words of the gospels'. It is rather a matter of profound presence and transformation through personal contact with Christ in his mysteries.

Bill Barry in his book, *Finding God in All Things,* clearly rejects a false understanding of the use of imagination in prayer on the gospel mysteries:

> The point is that we are asked to trust that the Holy Spirit of God who dwells in us will use our imaginations in order to reveal to us who Jesus is. When I talk about imagination in prayer in this way, it often happens that people think that it's not for them. They think that I am talking about a kind of imagination that can create a movie inside their heads. There are people, of course, who have such imaginations, and I have often envied them their ability to produce such interesting stories. But I believe that each of us has an imagination. Only we have different kinds of imaginations. For example, I say, and believe that Jesus is my companion and leader. I stake my life on my commitment to him. But I have no idea what he looks like. Yet I sense how he feels at times and have had some idea of how he feels about me. For many years as a Jesuit I thought that I was somehow deficient in my prayer life because I could never produce a picture of Jesus. I have come to realize that each of us has a different way of imagining. If you can read a novel and get involved in the characters, then you have an imagination. If you can be moved by a play or by music or by painting, you have an imagination. If you can weep for someone who tells you about the loss of a loved one, you have an imagination. As I put it once, if you can wince when someone tells you about hitting his thumb with a hammer, you have an imagination. Imaginations differ; we need to let God use the one we have and not bemoan the one we do not have.[30]

---

29. Brou, *La Spiritualite de S. Ignace*, 64: 'Nous avons là un bon example de ce que les Exercises appellent une contemplation, série de considerations affectueuses sur les faits, les personnes, les paroles évangeliques.'
30. W Barry, *Finding God in All Things* (Notre Dame, Ind: Ave Maria Press, 1991),

Barry's earlier experience of deficiency in praying with the gospel mysteries because of a supposed 'lack of imagination' is a frequently heard complaint, and one which goes right back to Teresa of Avila who, like Barry, was led to go beyond her supposed lack of imagination to the reality of what is involved in presence to the Lord: 'I had such little ability to represent things with my intellect that, if I hadn't seen the things, my imagination was not of use to *me*, as it is to other persons who can imagine things and thus recollect themselves.' This is the classic, oft-repeated complaint, in the form of a psychological projection, imagining that other people have imaginations which present clear pictures. Teresa continued: 'I could only think about Christ as He was as man, but never in such a way that I could picture Him within myself no matter how much I read about His beauty or how many images I saw of Him. I was like those who are blind or in darkness; they speak with a person and see that that person is with them because they know with certainty that the other is there. I mean they understand and believe this, but they do not see the other; such was the case with me when I thought of our Lord.'[31]

We are not concerned here with the production of anything like a still picture or a film of the incident involved in the mystery. This kind of exaggeration of the importance of forming clear imaginative pictures is not uncommon among commentators on the Exercises. Aloysius Ambruzzi wrote: 'The work of the imagination is to place before the Exercitant a really living picture—a movie, we might say —of some incident of our Lord's life.'[32] He then cites Joseph Rickaby: 'The contemplation that St Ignatius teaches in the Exercises is,' says Fr Rickaby, 'what an artist would call a study of a scene in our Lord's life.' We may call such a contemplation a 'mind painting.'[33] A similar idea is proposed by John English: 'This ability to enter personally into a novel, a movie, or a stage production is what Ignatius wants us to exercise in contemplating the mysteries of Christ's life. If a particular retreatant is unable to do this, at least to some degree, then the one

---

83–4.
31. St Teresa of Avila, *The Book of Her Life*, chapter 9.6, in *The Collected Works volume 1*, 102.
32. A Ambruzzi, *The Spiritual Exercises of St Ignatius with a Commentary by Aloysius Ambruzzi* (Mangalore: Codialbal, 1931), 187.
33. Ambruzzi, *The Spiritual Exercises of St Ignatius*, 190.

who gives the Exercises should introduce the retreatant to another method of prayer.'[34]

What we are concerned about is the quality of presence of the person to the mystery. The imagination is essentially a way into that presence. It may continue to operate actively, as in the example cited above (p 47), of the man who returned to the site of the Coral Sea battle, but the essence of the exercise is that one be put in touch with the in-depth, personal meaning here and now for one's life of what is being contemplated. Did Ignatius understand this clearly? Perhaps he would be unable to articulate it as clearly as someone who has had the advantage of a well-developed theology of the resurrection and the activity of the risen Lord in the life of his Church in every age and specifically in the present moment. But, while not having the advantage of this kind of formal theological education, Ignatius had the different and more significant advantage of having had mystical experiences like that of the Cardoner where 'the eyes of his understanding were opened'. Clearly such experiences did not allow him to anticipate and articulate future theological development, but they did give him such an intuition and seminal understanding of the mysteries of faith in the line of the *sentir* of his second Annotation that his writings were open to future developments and not, as the test of time has proven, at variance with them.

Essence of this form of contemplation

What, then, is the essence of the contemplation of the mysteries of Christ in the Second Week of the Spiritual Exercises?

This question was addressed in two articles in *Christus* in the 1950s. The first of these is by Henri Holstein,[35] and the second by Pierre Voulet.[36]

In his article Holstein rightly dates the beginning of the contemplation of Christ's mysteries for Ignatius at the time of his conversion at Loyola. There he pondered not only the text of

---

34. English, *Spiritual Freedom*, 134.
35. 'Gospel Contemplation' *(La Contemplation Évangelique)* in *Christus* 2 (1955): 451–65.
36. 'Contemplation of the Mysteries of Christ' *(La Contemplation des Mystères du Christ)* in *Christus* 5 (1958): 458–76.

Ludolph of Saxony, but the illustrations that accompanied that text in the translation of Ambrosio de Montesino. The contemplation became habitual for Ignatius, as we saw Ludolph recommend in his Introduction above so that, from the start of his time at Manresa, Ignatius was able to say: 'Besides his seven hours of prayer, he was occupying himself in helping some souls who would come and find him there in spiritual matters, and all the rest of the day remaining he would give to thinking about things of God, based on what he had read.'[37] Holstein declared that it was through the contemplation of the mysteries that 'in this light, little by little, his vocation was affirmed and the will of God for him became defined.'[38] This leads in the Exercises to 'a spiritual familiarity with the gospel, climate of the election and school of union with the incarnate Word, through presence to the mysteries of his life, of his passion and of his resurrection.'[39] In the text of the Exercises Ignatius sets the election firmly in the context of the gospel contemplations. These continue right through the time the retreatant spends in making the election. 'Among the three ways of making an election, if God does not move him in the first, he ought to give his attention to the second, so that he may clearly know his vocation through the experience of both consolations and desolations. In this way, as he continues with his meditations on Christ our Lord, let him see in which direction he is moved through the consolations which present themselves. Similarly, with the desolations.'[40]

Regarding the role of the memory in these contemplations, Holstein wrote that, whereas it had an active role in the meditations of the First Week, here it appears only as introductory (first prelude). This does not minimise its importance, for it situates the praying

---

37. J Munitiz and P Endean, *Reminiscences*, (26) 24.
38. Holstein, *'La Contemplation Évangelique'*, 452: 'à cette lumière, peu à peu, s'affermit sa vocation et se précise la volonté de Dieu sur lui.'
39. Holstein, *'La Contemplation Évangelique'*, 452: 'Il initiera ainsi les âmes a une familiarité spirituelle avec l'Évangile, climat de l'élection et école d'union au Verbe incarné par presence aux mystéres de sa vie, de sa passion et de sa resurrection.'
40. MHSI 76, *First Autograph Directory* of *Ignatius*, (18) 77: 'Inter tres modos electiones instituendi, si in primo modo Deus non moveat, insistat secundo, ut vocationem suam manifeste cognoscat, cum per consolationes tum per desolationes: hoc modo in meditationibus de Christo Domino nostro sese exercens, offerentibus sese consolationibus videat in quam a Deo partem moveatur. Idem in desolationibus faciendum.'

person in the reality of the historic salvation which Christ brought to our world. Similarly the second prelude fixes the imagination on a definite place, so that the incarnate Word is present for the retreatant both in time and in place. The third prelude, the all-important prayer for 'an intimate knowledge of our Lord, who has become man for me, that I may love Him more and follow Him more closely'[41] is interpreted by Holstein: 'That the Eternal Father, through his Spirit, grants us to know his beloved Son and conforms us to him. This conformity to Christ will only be obtained through a prolonged effort of *presence* to the mystery; and that is what constitutes contemplation as taught by the Exercises.'[42]

In presenting the Exercises of the Second Week, Ignatius repeatedly gives the instruction to reflect and draw profit: 'I will reflect on myself and draw profit from what I see.'[43] The contemplative, active participation in the mystery necessitates personal involvement of the praying person in their authentic here and now reality. As John Wickham put it: 'the one praying should carry an awareness of his whole life-world into the mystery; so that the divine Lord in the power of the mystery may pour himself into the life-world of the one praying.'[44] 'Reflect on myself' means to bring the real me as I now am into the mystery, so that my presence to the risen Lord, for Ignatius 'God our Lord', 'the Divine Majesty', 'the Eternal Son' brings my present life into the stream of salvation history, and God's self-revelation through the mystery of the Word-made-flesh. In the context of the Spiritual Exercises this revelation is not a revelation 'out there', but a revelation to this praying person in their life, lived with its whole history up to this point in time and open to the Lord's action now and into the future. The colloquy before the crucified Christ in the First Week has not been 'left behind'. That colloquy made very clear the movement of salvation history that was Ignatius's focus: 'Imagine Christ our Lord present before you upon the cross, and begin to speak with him, asking how it is that though He is the

---

41. SE 104.
42. H Holstein, 'La Contemplation Évangelique', 453: 'Cette conformité au Christ nes obtiendra que par un effort prolongé de *presence* au mystère; et c'est là, proprement, la contemplation telle que l'enseignent les Exercices.'
43. SE 106.
44. J Wickham, 'Ignatian Contemplation Today', in *The Way Supplement*, 34 (Autumn 1978): 37.

Creator, He has stooped to become man, and to pass from eternal life to death here in time, that thus he might die for my sins. I shall also reflect on myself and ask: 'What have I done for Christ? What am I doing for Christ? What ought I to do for Christ?' And so, beholding him in this plight, nailed to the cross, I shall ponder on what presents itself.'[45]

The 'ought' involved in this colloquy is not a question of making some moral 'resolution', but is a radical response to the invitation of the gospel. Pietro Schiavone sees it in Lucan terms: the question 'What are we to do?' of Luke 3:10, and of Acts 2:37, 16:30.[46] The threefold question about response to the love of Christ does not end with the first exercise of the First Week, but is an important aspect of the ongoing dynamic of the whole of the Exercises.

To take 'reflect on myself' in a too literal and narrow sense could result in distraction from the essence of contemplative presence to Christ and in drawing a multiplicity of mini-lessons of passing value from various parts of the contemplations. But there is something far more important at stake here, namely: the insertion of the retreatant into Christ in discipleship, which is going to affect the whole course of their life, and, in terms of the Spiritual Exercises, the election.

Dealing with the phrase 'reflect on myself' Holstein situates the contemplations in the context of their end of being 'conformed' to Christ:

> 'It is not matter or dreaming, of abandoning oneself to the spontaneous movements of sensibility, of being content with inconsistent, pious imaginings. Hence, the need to return in reflection upon oneself. This reflection must retain its proper place; it is only a secondary activity, and the absorption of a gaze fixed at length on Christ can make the reflection barely conscious. It is not a matter of turning the contemplation into meditation, and restricting by inappropriate considerations the movement of that grace which often leads the retreatant into a prayer that is very simple rather than discursive. It is often better to forget oneself and allow oneself to be

---

45. SE 53.
46. Schiavone, *Esercizi Spirituali*, 137.

carried along by the mystery, rather than lose one's peace in constructing beautiful programmes of perfection.'[47]

Voulet goes further in assigning a spiritual meaning to 'reflect on oneself': 'the exercise consists in looking and, listening, in order to then reflect on oneself and to draw from that a spiritual profit, that is to say a more intimate knowledge of the Saviour.'[48]

Throughout his article Holstein insists on the capital importance of the discernment of spirits in order to make the contemplations of the Second Week profitably: 'The Second Week, still more than the First Week is a privileged time when interior movements follow one another and struggle against one another; nothing is less peaceful than these contemplations.'[49] The main foci for the discernment are the real insertion of the retreatant into the great salvific plan of God revealed in Christ, and the 'childish' illusion of indulging the imagination in a peaceful lingering on the events, divorced from the reality of the challenge of an authentic response.

Holstein describes the process by which the contemplations attain their goal of knowing, loving and following Christ as 'a kind of osmosis', an evocative word, suggesting the avoidance of taking 'reflect on oneself' too literally. The fruit will be received gradually through contemplative presence over time, which is accompanied by authentic facing up to the real personal issues each one brings to the effort to follow Christ. Holstein makes a strange distinction in which he claims that it is the colloquy which deals with these

---

47. Holstein, *La Contemplation Évangelique*', 455: 'Il ne s'agit pas de rêver, de s'abandonner aux mouvements spontanes de la sensibilité, de se contenter de pieuses imaginations inconsistantes. D'où la necessité d'un retour reflexif sur soi. Cette reflexion demeurera discréte; ce n'est qu'une activité secondaire, et que le receuillement d'un regard longuement fixé sur le Christ Jésus peut rendre à peine consciente. Il ne faut pas transformer la contemplation en meditation, et gener par des reflexions intempestives le mouvement de la grace, qui souvent porte le retraitant à une oraison très simple et très peu discursive. Il vaudra mieux souvent s'oublier et se laisser prendre par le mystère que s'inquiéter de soi et de parfaire un beau programme de perfection.'
48. Voulet, '*La Contemplation des Mystères du Christ*', 458: 'l'exercice consistè a regarder et écouter, pour réfléchir ensuite sur soi-même et en tirer un profit spirituel, c'est-à-dire une connaissance plus intime du Sauveur.'
49. Holstein, '*La Contemplation des Évangelique*', 456: 'La seconde semaine, plus encore que la première, est un temps privilegié où les mouvements interieurs se succedent et se heurtent; rien de moins paisible que ces contemplations.'

issues rather than the contemplation itself: 'The colloquy... is more explicitly oriented towards the future (the election, and its execution in a changed living) than the contemplation itself, which is concerned with presence to the mystery alone.'[50] While 'presence to the mystery' expresses well the essence of this kind of contemplation, awareness of 'the election and its execution' need not be excluded from the contemplations. In any case, what happens in the contemplations is response to a divine gift, and for Ignatius will always be subject to a discernment which will be oriented to the practicalities of one's living.

The knowledge of Christ that is being sought in the contemplations is seen by Holstein to be a divine illumination. In his instructions for the repetitions Ignatius includes in this Second Week 'understanding'. 'In doing this (repetition), attention should always be given to some more important parts in which one has experienced understanding, consolation, or desolation.'[51] This leads Holstein to write: 'He insists on the spiritual illumination of these days of the 'contemplations'. The intellect is enlightened, not by a reasoning which would decide on the need to practise a certain virtue in imitation of Jesus, but by the intimate light which emerges from the mystery lived in prayer.'[52] And Holstein perceptively remarks that 'this light transforms the retreatant into the likeness of Christ.'[53] This likeness is an interior one: 'In sharing his earthly condition, the retreatant adopts the feelings of Christ; he shares his preferences, he brings his affectivity and his heart into harmony with the Heart of the Saviour.'[54] Later, in treating of the passivity involved in these contemplations, Holstein writes that 'it is necessary to allow oneself to be taken and moulded by the

---

50. Holstein, 'La Contemplation des Évangelique': 'Le colloque ... est plus nettement orienté vers l'avenir (l'election, et son execution dans une vie changée) que la contemplation elle-même, qui agit par la seule presence au mystère.'
51. SE 118.
52. Holstein, 'La Contemplation des Évangelique', 457: Il insiste sur l'illumination spirituelle de ces journées de 'contemplations'. L'intelligence est éclairée, non par un raisonnement qui conclurait à la necessité de pratiquer telle vertu, à l'imitation de Jésus, mais par la lumière intime qui se dégage du mystère vécu dans l'oraison.'
53. Holstein, 'La Contemplation des Évangelique', 457: 'cette lumière transforme le retraitant et le change à la ressemblance du Christ.'
54. Holstein, 'La Contemplation des Évangelique', 459: 'En partageant sa condition terrestre, le retraitant prend les sentiments du Christ Jesus; il partage ses preférences, il accorde sa sensibilité et son coeur au Coeur du Sauveur.'

mystery, to allow oneself to be invaded by the Saviour who grants us 'an intimate knowledge' of his Person.[55]

In dealing with the danger of pious sentimentality, what he calls 'childishness and excessive familiarity', Holstein has recourse to the importance of faith. This is the occasion of his referring to the gifts of the Holy Spirit (something that Voulet will develop more significantly in his article). If childishness is to be excluded, childlikeness is to be encouraged. 'The contemplations of the Second Week require a great spirit of faith, which seizes, so to speak, all the faculties of the retreatant, and which, with the help of the gifts of the Holy Spirit, concentrates his whole being to commune with the Gospel mysteries.'[56]

Holstein then declares that through 'presence in faith' a person contemplating can be present in time to something that took place in the past: 'Presence in faith which makes the soul contemporaneous with the mystery. It does not suppress the activity of the mind which reflects and draws profit from what the eyes see and the ears hear: in that, we think that contemplation is distinguished from the application of the senses where the superior faculties experience a quasi-mystical silence.'[57] Holstein's explanation of 'contemporaneity with the mystery' will remain unsatisfying. He seems here to change his previous stance in which he saw contemplation in contradistinction to colloquy as concerned with presence alone. His view of the Application of the Senses is an extremely exalted one, and makes no acknowledgement of the fact that Ignatius invites people to reflect and draw profit in that exercise as well as in the preceding contemplations.

After asking the question whether the contemplations involve a pious reconstruction of the pastoral vision of faith, Holstein fails to come to grips with the problem of the contemporaneity of the

---

55. Holstein, *La Contemplation Évangelique*, 461: 'il faut se laisser prendre et modeler par le mystère, se laisser envahir par le Seigneur qui nous accorde, de sa Personne une "connaissance intime."'
56. Holstein, *La Contemplation Évangelique*, 459–60: 'Les contemplations de seconde semaine exigent un grand esprit de foi, qui saisisse, pour ainsi dire, toutes les facultés du retraitant, et qui, avec l'aide des dons du Saint-Ésprit, concentre tout son être pour communier aux mystères évangeliques.'
57. Holstein, *La Contemplation Évangelique*, 460: 'Presence de foi qui rend l'âme contemporaine au mystère, Elle ne supprime l'activité de l'ésprit qui reflêchit et fait son profit de ce que voient ses yeux et entendent ses oreilles: par la, pensons-nous, là contemplation se distingue de l'application des sens, ou les facultés superieures connaissent un silence quasi-mystique.'

mysteries with the life of the praying person today. He does declare that the Risen one lives in us, and 'it is this actual presence of Christ in his faithful that, the contemplations bring to 'realisation' for the retreatant.'[58] He appeals to the Christmas Liturgy and its words: 'Today Christ is born for us *(Hodie Christus natus est nobis)*', but seems quite oblivious of the question whether these words are meant to draw attention to a birth of Christ *today* or *on this date*... Holstein rightly declares that 'the historical events of our salvation in Christ only truly become for us a spiritual reality at the moment when we welcome them through a personal union.'[59]

Towards the end of his article Holstein shifts the perspective from our presence to the mysteries of Christ to Christ's presence to us:

> Gospel history only truly becomes our history when we consent to become present to it, to consider it no longer as an account of past events, but as a presence of Christ to our own existence... Becoming in prayer immediate and compelling, this life of Christ will bear from now on, if we are faithful to grace, all its fruit... In prayer a presence of Christ in whom we live becomes clearly manifest.[60]

Holstein again fails to explain fully how it is that through contemplation Christ is present in time to us. He suggests our formation by the contemplation of gospel mysteries, without naming it as formation. At the end of his article he writes that daily Jesuit prayer is a sign of a need to allow ourselves to be always more transformed by the mysteries.

Early in his article Voulet declares, as many had done before him, that contemplation in the Second Week of the Exercises is not to be understood according to the usual terminology of spiritual authors, that is, as infused prayer. He acknowledges the general link

---

58. Holstein, *La Contemplation Évangelique*, 462–3: 'C'est cette actuelle presence du Christ en ses fidèles que les contemplations de seconde semaine font 'realiser' au retraitant.'
59. Holstein, *La Contemplation Évangelique*, 463–4: 'les evenements historiques de notre salut dans le Christ ne deviennent veritablement *pour nous* une realité spirituelle qu'à l'heure ou nous les accueillons par une adhésion personnelle.'
60. Holstein, *La Contemplation Évangelique*, 464: 'Devenue, dans la prière, immediate et contraignante, cette vie du Christ portera désormais, si nous sommes fidèles à la grace, tout son fruit.'

between contemplation and mystery. The events of the life of Jesus are indeed mysteries, with a hidden meaning. Voulet refers to the link between these contemplations and *lectio divina*: 'We will use the key meditations of the Second Week of the Exercises, which give a method for making the reading of the Gospel a contemplation.'[61] He concludes his introduction with what will be a most important theme of his article: 'the life of Christ contemplated in this way, is able to transform our life.'[62]

Voulet makes the crucial point that the Christ whom we attain in his mysteries is involved in the work of salvation, and we can only attain him if we ourselves enter into this salvific work. He draws attention to Ignatius's proposing in the Kingdom consideration a Christ who is engaged in a universal plan for the glorification of the Father, and who invites each of us to take part in this plan.

The incarnation is salvific, but only acquires its full meaning through the passion and resurrection. The historical character of the redemptive mystery and the long preparation God made for humanity to receive this gift throw light upon the importance of the temporal life of Christ. All of the acts of the life of Christ are mysteries because they participate in the fundamental mystery of incarnation, passion, resurrection. For the Gospel of John the profound significance of the actions and words of Jesus comes to light through the religious experience of the first Christian generation. Voulet acknowledges that Paul, focused as he was on the mystery of the suffering and glorious Christ, did not attach the same importance to the events of his earthly life. To attain the richness of the mysteries of the life of Christ one must read the synoptics in the light of John and Paul and the patristic tradition. 'In each incident of the synoptics there are found the essential character of the incarnation that they are rooted in and of the paschal mystery that they proclaim.'[63] Voulet will take up again later the truth that every mystery of the life of Jesus participates in

---

61. Voulet, 'La Contemplation Mystères', 459: 'Nous nous servirons des meditations-clés de la seconde Semaine des Exercises, qui donnent une methode pour faire de la lecture l'Évangile une contemplation.'
62. Voulet, 'La Contemplation Mystères', 459: 'la vie du Christ, ainsi contemplée, peut transformer le nôtre.'
63. Voulet, *La Contemplation Mystères*, 463: 'On retrouve en chacun d'eux les traits essentiels de l'Incarnation, où ils s'enracinent, et du mystère pascal qu'ils annoncent.'

the mystery of the divine plan—salvation through incarnation, death and resurrection. 'Each mystery contributes to the advancement of the Kingdom and finally to the glory of God. Although it is difficult to speak here of chronology, as each gospel has its own goal and its own order, yet there is, according to the saying of St Thomas, a 'progress' in the life of Christ.'[64] While affirming that the power of the gospel mysteries reaches us, Voulet does not attempt a full explanation of their eternal' character: 'Finally, the contemplation of the gospel mysteries supposes that their efficacity extends right to us. Without seeking to give an explanation of this 'perpetuity' which makes them communicable. It is useful to recall some spiritual aspects.'[65] Some of these 'spiritual aspects' are: the eternal love of God, revealed in the mysteries, the eternal nature of the Word and the doctrine of the mystical body of Christ. Regarding the feast of Christmas, Voulet cites Augustine: 'The eternal character of the Word consecrates as eternal the event of today;' and Leo the Great, who wrote in his sixth sermon for Christmas: 'For the birth of Christ is the origin of the people of Christ, and the birthday of the head is the birthday of the body.'[66]

Voulet sees the importance of the resurrection In making gospel contemplation possible because it is through' the resurrection that the Holy Spirit is active. 'Penetrated by the Holy Spirit; the body of Christ become the spiritual and mystical body.'[67] Through the incorporation into Christ that the Spirit effects, the whole of the incarnation, with the redemptive acts that Christ performed, is extended to all the faithful. 'It is by the Spirit that is applied to each of us the virtue of the

---

64. Voulet, *La Contemplation Mystères*, 463: 'Chaque mystere contribute à l'avancement du Royaume et finalement à la gloire de Dieu. Bien qu'il soit difficile de parter ici de chronologie, chaque évangile ayant son but et son ordonnance propre, il y a cependant, selon Saint Thomas, un 'progrès' au un développement dans la vie du Christ.'
65. Voulet, *La Contemplation Mystères*, 464: 'Enfin, la contemplation des mystères évanqgeliques suppose que leur efficacité s'étend jusqu'à nous. Sans chercher à donner une explication de cette perpetuité qui les rend communicables, il est utile d'en retenir quelques aspects spirituels.'
66. St Leo the Great, 'Sermon 6 on the Nativity' in *The Divine Office* I (Sydney: EJ Dwyer, 1974), 243.
67. Voulet, *La Contemplation Mystères*, 465: 'penetré par l' Éspit Saint, le corps du Christ devient corps spiritual et mystique.'

acts of the incarnate Word, through which is handed on the eternal love of the Father.[68]

Personal participation in the mysteries of the Gospel requires for Voulet personal faith. He fittingly draws attention to the attitude of Mary, who was so important for Ignatius, in her *fiat* at the Annunciation: 'The *fiat* by which she consents to the mystery ought to 'remain at the heart of all Christian contemplation.'[69]

The importance of faith for the contemplations corresponds to the role of the understanding in penetrating the gospel mysteries. Jesus reproached the Apostles for their lack of understanding: 'Why are you talking about having no bread? Do you still not perceive or understand? 'Do you have eyes, and fail to see? Do you have ears and fail to hear? And 'do you not remember?'[70] As for Holstein, the reflection on faith and understanding leads Voulet to write of the 'essential role' of the gifts of the Holy Spirit for contemplation. He invokes the teaching of St Gregory and of St Thomas Aquinas: 'According to St Gregory, followed by St Thomas, the gift of understanding makes us penetrate the divine words and the mysteries of faith.'[71] Closely linked to understanding is the Spirit's gift of wisdom. 'The gift of wisdom puts the finishing touch to the work of the intellect, to which is attributed the principal role in contemplation. In practice one can distinguish two characteristics of this wisdom. As the 'organising' Wisdom from which it originates, which conducts the whole history of salvation, it raises us up, via the events of the gospels to a view of the overall plan of God, and it fixes our affections on this redemptive work. On the other hand, it is a taste of spiritual realities, thanks to which a person experiences in some way, in Christ and in his mysteries, the divine presence. Interior savour and experience, which enter into every authentic contemplation.'[72]

---

68. Voulet, *La Contemplation Mystères*, 465: 'C'est par l'Esprit qu'est appliqué à chacun de nous la vertu des actes du Verbe incarné, par lesquels s'est traduit l'amour éternel du Pere.'
69. Voulet, *La Contemplation Mystères*, 467: 'Le *fiat* par lequel elle consent au mystère soit rester au coeur de toute contemplation chretienne.'
70. Mk 8:17–18.
71. Voulet, *La Contemplation Mystères*, 468: 'D'après saint Gregoire suivi par saint Thomas, le don d'intelligence nous fait pénétrer les paroles divines et les mystères de la foi.'
72. Voulet, *La Contemplation Mystères*, 468: 'Le don de sagesse achève l'oeuvre

These two gifts of the Holy Spirit are of very practical help in the goal that Ignatius proposed in the Second Week of the Spiritual Exercises: 'Understanding and spiritual wisdom will help us then to discern in the Gospel the Lord's will for us, in order to conform our life to it through a more faithful adherence to the plan of redemption.'[73] Voulet sees the words of Colossians as being specially applicable to the role of wisdom and knowledge in the Exercises: 'For this reason, since the day we heard it, we have not ceased praying for you and asking that you may be filled with the knowledge of God's will in all spiritual wisdom and understanding, so that you may lead lives worthy of the Lord, fully pleasing to him, as you bear fruit in every good work and as you grow in the knowledge of God.'[74] As Holstein had done, Voulet draws attention to the role of understanding for Ignatius in the repetitions of the Second Week. This leads him to make the strange remark that 'the repetitions . . . prolong the prayer and make it contemplative.'[75] The repetitions deepen the contemplation, but the whole thesis of the articles of Holstein and Voulet is that the contemplation of the gospel mysteries is indeed authentic contemplation.

The 'transformation of our life' brought about by gospel contemplation was suggested by Holstein, and is developed more fully by Voulet. He rightly sees it not only as the goal of the Exercises, but as the end of all authentic contemplation. Again there is the insistence that the contemplation of the Word-made-flesh is not only of a model to be imitated, but is the means to divinising our life, and in this context cites St Cyril of Alexandria. Just as the Apostles developed familiarity with Jesus over a long period, our contemplation is to be a pedagogy

---

de l'intelligence. C'est à lui qu'on attribue, on le sait, le rôle principal dans la contemplation. Pratiquement, on peut retenir deux traits de cette sagesse. Comme la Sagesse organisatrice dont elle dérive et qui conduit toute l'histoire du salut, elle nous éleve, à travers les faits évangeliques, a une vue d'ensemble du plan de Dieu et nous affectionne a cette oeuvre redemptrice. D'autre part, elle est un gout des réalites spirituelles, grace auquel l'ame expérimente en quelque sorte, dans le Christ et dans sans mystères, la présence divine. Gout interieur et experience qui entrent dans toute vrai contemplation.'

73. Voulet, La Contemplation Mystères', 469: 'Intelligence et sagesse spirituelles nous aideront donc à discerner dans l'Évangile la volonté du Seigneur sur nous, pour y conformer notre vie par une adhesion plus fidéle au plan redempteur.'
74. Col 1:9–10.
75. Voulet, La Contemplation Mystères', 470: Cette connaissance intervient encore dans les 'repetitions' qui prolongent la priere et la rendent contemplative.'

and a formation: 'Every mystery is a pedagogy. To keep oneself in the presence of Christ and to take part in the gospel events is to submit to a formation of which one can say in summary that it is a transition from the flesh to the spirit.'[76] Voulet gives a mystical interpretation of entry into Gospel history: 'We ought to enter into gospel history, each one following our own vocation: between this history and ours there exists a correspondence, not a material coincidence, but an internal and mystical harmony, the work of the Holy Spirit.'[77]

The result of our assimilation to Christ through contemplation of the mysteries is the election, which confers on each one their proper place within the history of salvation.

> Thus the existential choice which is the outcome of faith and through which we commit ourselves to God's service inserts us personally into the history of salvation and associates us with the Mystery . . . Our unique place in the Kingdom, our proper place in the Church of Christ, that is what we are finally seeking in the contemplation of the Gospel.[78]

Voulet cites Romans 8:29 in repeating Holstein's phrase of 'conformity to Christ', without attempting an exegesis of what that conformity means; but it is clear that for him it is to be understood in the context of our divinisation and assimilation to Christ: 'It is to Christ, living expression of the Mystery, as of the Kingdom, that the Holy Spirit will, assimilate us, to render us conformed to his image (Rom. 8, 29).'[79]

---

76. Voulet, 'La Contemplation Mystères', 471: 'Tout mystère est une pédagogie, Se tenir en la compagnie du Christ et prendre part aux episodes évangeliques, c'est se soumettre à une formation dont on peut dire qu'elle est une passage de la chair à l'ésprit.'
77. Voulet, 'La Contemplation Mystères', 472: 'Nous devons entrer dans l'histoire évangelique, chacun suivant notre vocation: entre cette histoire et la nôtre, il existe une correspondance, non point coincidence materielle, mais harmonie interne et mystique, oeuvre du Saint Ésprit.'
78. Voulet, 'La Contemplation Mystères', 474: 'Ainsi le choix existentiel auquel aboutit la foi et par lequel nous nous engageons au service de Dieu, en nous insérant personellement dans l'histoire du salut, nous associe au Mystère . . . Notre destinée prend par la son sens et son unité. Notre place unique dans le Royaume, notre vocation propre dans l'Église du Christ, voilà finalement ce que nous cherchons dans la contemplation de l'Évangile.'
79. Voulet, 'La Contemplation Mystères', 474: 'C'est au Christ, vivante expression du Mystère, comme du Royaume, que le Saint Ésprit nous assimilera pour nous

The Mystery for Voulet is clearly the mystery of the eternal salvific plan of the Trinity, and it is into the life of the Trinity itself that Gospel contemplation leads. 'Called to reproduce the sentiments of his Heart and of his intentions as Redeemer, will enter into participation with his interior life, that is, his consciousness of divine sonship'[80] The Trinity is present in every Gospel mystery. 'The Trinity is present everywhere... and all the mysteries are really Trinitarian mysteries.'[81] This presence to the Trinity throughout the Spiritual Exercises was affirmed by Karl Rahner, when he declared: 'The Spirit, in Whom we cry: 'Abba, Father (Rom 8:15), has been sent to us from the Son. Thus, we must familiarize ourselves with the way to the Father from the Son in His Spirit. This Trinitarian way was essential to the attitude to life of St Ignatius; it was the basis of his piety, and we meet it at every turn in his Spiritual Exercises.'[82]

The trinitarian and apostolic dimensions that Ignatius presented in the first contemplation of the Second Week on the incarnation cannot be separated from any of the contemplations of the Second Week. As William Peters put it: 'First, from now onward, the Spiritual Exercises are explicitly trinitarian. There can be no contemplation which is not first and foremost a contemplation of the Blessed Trinity. There is no great danger of losing sight of this fact, provided the contemplation on the Incarnation is taken as an example, as are the contemplation on the Nativity and first contemplations of the third and fourth weeks.'[83] Peters quite rightly understands the two contemplations presented by Ignatius, the incarnation and the nativity, as examples. The style of contemplation Ignatius proposed for the incarnation should not be simply left behind, and all subsequent contemplations modelled on the nativity contemplation:

> The two examples provide different methods of making a contemplation, and the exercitant is expected to employ them

---

rendre conformes à son image, (Rom 8:29).'
80. Voulet, 'La Contemplation Mystères', 474: 'Appelés à reproduire les sentiments de son Coeur et ses intentions de Redempteur, nous entrerons en participation de sa vie interieure, c'est-à-dire de la conscience de sa filiation divine.'
81. Voulet, 'La Contemplation Mystères', 474–5: 'La Trinité... est partout présente et tous les mysteres sont, à vrai dire, des mystères trinitaires.'
82. K Rahner, *Spiritual Exercises*, 16.
83. W Peters, *The Spiritual Exercises of St Ignatius*, 83.

> both. Traditionally, the contemplations on the Incarnation and the Nativity have been considered introductions rather than examples. Consequently, the proper method of contemplating has been derived in a very one-sided way from the contemplation on the Nativity. This one-sided view has eliminated from the Spiritual Exercises not only the mystery of the Trinity as subject matter of all the contemplations, but also that wide sweep of mankind that should play a part in every contemplation. The result has been that contemplation has often been reduced to a reflection upon the people encountered in the incident, or more accurately, upon the incident itself.[84]

The same presence of the Trinity in the contemplation of every mystery was emphasised by Michael Ivens when he wrote:

> The spirituality of the Second Week, as of the Exercises in their entirety, is both Christocentric and Trinitarian. The immediately obvious aspect of Christology in the Second Week is of course the human reality of the Incarnation. Less obvious on a perfunctory reading, yet fundamental to the spirituality of the Exercises, is the relationship of Christ to the Trinity. The salvation of the human race is the work of the Trinity (107), which decides on the Incarnation (102). Christ is our mediator with the Father (Triple Colloquy). The work of Christ is the work of the Father (95). The exercitant contemplates the life of Christ in the consciousness that the trinitarian God is manifest in that life. Thus one is conscious that to share in the life of Christ is to share the life of the Trinity; to be involved in Christ's mission is to be involved in the work of the Trinity in the world.[85]

Citing the traditional teaching that contemplation is perfect prayer, Voulet declares that

> the contemplation of the mysteries helps us grasp what is meant by that, and gives as a true idea of what contemplation is. It is a knowledge that is 'experimental' of divine things; different from reasoning intelligence which moves through

---

84. W Peters, *The Spiritual Exercises of St Ignatius*, 86.
85. M Ivens, *Understanding the Spiritual Exercises*, 76–7.

successive objects, it is an intuition which simplifies and grasps the whole; coming from the heart, it is affective; it tastes the word of God, which it depths, remaining sometimes on the same object for a long time; it is generally accompanied by a light and a peace that will fill the soul.

This is the nature, at least in its tendencies, of the contemplation that Ignatius implies. But it is not necessarily a passive prayer (the Exercises are not reserved for those favoured with the highest states of prayer); and it can be obtained with the help of ordinary grace. However, by its nature it tends towards the mystical and is an admirable preparation for it for those who should be called to it.'[86]

Voulet ends by emphasising the realism of this contemplative prayer. Like the prayer of Christ, the prayer of the retreatant must continually insert them more into the work of redemption, which is that of the Church. So, he very fittingly concludes: 'It disposes the Christian to receive, according to the desire of the Heart of Jesus, in the depth of their soul the fruit of the Eucharist: this mystical assimilation to Christ which unites the love of the Trinity and the salvific work of the Church of today.'[87]

---

86. Voulet, 'La Contemplation Mystères', 475–6: 'La contemplation des mystères nous aide à comprendre ce qu'il faut entendre par la et nous faire une idée juste de la contemplation. Elle est une connaissance pour ainsi dire experimentale des choses divines; a la difference de l'intelligence raisonnante qui parcourt des objets successifs, elle est une intuition qui simplifie et saisit les ensembles; procedant du coeur, elle est affective; elle goûte la parole de Dieu qu'elle approfondit, en demeurant parfois longuement sur le meme objet; elle s'accompagne en général d'une lumèire et d'une paix qui rassasient l'âme.

Tels sont bien les caracètres que presente, au moins dans les tendances, la contemplation que suppose saint Ignace. Or, celle-ci, remarquons-le, n'est pas necessairement une oraison passive (les Exercises ne sont pas resréves aux âmes favorisées des plus hauts états d'oraison) et elle peut s'obtenir avec le secours de la grace ordinaire. Cependant, par sa nature, elle tend a l'oraison mystique et y prépare admirablement ceux qui y seraient appelés.'

87. Voulet, 'La Contemplation Mystères', 476: 'Elle dispose le chrétien à reçevoir, selon le dèsir du Coeur de Jésus, dans l'intime de son âme et dans sa vie concrète, le fruit de l'Eucharistie: cette assimilation au Christ mystique, qui rejoint d'une part l'amour trinitaire, et de l'autre l'oeuvre salvifique de l'Église d'aujourd'hui.'

Contemporaneity of the mysteries

Ignatius certainly understood that for the personal prayer the mysteries of our Lord's life are happening *now*. In the colloquy for the contemplation of the incarnation he wrote: 'According to the light that I have-received, I will beg for grace to follow and imitate more closely our Lord, who has *just* become man for me.' (*ansi nuevamente incarnado*).[88] And again, in the first contemplation of the Third Week: 'Here it will be to ask for sorrow, compassion and shame because the Lord *is going* to His suffering for my sins.'[89]

In a series of addresses, and articles and books, from 1964 to1984, David Stanley repeatedly addressed, from the perspective of a New Testament exegete, the question of contemplation of the mysteries of the life of our Lord.[90] A question that particularly fascinated Stanley was that of the contemporaneity of the gospel mysteries with the prayer of the modern person contemplating them. He repeatedly questions the possibility of such simultaneity, never seeming to be quite satisfied with his own answer. Stanley had available to him a more developed theology of the resurrection than either Holstein or Voulet. Like them he rightly looks for the solution of his puzzle in the Lord's resurrection: 'the ultimate answer lies, of course, in the central event of Christian faith, Jesus' resurrection.'[91] It is not just the event of the resurrection, but the activity of the Spirit that makes this contemplation possible: 'What in fact did empower the inaugurators of the Christian tradition (and subsequently the evangelists) with

---

88. SE 109.
89. SE 193.
90. D Stanley, 1). 'Sagrada Escritura y Ejercicios Espirituales', in *Los Ejercicios a fa Luz del Vaticano II*. 2). 'Contemplation of the Gospels, Ignatius Loyola, and the Contemporary Christian', in *Theological Studies* 29/3 (Sept 1968). 3). 'A Suggested Approach to *Lectio Divine*' in *The American Benedictine Review* 23 (1972). 4). 'Revitalizing our Prayer Through the Gospels', in *The Way Supplement* 19 (Summer 1973). 5). 'Contemporary Gospel-Criticism and "The Mysteries of the Life of Our Lord" in *The Spiritual Exercises*' in *Ignatian Spirituality in a Secular Age*, G Schner (ed) (Waterloo, Ontario: Wilfred Laurier University Press, 1984). 6). *A Modern Scriptural Approach to the Spiritual Exercises* (Chicago: Institute of Jesuit Sources, 1967). 7). 'The Call to Discipleship The Spiritual Exercises with the Gospel of Mark', in *The Way Supplement* 43/44 (January 1982). 8). 'I Encountered God!' The Spiritual Exercises with the Gospel of John (St Loius: Institute of Jesuit Sources, 1986).
91. Stanley, 'Contemporary Gospel-Criticism and the Mysteries', 39.

the capacity to evoke faith in Jesus as Son of God was the privileged experience of the dynamic action of the risen Lord through his Spirit. It is because our gospel narratives are 'Spirit-filled' that they can enable the believer to be present to Jesus in the mysteries of his earthly life.'[92] Not only are the gospels 'Spirit-filled', so is the whole of the Word of God. So, Stanley commented when dealing with *Lectio Divina*: 'Israel's deep sense of how through the Scriptures the event of the past becomes a contemporary experience has been articulated in a striking way by the author of Deuteronomy. This writer composed his book five or six hundred years after the striking of the covenant on Mount Sinai. Yet he can represent Moses as speaking through the centuries to his own (the author's) contemporaries: "Hear, O Israel, the statutes and ordinances which I am delivering in your hearing *today*... The Lord our God made a covenant *with us* at Horeb. It was not with our forefathers that the Lord made this covenant, but *with ourselves, who are all here alive today*" (Deut 5:1–3). It is just such a contemporary experience, personal to me as a member of the people of God, that *lectio divina* was designed to create.'[93]

Stanley carries a long way forward the argument from the resurrection for the contemporaneity of the mysteries to the praying person: 'Faith is the *engagement* of the whole man to the person of Christ: it is nothing if it is not actually a profound inter-personal relationship with Him who through death and resurrection has acceded to universal power as the Master of history, the Lord of the universe.'[94] A text to which Stanley appeals more than once is Revelation 5:6: 'Then I saw between the throne and the four living creatures and among the elders a Lamb standing as if it had been slaughtered, having seven horns and seven eyes, which are the seven spirits of God sent out upon the earth.' From this text Stanley concludes to the *actuality* of all the mysteries of the earthly life of Jesus: 'If he depicts the Lord Jesus as eternally adorned with the stigmata of his passion, the seer thereby calls our attention to this significant theological truth by selecting the one most striking event in Jesus' mortal life: His passion and death. What our author clearly implies, however, is that all the mysteries of Jesus' earthly history

---

92. Stanley, 'Contemporary Gospel-Criticism and the Mysteries', 39–40.
93. Stanley, 'A Suggested Approach to *Lectio. Divina*', 455.
94. Stanley, 'Contemplation of the Gospels', 423.

from the cradle to the grave, have been mysteriously endowed in His glorified humanity with a totally new and enduring *actuality?*[95]

Another reflection on the text of the Lamb in Revelation 5:6; leads Stanley to conclude:

> They (the evangelists) equivalently tell their readers: the kind of Lord who imperiously demands your faith and love is a Lord who still carries the marks of the nails in his risen flesh, a Lord who consorts with sinners, even in table-fellowship, to make credible, visible, lovable the compassion of God. He is in truth a Lord who took pity on the pariahs, the ostracized, the alienated. He accepted women as well as men for disciples, displayed a loving concern for children, regarded as 'nothings' in the ancient world, introduced slaves into his parables as persons endowed with human rights.[96]

In other words, the gospels are not to be regarded as simply an historical record of events that happened in the past, but as normative for human life in every age, because they transmit the values and the life of the risen Lord, Jesus.

A favourite argument of Stanley's often repeated in the books and articles referred to above is that the process of contemplation of the gospel mysteries is analogous to the process of composition of the gospels in reverse. The disciples had an experience of Jesus, which led to theological reflection on the part of the early Church, which led to the writing of the gospels:

> This (the creation of our sacred literature) will be seen upon analysis to consist of three principal moments: (1) *experience* of God's working from within history (and this involves the reaction of faith on the part of the individual or the collectivity, vouchsafed such a privileged revelation); (2) a period of *theological reflection,* animated by faith, upon the data thus revealed; and (3) the *formulation* of *the experience* with its concomitant reflection, in an attempt to communicate this revelation inwriting to the present and particularly future generations of believers.[97]

---

95. Stanley, 'Contemplation of the Gospels', 430.
96. Stanley, 'Contemporary Gospel-Criticism and the Mysteries', 46.
97. Stanley, 'Contemplation of the Gospels', 435.

Today the person seeking a contemplative experience of Jesus takes up the gospels, and proceeds to theological reflection, leading to contemplative experience. Stanley correctly identifies the goal of gospel contemplation as 'collaboration in the saving event': 'In order, then, to collaborate in the saving event which is the intended goal of the Ignatian *contemplatio*, the Christian of the twentieth century must begin with the sacred text itself, the inspired expression of the religious experience of the Evangelist, the result of his personal confrontation and that of the apostolic Church, whose special witness he is with the exalted Lord Jesus.'[98] For Stanley this openness to the Word of God in the gospels rightly involves labouring to grasp, as far as possible, the literal meaning of the text and its 'Christological import'. The second step in the contemplation process is personal theological reflection, which for Stanley, in this context, consists of 'one simple searching question: 'What is the Lord Jesus attempting to say to *me now* through this particular text of the gospel?'[99] The third and final step in the contemplation process is 'the religious experience, the saving event'.

John Ashton was critical of this proposal of Stanley's, principally on the grounds that there is no explanation of the different kinds of 'theological reflection' on the part of the early Church in the process of the writing of the gospels and on the part of the person praying in the process of contemplation.[100] While the similarity in reverse of the two processes should not be pushed too far, the schema presented by Stanley certainly throws light on the use of the gospels as a way into a here and now meeting with the risen Lord through the contemplation of his mysteries set forth through the words of the gospels.

On the question of the contemporaneity of the gospel mysteries Thomas Merton wrote:

> To make this experience deeper and more personal, meditation seeks to read the *inner meaning* beneath the exterior, and also, (most important of all) to *relate the historical events given us in the Gospels with our own spiritual life here and now.*

---

98. Stanley, 'Contemplation of the Gospels', 439.
99. Stanley, 'Contemplation of the Gospels', 440.
100. J Ashton, 'The Imitation of Christ' in *The Way Supplement*, 6 (Summer 1972): 34–5.

> In simple terms, the Nativity of Christ the Lord in Bethlehem is not just something that I make present in fantasy. Since He is the eternal Word of God before whom time is entirely and simultaneously present, the Child born at Bethlehem 'sees' me here and now. That is to say, I 'am' present to His mind 'then'. It follows that I can speak to Him as to one present not only in fantasy but in actual reality. . . This enters into our meditations on Christ and His life; for He desires and intends to live in us. The Christ-life has, as its most important aspect for each of us, His actual presence and activity in our lives.[101]

In his 1947 encyclical letter on the Liturgy, *Mediator Dei*, Pius XII had already stressed the importance of understanding the mysteries of Christ as being really present here and now to the person at liturgical prayer:

> Therefore the liturgical year, animated throughout by the devotion of the Church, is no cold and lifeless representation of past events, no mere historical record. It is Christ Himself, living on in His Church, and still pursuing that path of boundless mercy which 'going about and doing good' He began to tread during his life on earth. This He did in order that the souls of men might come into contact with His mysteries and, so to speak, live by them. And these mysteries are still now constantly present and active, not in the vague and nebulous way which certain recent writers describe, but as the Catholic doctrine teaches us.[102]

To know, love and follow

'Third Prelude. This is to ask for what I desire. Here it will be to ask for an intimate knowledge of our Lord, who has become man for me, that I may love Him more and follow Him more closely.'[103] This is the 'preparatory prayer for the first exercise of the Second Week, on the

---

101. T Merton; *Spiritual Direction and Meditation* (Collegevill: Liturgical Press, 1960), 86–8.
102. Pope Pius XII, *Christian Worship* (London: Catholic Truth Society,1959), No 176, 65.
103. SE 104.

incarnation. The perfect tense 'who has become' *(que se ha hecho)* is an indication of the present reality of the mystery, available now to the person praying. The term 'preparatory' in no way implies that this prayer is to be made and then left behind as the contemplation continues. The prayer, in fact, permeates all the contemplations, and gives a summary of the goal of the Second Week contemplations. The whole of each exercise is aimed at a deepening of a personal relationship with the risen Lord, through the gift of knowledge (understanding) from the Holy Spirit, geared to love and to an authentic and effective following of Christ in discipleship The same prayer runs through every exercise of gospel contemplation in the Second Week. In the second contemplation, on the Nativity, Ignatius wrote: 'Third Prelude. This will be the same as in the preceding contemplation and identical in form with it.'[104] When gospel contemplation resumes on the fifth day of the Second Week, after the 'Ignatian day' of the Two Standards and the Three Classes of Persons, Ignatius wrote: 'In each of these five exercises, there will be at the beginning, the preparatory prayer and the three preludes as was fully explained in the contemplations on the Incarnation and Nativity.'[105] Though there is a logical sequence from knowing to loving to following, in reality the three are never separate, and are simply three aspects of the process of discipleship, of assimilation to Christ.

The Imitation of Christ

Closely bound to the idea of following Christ in discipleship is the notion of following him as an exemplar. A right understanding of the imitation of Christ in the Spiritual Exercises demands that it always be seen in the context of discipleship, as a function of knowing, loving and following the Lord. Ignatius uses the verb 'to imitate' *(imitar)*, as applied to Christ, nine times in *The Spiritual Exercises,* and never the noun 'imitation' *(imitacion)*;[106] 'to follow' *(seguir)* appears twelve times.'[107] And the prayer to know, love and follow Christ is at the heart of every contemplation. In the light of this it hardly does justice to

---

104. SE 113.
105. SE 159.
106. Echarte, *Concordancia Ignaciana*, 641.
107. Echarte, *Concordancia Ignaciana*, 1151.

Ignatius simply to attribute to him the medieval idea of 'imitation of Christ'. Bill Dalton wrote: 'Ignatius shared with the medieval world before him a simple idea of the inspiration of the gospels ... Thus, for Ignatius, the gospels were a sort of flashback into the past, revealing the actual story of Jesus' birth, life, death and resurrection, just as they occurred. The believer was enabled to live again those privileged days, by entering, through his imagination, into the scenes. And the chief purpose behind this exercise was to learn how to love: Jesus was the great moral model of Christian life. The imitation of Christ, his poverty, his love for others, his heroism in death, the joy he experienced in his resurrection, all provided a model for the Christian life of the retreatant.'[108] The constant repetition in the contemplations of the Second Week of the prayer to know, love and follow our Lord is an indication that Ignatius was at least intuitively aware that there is far more involved here than external and moralistic imitation.

Henri Holstein addressed the attitude that had become prevalent among Jesuits in the first half of the twentieth century, of stressing the moral imitation of Christ, to be sought in the Second Week exercises, rather than the interior transformation these exercises were aimed to bring about. He calls this moral imitation 'mimetism', or mimicry: 'Another danger waylays the retreatant. One makes one's own the presumed sentiments of Christ, of Mary and other persons. One will clothe oneself with them, as with a shell without any true effort of interior assimilation, of 'intrasusception' as Blondel would have put it. Hence, there is the reduction of the gospel scenes to moral and ascetical attitudes, which one imposes on oneself by a kind of voluntarism, more generous than enlightened. Thus, for generations of Jesuits (and other religious, I should think!), the contemplation of the hidden life of Nazareth became a command to obedience, silence and acceptance of the gloomy years of formation.'[109] In this

---

108. W Dalton, How to Use the Bible in the Exercises', in *The Word of God in the Spiritual Exercises*, 17.
109. H Holstein; 'Entendre la Parole de Dieu dans les Exercices', in *Christus* 14 (1967): 83: 'Un autre danger guette alors le retraitant: le *mimétisme*. On fera siens les sentiments présumés du Christ, de la Vièrge et des autres personnages; on s'en revêtira comme d'une cuirasse, sans effort vrai d'assimilation interieure, d'une 'intrasusception' comme aurait dire Blondel. D'où la reduction des scenes évangeliques à des attitudes morales et ascetiques, que l'on s'impose par une sorte de volontarisme plus généreux qu'éclairé, C'est ainsi que, pour des generations de Jésuites (et d'autres religieux, je pense!), la 'contemplation de

attitude of 'mimetism' 'Christ was envisaged uniquely as a model. No consideration was given to the work of redemption for which he became obedient, nor to the perspective of grace which enables us to 'put on his mind' because it incorporates us into him, nor even the apostolic dimension of the Jesuit vocation. It is necessary to 'make a tracing' of the sentiments and attitudes of the great Model, Jesus Christ.'[110]

A more positive exposition of the imitation of Christ was given by David Stanley in an address to the 1966 conference on the Spiritual Exercises, held in Loyola. Stanley commenced by declaring that 'it is difficult to give a definitive response to the second problem, which deals with the 'imitation of Christ' in his earthly life.'[111] He ascribes to Ignatius a nicely balanced concept of following and imitation: 'It forces us, naturally, to study the end which St Ignatius proposes to attain in the contemplations of the Second Week. This end is to follow more closely, *sequi studiosius*, this Jesus who is the exemplar type and also the historical model of Christian Life. After rejecting mimetism, Stanley declares that what is being dealt with is 'an arduous, prolonged process, through which the risen Christ acts in the heart of the person.'[112] This will lead to a free and total surrender to the risen Christ.

Stanley reflects on the New Testament usage, in which the verb 'to follow', as a synonym of 'to imitate' is used only of the immediate disciples of Jesus. 'Imitate' and 'imitation' are often used by St Paul, notably in writing to the churches he had founded, as in his saying to

---

       la vie cachée de Nazareth' est devenue un imperatif d'obéissance, de silence et d'acceptation des mornes annees de formation!

110. Holstein, 'Entendre la Parole de Dieu dans les Exercices', 84: 'Christ soit uniquement envisagé comme modèle. Ni la consideration de l'oeuvre redemptrice, pour laquelle il s'est fait obéissant, ni la perspective de la grace qui nous permet de 'prendre ses sentiments' parce qu'elle nous incorpore a Lui, ni meme la dimension apostolique de la vocation du Jésuite n'interviennent. Il faut simplement 'calquer' sentiments et attitudes sur le grand Modèle qu'est Jésus Christ.

111. Stanley, 'Sagrada Escritura y Ejercicios', 224: 'Es dificil dar una respuesta definitiva al segundo problema, que trata de la 'imitacion de Cristo' en su vida terrena.'

112. Stanley, 'Sagrada Escritura y Ejercicios', 225: 'un arduo y prolongado proceso, a traves del cual Cristo resuscitado actua en el interior del hombre.'

the Corinthians: 'Be imitators of me, as I am of Christ.'[113] This is to be no external imitation, but the discerning of the activity of the Holy Spirit, who is leading Paul.

> If Paul exhorts to this imitation of himself, it is in order to become profoundly conscious of the fact that the glorified Son of God is mysteriously present in him, through the Holy Spirit, as the dynamic source of his own Christian life (a truth that he learned in his conversion, according to Galatians 1:16). In the role of apostle, he has a lively consciousness of the responsibility that makes it incumbent on him to develop in his converts an ever more profound experience of the Mystery par excellence 'Christ among you, the hope of glory' (Col 1:27).[114]

Karl Rahner added his weight to the argument against a mere moral imitation of Christ. When preaching on the Spiritual Exercises, he said:

> The imitation of Christ does *not* consist in the observance of certain moral maxims which may be perfectly exemplified in Jesus, but which have an intrinsic value in themselves independently of Him and can be known as such. The imitation of Christ consists in a true entering into *His* life and *in Him* entering into the inner life of God that has been given to us.[115]

And again:

> We should be careful not to consider the meditations on the various events of Jesus' life as an excellent opportunity to draw moral lessons. Ethical maxims are treated much more exactly in moral handbooks. The purpose here in these meditations is to place ourselves in a real, not just abstract, relationship to the event of Jesus' life being considered by means of a salvation-historical and salvation-bringing remembrance. This relationship will bring us the grace necessary to follow

---

113. 1 Cor 11:1.
114. Stanley 'Sagrada Escritura y Ejercicios', 226.
115. Rahner, *Spiritual Exercises*, 118.

> Christ. We must always keep this fact before our eyes when we are meditating on the life of Jesus, otherwise our meditations can rapidly become boring and useless. What takes place in a narrower, sacramental sense in the sacrifice of the Mass, also occurs in a very true sense in the faith-penetrated remembrance of the other events of Jesus' life: And this remembrance is not a mere speculative treatment of Jesus' history—in it, the grace of a definite mystery is revealed and offered to the one praying.[116]

It is the entry into 'a salvation-historical and salvation-bringing remembrance' that is at the heart of understanding the contemplations of the life of Christ in the Spiritual Exercises.

A nicely balanced treatment of the imitation of Christ has been provided by EJ Tinsley.[117] He commenced his article on this subject with the objection of Luther to the notion of imitation as concealing a doctrine of works rather than of faith and grace. So, Luther preferred the term of the Letter to the Romans, 'conformity' *(conformitas)* to 'imitation' *(imitatio)*. The relevant text is Romans 8:29: 'For those whom he foreknew, he also predestined to be conformed to the image of his Son, in order that he might be the first of many brothers.'[118] For Holstein this conformity was an important fruit of the contemplation of the mysteries of Christ,[119] and in the same context Voulet drew explicitly upon Romans 8:29, as mentioned on above. The text clearly emphasises the divine foreknowledge and activity in bringing about the conformation to Christ, without, of course, minimising the importance of a human response in faith.

Another text suggestive of the kind of union with Christ brought about through contemplation of the gospel mysteries is Romans 13:14: 'But put on the Lord Jesus Christ and make no provision for the flesh to carry out its desires.' Moo comments:

> The exact meaning of what Paul intends to say is not easy to pinpoint. But perhaps we should view the imperative of

---

116. Rahner, *Spiritual Execercises*, 162.
117. E Tinsley, 'Some Principles for Reconstructing a Doctrine of the Imitation of Christ' in *Scottish Journal of Theology*, (1972): 25.
118. The translation is that of D Moo, *The Epistle to the Romans* (Grand Rapids: Eerdmans, 1996), 508.
119. Holstein, *'La Contemplation Évamgelique'*, 453.

his understanding of Christ as a corporate figure. As a result of our baptism/conversion, we have been incorporated into Christ, sharing his death, burial and (proleptically) his resurrection (Rom 6:3-6). Our 'old man,' our corporate identity with Adam, has been severed (Rom 6:6); and in its place, we have become attached to the 'new man' (Col 3:10-22; Eph 2:16), Jesus Christ himself (cf Eph 4:13), whom we have 'put on' (Gal 3:27). But our relationship to Christ, the new man, while established at conversion, needs constantly to be reappropriated and lived out, as Ephesians 4:25, with its call to 'put on the new man' makes clear. Against this background, Paul's exhortation to 'put on the Lord Jesus Christ' means that we are consciously to embrace Christ in such a way that his character is manifested in all that we do and say. This exhortation appears to match the exhortation at the beginning of this section, 'be transformed by the renewing of the mind,' suggesting that it is into the image of Christ that we are being transformed (cf 8:29).[120]

Again Paul urges likeness to Christ on his readers in Philippians 2:5[121] Peter O'Brien translates this verse: 'Adopt towards one another, in your mutual relations, the same attitude that was found in Christ Jesus.'[122] O'Brien summed up his reflections on this verse:

> Accordingly, the Christ-hymn presents Jesus as the ultimate model for Christian behaviour and action, the supreme example of the humble, self-sacrificing, self-giving service that Paul has just been urging the Philippians to practice in their relations one towards another (vv 1-4). There is a relationship between the saving . . . events of the gospel and the conduct appropriate to those who are in Christ. Because of the later connotations' of the term, it is better to speak of 'conformity' to Christ's likeness rather than of an 'imitation' of his example. The hoped-for attitude set forth by Paul in vv 2-4 corresponds with that exhibited by Christ Jesus, especially vv 6-8.[123]

---

120. Moo, *Romans*, 825-6, 202.
121. P O'Brien, *The Epistle* to *the Philippians* (Grand Rapids: Eerdmans, 1991)
122. O'Brien, *The Epistle* to *the Philippians*, 202.
123. O'Brien, *The Epistle* to *the Philippians*, 205.

There are three texts from Galatians that need to be considered in terms of Paul's giving expression to the kind of union with Christ that is the basis for Gospel contemplation, and which grows and develops through that contemplation: Galatians 1:16; 2:20; 3:27.

Galatians 1:16 Ronald Fung has translated: '15 But then in his good pleasure God, who had set me apart from birth and called me through his grace, 16 chose to reveal his Son to me and through me, in order that I might proclaim him among the Gentiles.'[124] In commentary Fung wrote:

> 'chose to reveal his Son to me and through me': Here the simplest and most natural translation probably also gives the most apposite meaning: 'in me' (AV, RV, NIV), that is, 'within me' (Phillips) or 'in (the sphere of) my soul,' Paul thus stressing by the phrase 'the inward and intensely personal character of God's revelation to him of the risen Jesus.
>
> The phrase should not, however, be taken to suggest a merely inward revelation without a corresponding external object, for there is little doubt that the preceding phrase ('to reveal his Son') refers to Paul's vision of Christ (also attested in 1 Cor. 9:1; 15:8) on the road to Damascus (cf v 17). 'In me' underscores the idea of inwardness already implied by the verb 'reveal', which connotes a disclosure involving perception and understanding on the part of the recipient.'[125]

James Dunn translated the relevant phrase of Galatians 1:16: 'to reveal his Son in me,'[126] and then explained:

> 'Several argue for the dative 'to me', but when Paul wanted to use a dative with the verb 'reveal' he did so (1 Cor 2:10; 14: 30; Phil 3:15). The implication is rather that he wished at this point to express the personal transformation effected by this revelation from heaven (cf 2 Cor iv.:6—'in our hearts'; Gal 2:20—'Christ in me')... but as transformation not so much of the person as of purpose and commitment (no longer 'to destroy the church', but now 'to preach Christ among the

---

124. R Fung, *The Epistle to the* to *the Galatians* (Grand Rapids: Eerdmans, 1990), 202.
125. Fung, *The Epistle to the* to *the Galatians*, 64.
126. J Dunn, *The Epistle* to *the Galatians* (London: A& C Black, 1993), 62.

Gentiles'); hence, presumably, the Revised English Bible's 'in and through me'.[127]

Galatians 2:20. Fung's translation is: 'I have been crucified with Christ: the life I now live is not my life but the life which Christ lives in me; and my present bodily life is lived by faith in the Son of God, who loved me and gave himself up for me.'[128] And he commented:

> The life Paul now lives is not lived by him—by the 'I' of v 19, the self-righteous Pharisee who based his hope for righteousness and salvation on strict observance of the law—but by Christ the risen and exalted One, who dwells in him. It is sometimes said that these words show the mysticism of Paul's experience; but if the mode of expression may be somewhat 'mystical', the meaning is clarified by the completely rational statement that follows. Now that Paul's natural self has come to an end, his earthly existence is no longer an independent life of his own; but a life of believing dependence on the Son of God, who loved him and gave himself for him. To have Christ living in Paul, therefore, does not mean some kind of mystical depersonalization, as though the human 'I' of Paul were absorbed into the pneumatic 'I' of Christ; on the contrary, Paul fully retains his identity as an 'I' who sustains an 'I-Thou' relationship with Christ.[129]

Dunn translated: 'I have been crucified with Christ; (20) and it is no longer I that lives, but Christ lives in me. And the life I now live in the flesh, I live by faith which is in the Son of God who loved me and gave himself for me.'[130] He commented:

> 'it is no longer I that lives, but Christ lives in me. The language is startling, and of course exaggerated... But the exaggeration was obviously to make a point. And the 'point was to bring out the very radical nature of the personal transformation effected by Paul's encounter with the risen Christ. The old 'I' was dead, and had been replaced by a new focus of personality.

---

127. Dunn, *The Epistle to the Galatians*, 64.
128. Fung, *Galatians*, 122.
129. Fung, *Galatians*, 124.
130. Dunn, *Galatians*, 131.

The idea of 'Christ indwelling' the believer (Rom viii. 10; 2 Cor xiii. 5: Col i. 27; Eph. iii.17) is much less common in Paul than its reverse, the believer 'in Christ' (see on i. 22 and ii.17). More typical of Paul is the thought of the Spirit indwelling or acting in the 'believer (Rom v, 5; viii, 9, 11, 1 5-16, 23, 29 etc.; see on iii.2). Experientially, it comes to the same thing: the awareness of a new focus of identity expressed in different goals and new inner dynamic, with Christ as the inspiration and Christ-likeness the paradigm ('mystical' if you like, though many are suspicious of the word's connotations). Theologically, it means that for Christians the Spirit of God is also now to be recognized as the Spirit of Christ and the personal existence of the post-resurrection Christ cannot be thought of simply as having an individual bodily focus.[131]

Galatians 3:27. Fung translated: 'Baptized into union with him, you have all put on Christ as a garment.'[132] His comment is:

'Baptism is here regarded as the rite of initiation into Christ, that is, into union with Christ, or what amounts to the same thing, of incorporation into Christ as the Head of the new humanity. This sense of the expression 'baptized into' as 'baptized so as to become a member of' is required by the context on each of the three occasions which are decisive for its meaning: here, 1 Corinthians 12:13, and Romans 6:3.

Baptism is also regarded as 'putting on' Christ, who is thought of as a garment enveloping the believer and symbolizing his new spiritual existence. (cf. Rom 13:14, where the ethical aspect is primarily in view). The metaphor is probably derived from Hebrew tradition where the figure of changing clothes to represent an inward and spiritual change was common (cf Isa 61:10; Zech 3:3f.).'[133]

Dunn's translation was: 'For as many of you as were baptized into Christ have put on Christ.'[134] And he commented:

---

131. Dunn, *Galatians*, 145-6.
132. Fung, *Galatians*, 167.
133. Fung, *Galatians*, 172.
134. Dunn, *Galatians*, 202.

'For, as many of you who were baptized into Christ. The phrase is more or less exactly the same as in Rom vi. 3, ... It was by being baptized into Christ (27) that they had become 'in Christ' (26)... But 'into Christ' has more the sense of 'into' so as to become 'in', as describing the moment in which and action by means of which their lives and destinies and very identities became bound up with Christ.'[135]

'That Paul was thinking in metaphors is further suggested by the next phrase—all who were baptized into Christ have put on Christ. Paul rings the changes in his attempts to express the reality which he and the first Christian experienced – a reality which we can describe most simply as a profound sense of identification with Jesus. Hence the talk of 'in Christ' and 'into Christ' (i. 22 etc. and above), of crucifixion with Christ and Christ living within (ii. 19-20), and now of 'putting on Christ'. The imagery is obviously of putting on clothes. It could be a further allusion to a ceremony of initiation, if indeed baptisands did put on a fresh robe or tunic after baptism. Elsewhere in the Pauline letters the metaphor appears as an exhortation to Christians: 'put on Christ', as the epitome of ethical paraenesis (Rom. xiii.14; cf. Col. iii.10–13; Eph iv. 24) with a view to eschatological completion (Rom. xiii. 11–14; cf. 1 Cor xv. 49–54; 2 Cor v 3). So Paul could have in mind the thoroughgoing transformation of personality which a good actor could achieve by immersing himself in a character, by 'living a part' (not to be parodied as 'mere play-acting'), or may specifically have recalled the personality transformations which the coming of the Spirit had wrought among the Galatians during his ministry (iii. 2-5; cf. 1 Cor vi. 9–11; 2 Cor. iv. 16–v. 5). That is what the act of believing into Christ (ii.16), of being baptized (in the Spirit?) into Christ (iii. 27) involved; 'it affects something within me so deeply that Christ himself becomes my own self (ii.20)' [G Ebeling, *The Truth of the Gospel, An Exposition. of Galatians* (Fortress, Philadelphia, 1985), 212]. By such variation of metaphor Paul was thus able to bring out further aspects of what identification with Christ should mean for these first Christians.'[136]

---

135. Dunn, *Galatians*, 202.
136. Dunn, *Galatians*, 204-5.

The weight of this evidence from Paul certainly shows that the idea of conformity with Christ is scripturally well established. It is through God's initiative that the Christian is invited to respond to the grace of baptism by living out a personal relationship with Christ. This relationship will involve the gradual developing of more of the inner attitudes of Christ: in modern terms, 'putting on his mind and heart'.[137] The terminology of 'imitation of Christ' could be legitimately applied to all of this, but the term 'conformity' carries with it the allusion to the deeper roots of union, avoiding the possibility of misinterpreting the imitation as being merely moral, or even external.

Tinsley sees as an unfortunate consequence of Luther's critique the rejection of the whole idea of imitation of Christ, and argues for the retention of both terms, conformity and imitation. 'In a fully developed theology of the Christian life as imitation of Christ both the terms *conformitas* and *imitatio* would need to be used. The imitative life of the Christian involves both God's activity through the Spirit, in conforming man to his image in Christ *(conformitas)*, and man's focusing of his moral and spiritual attention on the exemplar, Christ *(imitatio)*.[138] Tinsley argues persuasively for understanding the imitation of Christ eschatologically, citing in this context Ephesians 4:13: 'until all of us come to the unity of the faith and the knowledge of the Son of God, to maturity, to the measure of the full stature of Christ.' And also 1 John 3:2: 'Beloved, we are God's children now; what we will be has not yet been revealed. What we do know is this: when he is revealed, we will be like him, for we shall see him as he is.' 'Growing into Christ ought not therefore to be conceived in terms of a constant looking back to a past model, but as a living process which attains its goal in the future.'[139]

Tinsley concludes in asking for a 'mimetic creativity': 'The *imitatio Christi* needs to be closely integrated with the Christian doctrine of man made in the image of God. This means among other things that man is capable of mimetic creativity which can be taken as a analogy of God's creativity in the incarnation of fashioning the new man in Christ. Man is a genuine pro-creator. The doctrine of man as made in the image of God (which Christ alone is) means that human beings are

---

137. See MHSI 27, 695 and 848–52.
138. Tinsley, 'Some Principles for Reconstructing', 47.
139. Tinsley, 'Some Principles for Reconstructing', 55.

inevitably, by their existence, potential imitations of Christ. Human life seen in terms of the work of the Holy Spirit in grace discloses to the believer Christ himself engaged in transforming these imitations into the real thing.'[140]

At the heart of the Spiritual Exercises, in the Two Standards meditation, Ignatius asks a person to pray earnestly through the threefold colloquy 'to be received under His standard, first in the highest spiritual poverty, and, should the Divine Majesty be pleased thereby and deign to choose and accept me, even in actual poverty; secondly in bearing insults and wrongs, thereby to *imitate* Him better, provided only I can suffer these without sin on the part of another, and without offence of the Divine Majesty.'[141] This had already been anticipated by Ignatius in the suggested offering in the exercise on the Call of the King: 'I protest that is my earnest desire and my deliberate choice, provided only it be for Thy greater service and praise, to *imitate* Thee in bearing all wrongs and all abuse and all poverty, both actual and spiritual, should Thy most holy majesty deign to choose and admit me to such a state and way of life.'[142]

The imitation of Christ that Ignatius is suggesting here is not an external one (the imitation of Christ is not generally a good motive for choosing carpentry as a trade) or a moral one, of the kind rejected by the authors referred to above. It is an imitation in the most radical of gospel values. As such, it cannot be achieved through thinking about it, or in any voluntaristic way. It must come from a deep, inner attitude, a 'conformity' that can only be the fruit of contemplation. Spiritual poverty is a radical gospel value that can be to some extent understood and readily appreciated, though it demands a contemplative relationship with Christ in order to be realised. The value of actual poverty and 'bearing insults and wrongs' is much more elusive, and can only be founded in love for the Lord who, through his own life, has proclaimed the value of this way of living. A person comes to the Call of the King after the contemplative experiences of the colloquies of the First Week and of the faith relationship involved in conversion. They come to the Two Standards after spending several

---

140. Tinsley, 'Some Principles for Reconstructing', 57.
141. SE 147.
142. SE 98.

days in earnest prayer to know, love and follow Jesus. But why should this knowing, loving and following necessarily involve imitation?

A retreatant may readily accept the invitation to radical spiritual poverty involved in the meditation on the Three Classes, and may be readily attracted to the spiritual freedom, or indifference, that is called for. The same is true of the second of the Three Kinds of Humility, which outlines the same freedom or indifference. But the Third Kind of Humility is not so readily understood or appreciated: 'If we suppose the first and second kind attained, then whenever the praise and glory of the Divine Majesty would be equally served, in order to *imitate* and be in reality more like Christ our Lord, I desire and choose poverty with Christ poor, rather than riches; insults with Christ loaded with them, rather than honours; I desire to be accounted as worthless and a fool for Christ, rather than to be esteemed as wise and prudent in this world. So Christ was treated before me.'[143]

The imitation proposed here is not just the fruit of conformity but is also the cause of it. It is through this imitation that we will 'be in reality more like Christ our Lord'. Imitation, then, is not something that is added from outside to knowing, loving and following, but is necessarily and intimately bound up with the following of Christ. It flows from union with Christ and deepens that union. There is a love relationship evoked in the disciple's response to the love of Jesus. Generally a lover wishes to share the lot, the lifestyle of the beloved. Characteristic of love is a sharing of life, and those who love grow to be more like each other. Yet, love does not necessarily involve each imitating the other. A wealthy lover certainly may not wish to share the poverty of the beloved, but rather raise the lifestyle of the beloved to their own level. In the case of the love between Christ and the disciple there is no question of the disciple raising the level of the life of Jesus to be more like their own. The contrary is true. Jesus is the source of all life; he is the one who is truly rich. As St Paul put it: 'though he was rich, yet for our sakes he became poor, so that by his poverty we might become rich.'[144] We must be drawn to share his poverty and self-emptying, which are the way to true riches. Ignatius wrote most cogently about the imitation of the poor Christ in the *Constitutions* of *the Society* of *Jesus*:

---

143. SE 167.
144. 2 Cor 8:9.

'to how great a degree it helps and profits one in the spiritual life to abhor in its totality and not in part whatever the world loves and embraces, and to accept and desire with all possible energy whatever Christ our Lord has loved and embraced. Just as the men of the world who follow the world love and seek with such diligence honours, fame, and esteem for a great name on earth, as the world teaches them, so those who are progressing in the spiritual life and truly following Christ our Lord love and intensely desire everything opposite. That is to say, they desire to clothe themselves with the same clothing and uniform of their Lord because of the love and reverence which He deserves, to such an extent that where there would be no offence to His Divine Majesty and no imputation of sin to the neighbour, they would wish to suffer injuries, false accusations, and affronts, and to be held and esteemed as fools (but without their giving any occasion for this), because of their desire to resemble and imitate in some manner our Creator and Lord Jesus Christ, by putting on His clothing and uniform, since it was for our spiritual profit that He clothed Himself as He did.'[145]

Knowing that he had not yet clinched the needed logic of the argument of imitation, Ignatius concludes with the words: *'and follow Him, since he is the way which leads to life.'* The relationship of the disciple to the Lord is not a relationship between equals. Rather it is the Lord who confers everything, including the power to respond, upon the disciple. Therefore, discipleship involves the sharing of the Lord's values and attitudes, and style of living, even in matters that may superficially seem 'indifferent'. Such matters do not remain indifferent when one has come to the degree of union with Christ through love that is involved in the ignatian Third Kind of Humility.

Presence to the humanity of Christ

Does the use of the term 'contemplation' as applied to the gospel mysteries need some qualification because it falls short of contemplation in the strict sense, having as its focus the humanity of

---

145. St Ignatius of Loyola, *Constitutions*, (101) 107–8.

Christ rather than the divinity or the life of the Trinity itself? On this point St Thomas Aquinas wrote as follows:

> Matters concerning the Godhead are in themselves the strongest incentive to love, and consequently to devotion, because God is supremely lovable. Yet such is the weakness of the human mind that it needs a guiding hand not only to the knowledge, but also to the love of divine things by means of certain sensible objects known to us. Chief among these is the humanity of Christ, according to the words of the Preface that knowing God visible we may be caught up to the love of things invisible. Wherefore, matters relating to Christ's humanity are the chief incentives to devotion, leading us thither as a guiding hand, although devotion itself has for its object matters concerning the Godhead.[146]

Again, reflecting on the Gospel of John, Thomas wrote:

> Since the humanity of Christ is for us a way of tending towards God, as is said below in 14:6, 'I am the way, the truth and the life', we should not rest in it, as in our end, but through it we should tend towards God. Therefore, lest the hearts of the disciples, moved with a carnal affection towards Christ should rest in him as in man, on that account Christ swiftly removed his bodily presence from them.[147]

---

146. St Thomas Aquinas, *Summa Theologiae, IIa IIae* (London: Blackfriars, 1964), q. 82 a. 3, ad 2, 40, 42: 'ea quae sunt divinitatis sunt secundum se maxime excitantia dilectionem, et per consequens devotionem, quia Deus est super omnia diligendus; sed, ex debilitate mentis humanae est quod sicut indiget manuductione ad cognitionem divinorum, ita ad dilectionem per aliqua sensibilia nobis nota; inter quae praecipuum est humanitas Christi, secundum quod in Praefatione dicitur *Ut, dum visibiliter Deum cognoscimus, per hunc in invisibilium amorem rapiamur.* Et ideo ea quae pertinent ad Christi humanitatem, per modum cuiusdam manuductionis, maxime devotionem excitant; cum tamen devotio principaliter circa ea quae sunt divinitatis consistat.'
147. St Thomas Aquinas, *Super Evangelium Joannis Lectura* (Turin: Marietti, 1952), 1074, 204: 'Cum enim Christi humanitas sit nobis via tendendi in Deum, ut dicitur infra XIV, 6: *Ego sum via, veritas* et *vita,* non debemus in ea quiescere ut in termino, sed per eam debemus in Deum tendere. Ne ergo corda discipulorum ad Christum carnaliter affecta, in eo ut in homine quiescerent ideo Christus corporalem suam praesentiam ab eis cito subtraxit.

The thought of Karl Rahner on the incarnation is quite the contrary. Rahner declared that,

> the ultimate reason why every man exists is that; by his life and existence with the Incarnate Word, he might make it possible for God to undertake the adventure of His love outside of Himself. In order to achieve this, God really does need humanity, because finite man (and that is what God himself became) is essentially related to and dependent on the other human 'Thou'. This means that all of humanity is concentrated around the Son of Man as its source of ultimate meaning. Humanity is 'the fullness of Christ.'
>
> Now if the concrete life of Jesus of Nazareth, and nothing else is the, appearance, the manifestation, the presence of the Word of God Himself and His life, and if in, this concrete life of Jesus the inner life of God is revealed to us in an unsurpassable way, then a personal entering Into this life of Jesus of Nazareth is a participation in the inner life of God; then the gaze into the face of Jesus of Nazareth is changed into the face-to-face vision of God, even if both the encounter with Jesus and the consequent vision of God only make their presence fully known when the confinement of our poor body is split open by death. 'Jesus said to him: Have I been with you for so long and you have not known me Phillip? He who sees me also sees the Father. How can you say: Show us the Father?' (Jn 14:9).[148]

We saw Ignatius in writing to Francis Borgia expressing a certain hierarchy in contemplation according to the objects contemplated '(tears) over one's own sins or the sins of others, in the mysteries of Christ our Lord in this life or in the other, in the consideration or love of the divine persons; these are to that degree more valuable and more precious, in so far as the thoughts and considerations are higher. And although in itself the third is more perfect than the second and the second more perfect than the first, that part is much better for a particular individual, where God our Lord communicates himself, displaying his most holy 'gifts and spiritual graces.' While allowing for this hierarchy, Ignatius never denied to the contemplation of the Gospel mysteries the fullness of contemplation. And we saw how in

---

148. Rahner, *Spiritual Exercises*, 114–15.

his catechesis on the sign of the Cross he emphasised that 'in Jesus our Saviour and Redeemer, there are the Father and the Son and the Holy Spirit, one only God our Creator and Lord, and that the divinity was never separated from the body of Christ in death.' As we saw in the reflections on the *Spiritual Diary*, it was presence to our Lady' and to Jesus as intercessors that led Ignatius into the contemplation of the heart of the mystery of the Trinity.

The exalted nature of the contemplation of the person of Christ is central to the spirituality of Pierre Berulle. In his *Discourse on the State and Grandeurs of Jesus*, he wrote:

> 'We need to contemplate in the exalted and sublime life of the only Son before his Father the life we should begin on earth and bring to completion in heaven: tracing the preliminary lines and sketches of our perfection based on such an accomplished model; forming ourselves in the life of the Spirit and in all that is virtuous by imitating such a divine life and such a rare and excellent exemplar. For as the eternal Word proceeds in his divine being and has God for Father, so also we proceed in our supernatural being (though in a different manner) and we should recognize the Son of God as our Father, from whom we draw existence and the life of grace. This gives him, among those titles and attributes announced in the prophecies of his coming, the name of Father of the world to come.
>
> As the Word and eternal Son of God always contemplates his Father, because he is his Father, so we should constantly contemplate the Son, because he has been established as our Father. Our gaze toward him should be a gaze of the greatest honour, the most powerful love, and total and absolute dependence. We should wish that our beings were nothing but vision and spirit so that we could be completely occupied and given over to this spiritual and divine contemplation of the new source and principle of our being, The only Son of God constantly refers all that he is to the Father. His being and his life consist in this relationship Even, strictly speaking, his life is nothing but a life that substantially and personally refers all that he is to his sole source. In the same way our being and our life should be totally dedicated to a perfect and absolute

referral of all that we are, in the order of nature and grace, because of his eternal mercy.'[149]

Another who recognised the possibility of contemplative union in the contemplation of Christ in his humanity was Thomas Gallus of Vercelli (dec 1246). In an article entitled, 'Thomas Gallus and the Contemplative Effort' James Walsh wrote:

> 'Some of the greatest spiritual authors have taught a form of affective prayer which raises itself towards unitive contemplation, but remains rooted in the imagination. Such are the contemplations of Christ incarnate which constitute the principal prayer of the Spiritual Exercises of Ignatius of Loyola. Ignatius is the heir of a long tradition which undoubtedly finds its clearest expression in the monastic spirituality of the twelfth and thirteenth centuries—with the Cistercians, the Carthusians and the Franciscans. Thomas Gallus, in spite of his predilection for Denis and of the strange nature of his spiritual vocabulary, is one with Teresa of Avila in affirming that affective meditation of the suffering humanity of Christ is a short cut to arrive at *unitive* contemplation.'[150]

Walsh backs up this statement with the following quotation from Gallus:

> That is to say, in the lengthy consideration of the wounds of the most blessed and most beautiful Christ. For among all the exercises capable of raising the spirit this is the most effica-

---

149. P Berulle, *Discourse on the State and Grandeurs of Jesus* in *Berulle and the French School* (W Thompson ed) (NewYork: Paulist Press 1989), 136–37.
150. J Walsh, 'Thomas Gallus et L'Effort Contemplatif' in *Revue d'Histoire de la Spiritualité*, 51 (1975): 41: 'En pratique, quelques-uns des plus grands auteurs spirituels ont enseigné une forme de prière affective qui s'élève vers la contemplation unitive, mais qui s'enracine également dans l'imagination. Telles sont les contemplations imaginatives du Christ incarné qui constituent la prière principale des *Exercices Spirituels* d'Ignace de Loyola. Ignace est l'heritier d'une longue tradition qui s'exprime le plus nettement, sans doute, dans la spiritualite monastique des douzième et treizième siècles—chez les cisterciens, les chartreux et les franciscains. Thomas Gallus, en dépit de sa predilection pour Denys et du caractère étranger de son vocabulaire spirituel, se rencontre avec Thérèse d'Avila pour affirmer que la meditation affective de l'humari té souffrante du Christ est un raccourci pour arriver à la contemplation unitive.'

cious. In fact, the more we are inflamed by his sweet love in representing him imaginatively, in a way that is holy and full of piety and devotion, the more our apprehension of divine realities will Increase.[151]

In *The Book of Her Life,* chapter 22 and again in *The Interior Castle;* 6.7.5 to 6.7.12, St Teresa makes it clear that the contemplation of the humanity of Christ is the normal way of prayer, even for those who have advanced to contemplative union, and that this contemplation can never be abandoned on the grounds that one has passed beyond it. While wisely allowing for individual personal differences, she returns constantly to the need to contemplate Christ in his humanity. Even in times when concentration on the mysteries of the Passion, for instance, is not possible, personal presence to Christ does remain possible: 'If our health doesn't allow us to think about the Passion, since to do so would be arduous, who will prevent us from being with Him in His risen state? We have Him so near in the Blessed Sacrament, where He is already glorified and where we don't have to gaze upon Him as being so tired and worn out, bleeding, wearied by His journeys, persecuted for those for Whom He did so much good and not believed in by the Apostles.'[152] In very strong language she laments her earlier attempts to abandon the contemplation of the humanity. She powerfully sums up her argument for the contemplation of the humanity in this paragraph from *The Life:*

> 'Thus your Reverence and lordship should desire no other path even if you are at the summit of contemplation; on this road you walk safely. This Lord of ours is the 'one through whom all blessings come to us. He will teach us these things. In beholding His life we find that He is the best example. What more do we desire than to have such a good friend at our side,

---

151. Walsh, 'Thomas Gallus et L'Effort Contemplatif', 41. Walsh is citing B Pez (ed), *Commentarium Hierarchicum in Cantica Canticorum* (Florence: Biblioteca Media Infimae Latinitatis, 1809), 551: 'Hoc est: in intima consideratione vulnerum beatissimi et formosissimi Christi. Nam inter omnes actiones mentis haec efficacissima est ad intelligentiam elevandam . . . Re enim vera quanto in eius amore superdulcissimo fuerimus ardentiores, per iugem ipsius beatissimam, piam, devotam et venerandam imaginationem, tanto nimirum in apprehensione divinorum erimus altiores.'
152. St Teresa of Avila, *The Book of Her Life,* chapter 22. 6, in *The Complete Works,* volume 1, 1 93.

who will not abandon us in our labours and tribulations, as friends in the world do? Blessed are they who truly love Him and always keep Him at their side! Let us consider the glorious St Paul: it doesn't seem that any other name fell from his lips than that of Jesus, as coming from one who kept the Lord close to his heart. Once I had come to understand this truth, I carefully considered the lives of some of the saints, the great contemplatives, and found that they hadn't taken any other path: St Francis demonstrates this through the stigmata; St Anthony of Padua, with the Infant; St Bernard found his delight in the humanity; St Catherine of Siena—and many others about whom your Reverence knows more than I.[153]

The mysteries chosen for contemplation.

The gospels contemplations of the Second Week of the Spiritual Exercises fall into two parts: the contemplation of the infancy and growing to maturity of Jesus, and the contemplation of his public life up to and including Palm Sunday. Between the two Ignatius interposes what is generally called 'the Ignatian day', his meditation on the Two Standards with its repetitions and his meditation on the Three Classes of Persons. Like all other parts of the Exercises, the Second Week demands, for its understanding, careful attention to the dynamic of the whole Exercises. A person is presumed to emerge from the exercises of the First Week with a profound sense of being fully redeemed and loved by God in Christ. Such a one, full of gratitude, is ready to follow Christ as fully as possible in discipleship The Second Week for Ignatius will be dominated by two goals: that of growing in knowledge, love and discipleship of the Lord Jesus, and that of seeking and finding the will of God in the disposition of one's life. The two are always inseparably intertwined.

Inspired by the vision presented in 'The Call of the King' consideration, and wishing to make the offering of self suggested by Ignatius at the end of it, a person takes up the contemplation of the life of Jesus as revealed in the gospels. This contemplation is not just an attempt to follow through the gospels chronologically, but to respond to their dynamic call to growth in relationship with Christ.

---

153. Teresa of Avila, *The Book of Her Life* chapter 22. 7, 194.

In this process the narratives of the infancy of Jesus, presented by Matthew and Luke, have a specific part to play. Both gospels present the infancy in stories which are more notable for their appeal to the imagination than for their historicity. As a late development from the early kerygma of the Lord's resurrection and death and looking forward to his coming again, these stories are a reflection on who is this Jesus who had become Lord must have been from the beginning. In brief summary, one could say that Luke presents him as 'salvation for the peoples' and Matthew as 'God with us', the initial pronouncement that 'they shall call him Emmanuel' (Matt 1:23) being repeated in the gospel's last words, 'I am with you always, till the end of the age' (Matt 28:20).

There is, then, in the early part of the Second Week of the Exercises a time of delaying over the stories of the infancy to grow in knowledge, love and desire to follow the Word who has been made flesh. Ignatius is careful to direct a retreatant at this stage to remain in touch with the reality of their personal situation before God, not simply to enter a different, unreal world of allowing the imagination to take flight. Hence, his repeated instruction to reflect on oneself and draw fruit from what one is experiencing (SE 106, 107, 108, 114, 115, 116, 122, 123, 124, 125). Were one simply to regard the Second Week of the Exercises as a time to come to grips with the gospels, without due attention to the dynamic, the time Ignatius gives to the infancy narratives would seems grossly out of proportion. He proposes a 'week' of twelve days for the contemplation of the life of Christ up to Palm Sunday. Of these a whole three days are given over to the infancy contemplations. After the text of the four weeks, Ignatius gives points for the contemplation of the mysteries of the life of Christ our Lord. For the mysteries of the Second Week (SE 261–287), eleven are devoted to the infancy, and only fifteen to the whole of the public life.

In a note Ignatius, suggests the possibility of lengthening or shortening the Second Week as he had detailed it in the text of the Exercises: 'Everyone, according to the time he wishes to devote to the contemplations of the Second Week, and according to his progress, may lengthen or shorten this Week. If he: wishes to lengthen it, let him take the mysteries of the Visitation of our, Lady to Elizabeth, the Shepherds, the Circumcision of the Child Jesus, the Three Kings and also others. If he wishes to shorten the Week, he may omit even some of the mysteries that have been assigned. For they serve here to afford an introduction and a way for better and more complete contemplation later.'[154] In this note Ignatius suggests for the lengthening of the Week several more contemplations from the infancy, virtually exhausting the gospel material of the first two chapters of Matthew and Luke, and offers no further suggestions for contemplations of the public life.

How does one explain the apparent imbalance presented in this Second Week between the contemplation of the child Jesus and the contemplation of the public ministry of Jesus? As always in dealing with the Spiritual Exercises, the overriding consideration is their goal. There is a twofold aim in the Second Week: growth in heart knowledge, love and following of Christ, and seeking and finding the will of God for one's life. The narratives of the infancy are specially suitable for presence to the mystery of the incarnation and the mystery of the Trinity. Though the retreatant is often instructed to reflect on their own person and draw some profit, there is not the focus on self that will be later involved with regard to the election. In the second part of this Second Week, when Ignatius turns explicitly to the election in his text, there is far more 'space' for the retreatant to reflect on where God is leading them, with just one subject for contemplation each day. William Peters, commenting on the fact that in the second half of the Second Week Ignatius presented just one event of the public life for contemplation each day, drew attention to this double goal of the Second Week contemplations: 'It proves that any event is of relative unimportance, it always yields first place to the Person of Christ. Another point must be noted. If the exercitant returns over and over again to those parts of the contemplation where he felt consolation or desolation and where he experienced greater spiritual relish—this is of the essence of all repetitions (62, 118)—the supposition is that he is being moved by various spirits and more so now than in previous days. It is here that the meditation on Two Standards asserts its influence.'[155]

The mysteries of the public life actually chosen by Ignatius parallel very closely mysteries as presented by Ludolph in the *Vita Jesu Christi* and by John de Caulibus before him in the *Meditaciones*

---

154. SE 162.
155. Peters, *The Spiritual Exercises*, 108.

Vite Christi. In both those authors there is the combining of Jesus' journey from Nazareth and his baptism; and the combining of his retiring to the desert and being tempted. The order in which Ignatius presents his eight mysteries is the same as in John and in Ludolph. Ignatius presents the mystery of Jesus' rejection in the temple from the two brief verses of Luke 19:47-48, and has it out of order (before Palm Sunday). John and Ludolph presented it in the same position as Ignatius, but chose as the text John 8:59: 'So they picked up stones to throw at him, but Jesus hid himself and went out of the temple.'

It is difficult to provide any rationale for Ignatius's choice of the mysteries to be contemplated from the public life of Jesus. Peters attempted to show a series of parallels between the mysteries of each of three sets of four days of Ignatius's twelve-day Second Week.[156] The attempt seems very contrived, and Peters himself did not seem very convinced, referring to 'the somewhat frail outlines of a rhythm between the first and second quartets of days' and the need for 'treading carefully'.[157]

When he came to consider the mysteries recommended for contemplation by Ignatius in the Second Week, David Stanley prefaced his account of the suggested mysteries by indicating that there is a need to adjust the presentation of the Exercises to respect the modern understanding of the individual character of each of the gospels. There is certainly general agreement on this issue. Part of Stanley's outline of the deficiencies in Ignatius's understanding of the gospels reads as follows: 'Likewise he (Ignatius) has extracted from the Matthean Passion narrative the contemplation, 'The supper at Bethany' (Mtt 26:6-13), conflated it with two details from the story at John 12:1-8, the presence of Lazarus (Jn 12:2) and of Mary of Bethany (Jn 12:3), whom he calls Magdalene, and, under the influence of the Fourth Gospel, follows it with Matthew's version (for the most part) of 'Palm Sunday' (SE 287; Mtt 21:1-11). All these discrepancies, assuredly of minor importance, exemplify the medieval approach to the Gospels, and so indicate 'the need of adjusting the Spiritual Exercises for retreatants who are more sensitive to the individual character of each of the four Gospels.'[158]

---

156. Peters, *The Spiritual Exercises*, 110-12.
157. Peters, *The Spiritual Exercises*, 111.
158. Stanley, 'Contemporary Gospel-Criticism and the Mysteries', 30.

All that can be said in conclusion on the choice of mysteries to be contemplated is that the director of the Spiritual Exercises must make choices that are faithful to modern scripture scholarship, as well as to the twofold goal of enabling the retreatant to contemplate the person of Christ, so as to know, love and follow him ever more closely, and to discern the will of God for the living of their life in union with the Same Lord Jesus.

c) The Application of Senses.

No part of the Spiritual Exercises has been open to such a wide range of interpretation as the exercise which has been given the name 'Application of Senses'. At one end of the spectrum there is an opinion like that of William Peters who declared that this exercise in the Second Week was unimportant: 'Of greater importance is the fact that Ignatius does not insist on the application of the senses being made. He does not impose this exercise, which makes it unlikely that it is a very high form of prayer. It is a useful exercise, it may help (121).'[159] This hardly does justice to the text Ignatius recommends applying the senses in every exercise from the start of the Second Week contemplations. His use of the term 'it is helpful' *(aprouecha)*, far from being dismissive, is really a recommendation. It is the same word that he used concerning the supremely important fifth Annotation: 'it is very helpful' *(mucho aprouecha)* (SE 5).

Perhaps next on the ascending scale of value attached to the exercise of the Application of Senses come the comments of the official Directory of 1599. Under the chairmanship of Gil Gonzalez Davila the commission which prepared the Directory strove to avoid every taint of Illuminism. The contemplations of the Second Week of the Exercises were treated as meditations. The role of the 'spiritual (non-corporeal) faculties' of intellect and will was regarded as far superior to that of the sense (corporeal) faculties. As a result the Directory treated the exercise of applying the senses as one that consisted in an 'easy' use of the imagination: 'The fifth Exercise which is the application of the senses is very easy, and useful. We imagine that we see the persons, and hear their words, or any other sound that there is, or we touch or kiss the places or the persons; (which must be done with all reverence, modesty and fear). Our holy father Ignatius directs the sense of smell to smelling the fragrance of the soul coming

---

159. W Peters, *The Spiritual Exercises*, 87.

from the gifts of God, and the sense of taste to tasting its sweetness. Both of these signify a certain presence of the thing or the persons we are meditating upon, with a tender savouring and love for them.'[160]

In keeping with the presupposition out of which the editing of the Directory was functioning, the exercise of application of senses was regarded as inferior to the preceding exercises of meditation: 'How does the application of senses differ from meditation? The application of senses differs from meditation in that meditation is more intellectual, and is more concerned with reasoning and is altogether higher. Meditation thinks over the causes and effects of the mysteries, and in them it investigates the attributes of God: like his goodness, wisdom, love, and the others. But the application of senses does not think, but only rests in sensible things, like what one sees and hears, and other things of this kind, which it enjoys and delights in with spiritual profit.'[161]

The basic problem underlying these paragraphs of the Directory is that they were founded on an excessively analytic psychology. The knowing faculties of the human person were neatly divided, and the higher faculties of the soul, intellect and will, were the ones to which the word spirit could be strictly applied. This was exemplified in Gagliardi's remark, quoted above on page 21, that the lower faculties themselves do not pray. Prayer was seen as belonging only to the higher powers of the soul. A modern, much more integrated psychology sees the whole person as a unified being of body and mind, so that the Holy Spirit operates within all the faculties of the mind, as well as through the body itself. A higher form of prayer is

---

160. MHSI 76, 677: 'Exercitium quintum, quod est applicatio sensuum, est facile valde, et utile imaginando nos videre *personas*, et audire verba, aut strepitum si qui fit, vel tangere, aut osculari sive loca, sive personas; quod tamen fieri debet cum omni reverentia, et modestia, ac timore. Olfactum P N. Ignatius refert ad odorandam fragrantiam animae ex donis Dei et gustum ad gustandum eius dulcedinem, quod utrumque significat praesentiam quamdam rei, vel personarum, quas meditamur, cum gustu et amore earum tenere.'
161. MHSI 76, 681: 'In quo differt applicatio sensuum a meditatione? Differt autem applicatio ista sensuum a meditatione, quoniam meditatio est magis intellectualis, et magis versatur in ratiocinatione, et omnino est altior: discurrit enim per causas illorum mysteriorum, et effecta, et in eis investigat attributa Dei, ut bonitatem, sapientiam, charitatem, et reliqua. At vero applicatio non discurrit, sed tantum inhaeret in illis sensibilibus, ut in aspectu et auditu, et reliquis eiusmodi, quibus fruitur et delectatur cum profectu spirituali.'

not one in which the intellect is more in operation, but one in which the person is more open to the influence of God's Spirit.

By the time of the Directory, without reference to Ignatius' distinction in the Spiritual Exercises between meditation and contemplation, the exercises on the gospel mysteries were seen as meditations, and as such were higher than an exercise firmly rooted in the use of the senses of the imagination. With the proper acceptance of the contemplative character of all the exercises on the gospel mysteries, the question whether the Application of Senses is higher than meditation ceases to have any relevance. The question, however, which has tended to remain is whether the Application of Senses is a higher form of prayer than the prayer of the other exercises on the gospel mysteries. Certainly, what is relevant for a person making the Spiritual Exercises is: in what way, if any, is the Application of Senses different from the other exercises?

In the text of *The Spiritual Exercises* Ignatius presents three different ways to pray in which the five senses are to be used. The first of these is the meditation on hell (SE 65–71); the second is the exercise we are considering here, the last exercise of the day from the Second Week on (SE 121–126); the third appears in the text of the first of the three ways to pray (SE 247). The exercise on hell is a highly imaginative construct, which could be the reason for its being given the name 'meditation', rather than contemplation. Of the five senses hearing and smelling are the ones concerned with the most directly observable. Ignatius recommends hearing 'the wailing, the howling cries and blasphemies against Christ our Lord and His saints.' (SE 67). This is hardly the kind of sensation to be dwelt upon directly, without paying more attention to the fact 'that up to this very moment He has shown Himself so loving and merciful to me' (Ignatius's words in the colloquy of SE 71). The sense of smell is 'to perceive the smoke, the sulphur, the filth and corruption (SE 68). The other three senses are concerned with far less sensible realities, namely fires and flames that touch souls (SE 66, 70), and 'to taste the bitterness of tears, sadness and remorse of conscience.' (SE 69). It should be clear from all this that Ignatius is not writing here about a simple use of the 'imaginative senses', but is using the category of sense in a metaphorical way.

When Ignatius discusses the use of the senses in the first way to pray (SE 247), he is concerned with an attempt 'to imitate Christ our

Lord in the use of the senses' and 'to imitate our Lady in the use of her senses' (SE 248), Once again he is hinting at a reality that is not at all easy to grasp A simple, direct question, like 'how did Christ our Lord, or our Lady exercise their sense of taste?' has no simple, direct answer. What does one do in this exercise? One allows one's imagination free play and enters via the imagination into a depth of relationship with Christ or with our Lady.

From the analogy of these first and third ways of using the senses, it should be evident that when Ignatius directs a person to pray with the senses, he is entering into a realm that is very difficult to grasp in purely rational terms. The same will hold true for the Application of the Senses to the mysteries of the gospel. Ignatius did not, in fact, use an abstract term like 'application', but wrote in very concrete terms: to bring the senses *(traer los sentidos)*. As commentators continued to reflect on this apparently simple exercise of applying the senses to a gospel mystery, more and more complex analyses of what Ignatius intended began to emerge. Clearly opposing positions were taken, and attempts were subsequently made to synthesise them in such a way as to reconcile the opposites. The analyses tended to come under the heading of what kind of senses Ignatius was referring to in this exercise: the senses of the imagination, or the so-called spiritual senses, with a long history going right back to Origen in the third century. The solution to this question would provide the answer to the question whether Ignatius was intending this fifth exercise to be simply another kind of discursive, ordinary prayer or a truly mystical prayer. Controversies that arose in Jesuit circles about the Application of Senses were largely concerned with what kind of senses Ignatius had in mind. Was he simply giving a direction to take up again the use of the imagination, or was there something here more special, more oriented towards a deeper, contemplative form of prayer? In the first place, it would hardly seem sensible to introduce a new way of praying, with a new name into the Exercises of the Second Week, if there was nothing different intended from what had already been outlined in using the senses in the previous contemplations. Retreatants have already been encouraged to see the persons and hear what they are saying (SE 106, 107, 114, 115). Not only have they been encouraged to see and hear, but to do this as an exercise of contemplation.

Towards the end of his article on Application of Senses in the *Dictionnaire de Spiritualité* Joseph Maréchal wrote: 'The Exercises . . . do not have a 'method' for crossing the threshold of passive prayer. This reserve was necessary in a tactical manual: would it not have been a nonsense to prescribe, as the fifth exercise of the day of retreat, a mystical prayer?'[162] This is, indeed, a rhetorical question. Mystical prayer is sheer gift, and certainly cannot be 'prescribed'. However, this is hardly a valid argument against the possibility that Ignatius was wishing to encourage retreatants to go beyond the merely active use of imagination to an openness and receptiveness to an expected deeper gifting by God. Earlier Maréchal had written an article on the Application of Senses which was reproduced in his *Studies in the Psychology of the Mystics*. His writing on the subject is a clear example of an attempt to embrace and reconcile a vast range of different opinions. A hint of this is given in the, title of the article: 'An Essay on Meditation Oriented towards Contemplation'[163] While much of Maréchal's article can be read as a clever balancing of widely different opinions; in one sentence he declared: 'Moreover the application of senses, far from being inferior to discursive meditation, approaches contemplation strictly so called.'[164] Part of Maréchal's attempt at reconciliation involved introducing in his *Dictionnaire* article a third kind of senses, which he named 'metaphorical senses'. He saw this as an explanation of what Ignatius meant in his references to the senses of smell and taste: 'This is to smell the infinite fragrance, and taste the infinite sweetness of the divinity. Likewise to apply these senses to the soul and its virtues' (SE 124). For Maréchal words like 'to see a truth, to give ear to the inspirations of the Holy Spirit, to burn with charity' are examples of the use of the metaphorical senses.

M Ruiz, in an article in *Manresa*, took up the three types of senses, which he named as imaginative *(imaginativos)*, rational *(racionales)*, and mystical *(mysticos)*, and asked: 'to which kind is the holy father (Ignatius) referring in the Exercises? . . .' To all three. Absolutely and

---

162. J Maréchal, 'Application des Sens', in *Dictionnaire de Spiritualité, Tome 1* (Paris: Beauchesne, 1937), col 827.
163. J Maréchal, 'Un Essai de Meditation Orientee vers la Contemplation' in *Etudes sur la Psychologie des Mystiques, (Tome second)* (Paris: Desclee de Brouwer, 1937), 365°82.
164. Maréchal, 'Un Essai de Meditation Orientee vers la Contemplation', 370.

categorically.'[165] Ruiz's principal argument for the mystical senses is the witness of 'Polanco; Nadal, La Palma, Alvarez de Paz, Suarez and others'.

Not surprisingly, Maréchal is far more cautious in his answer to the question: 'Which of the three degrees did Ignatius have in mind in the Spiritual Exercises?' He answers: 'Certainly the first degree (the imaginative), that of 'beginners'; also up to a certain point, the second degree (the metaphorical), closely allied to the first, and dependent, like it, on human effort. As to the third (the spiritual), it is clear that the Exercises say nothing.'[166] Maréchal gave a very important role to the metaphorical senses, which 'provide, in different degrees, a feeling of objective presence or, at least attenuate the unreal, distant nature of the object thought of.'[167]

While, at one level, Marechal's introduction of a third kind of senses, the metaphorical, can seem like an unnecessary multiplying of entities, it is perhaps the term metaphorical that best captures what Ignatius was concerned about in the Application of the Senses. The sense of presence which these senses give was already emphasised in Maréchal's article' in *Studies in the Psychology* of *the Mystics*. 'If the variety and concreteness of the images is not of much importance, there is still in the direct or imaginary exercise of the senses something which has a more noteworthy value for prayer: namely, the *sense of presence*.'[168] And 'again: 'In the course of contemplation sensible imagery will readily become attenuated to the point of barely leaving, along with the intelligible object, only an impression of reality or of

---

165. M Ruiz, 'Aplicacion de Sentidos', in *Manresa* 68 (Sept 1946): 261–2.
166. Maréchal, 'Application des Sens', col. 827: 'Lequel de ces trois degrés saint Ignace eut-il en vue dans les *Exercices Spirituels?* Certainement le premier degré, celui des 'commençants'. Et aussi, jusqu'a un certain point, le second degre, lie d'assez près au premier et dependant comme lui de l'industrie humaine. Quant au troisieme degré, il est clair que les Exercices n'en disent rien.'
167. Maréchal, 'Application des Sens', : '... cette transposition symbolique des sens ... procure, à divers degrés, un *sentiment de presence* objective, ou du moins attenue le caractere irreel et lointain de l'objet conçu.'
168. Maréchal, 'Un essai de Meditation', 374: 'Si la varieté et relief des images n'importent pas beaucoup, il est toutefois, dans l'exercice direct ou imaginaire de la sensibilité, un caractère dont la valeur pour l'oraison apparâit plus notable: nous voulons parler du *sentiment de presence*.'

presence'.[169] It is this sense of being really present, which is more likely to be a deep feeling than a strong feeling, that opens the way to the reception of whatever gift of contemplation is given. On p 156 above we have already rejected any notion that the use of the imagination in contemplating the gospels is meant to produce something like a still picture or a film of a gospel incident. Apropos of the Application of the Senses Marechal comments on this point: 'sometimes they (retreat directors) present the application of the senses like an advanced school of the imagination, either by preaching vividness and concreteness, or by looking for minute detail, in the style a Dutch tableau; the retreatant is forced to paint or to model, when they ought to be occupied in loving.'[170]

René de Maumigny had advanced the theory that in writing about the senses of sight, hearing and touch Ignatius was referring to the imaginative senses, but in writing of taste and smell, he was alluding to the spiritual senses: 'St Ignatius, while allowing full liberty for the use of imaginative or the spiritual senses, counsels the use of the imaginative senses for sight, hearing and touch, and the spiritual senses for taste and smell.'[171] De Maumigny was not proposing a new theory, but repeating the line followed by Juan Polanco in his Directory *(circa* 1594).[172] Ignatius's strikingly different language about the senses of smell and taste certainly provided a difficulty for those who saw the whole exercise as one involving only the imaginative senses. Rather than look for an explanation in which the form of prayer has suddenly changed to something mystical in what Ignatius

---

169. Maréchal, 'Un essai de Meditation', 380: 'Facilement d'ailleurs, au cours de la contemplation, l'imagerie sensible s'attenuera, au point de ne laisser guère subsister, a côte de l'objet intelligible, qu'une impression de realité ou de presence.'
170. Maréchal, 'Un essai de Meditation', 382: 'parfois ils présentent l'application des sens comme une haute école d'imagination, soit qu'ils y prêchent vivacité et le relief, soit qu'ils y recherchent le detail minutieux, a la façon des tableaux hollandaise; le retraitant s'efforce de preidre ou de modeller, la ou il devarait surtout aimer.'
171. R de Maumigmy, *Pratique de L'Oraison Mentale, premier traite* (Paris: Beauchesne, 1907), 319: 'Saint Ignace, tout en laissant libre de faire usage des sens soit imaginalres, soit spirituelles, counseille de se servir des sens imaginaires pour la vue, l'ouïe, le toucher, et des sens spirituels pour le goût et l'odorat.'
172. See MHSI 76, 300–303.

gave as the 'third point', it would seem more reasonable to understand the use of all five senses as metaphorical.

Jesuit controversies around the Application of Senses had focused on the question of what kind of senses Ignatius had in mind for this fifth exercise of the day. We have seen that the 1599 Directory considered it a 'very easy exercise', where one descended from the loftier heights of meditation to a mere resting with sensible data. This way of thinking was reinforced by John Roothaan, who wrote in his notes on the Exercises: 'The exercise of Application of Senses according to the mind of St Ignatius, requires less stress; therefore he always puts it in the last place among the exercises to made each day, before supper, when the mind of the exercitant is rather weary from the exercises made throughout the day, and can and should be more in touch.'[173]

A diametrically opposite view on the point of being an easier, less tiring style of prayer was taken by Achille Gagliardi: 'This is a way that is higher and more difficult.'[174] More difficult, presumably, because more demanding of the person. Gagliardi saw the Application of Senses as a very contemplative form of prayer: 'through a kind of intuition of the matter, as if present, and without any movement or disturbance of the mind.'[175] This kind of prayer requires great commitment and concentration on the part of the praying person.

In these controversies much was made of the fact that Ignatius presented the Application of Senses as the last exercise of the day. Those who saw it as an easier and less exalted form of prayer appealed to the need of a retreatant to rest in the calm of evening after the efforts of the day's prayer. Those who saw it as an invitation to use the spiritual senses and enter into mystical prayer made much of the fact that that the person was well prepared by the previous meditations or contemplations and the repetitions to go to deeper levels in prayer.

---

173. J Roothaan, *Exercitia spiritualia:* cited in J Maréchal, 'Un Essai de Méditation', 367: 'Exercitium applicationis sensuum, ex mente S. Patris, minorem contentionem (requirit); quapropter illud etiam semper ultimo loco ponit, inter cuiusvis diei exercitia faciondum *ante cenam,* quando scilicet exercitantis animus exercitiis per diem factis jam fatigatior consert potest ac debet.'
174. A Gagliardi, *Commentarii seu explanationes in Exercitia spiritualia S. P Ignatii de Loyola,* cited by J Maréchal, 'Un Essai de Meditation', 369.
175. Cited by J Maréchal, 'Un Essai de Meditation', 369.

Moreover, the calm, gentle time of evening is found by many people to be the most 'contemplative' time of day. And Ignatius was one to make use of times and seasons, light and darkness and climate for his spiritual ends (SE 79, 130, 229). At the same time, the gift character of contemplative and mystical grace must always be borne in mind, and God gives those graces when God wills. While the formal structure of the exercises as Ignatius presents them seems to imply a progressive growth during the course of a day, and one could well expect some such development, it would be quite wrong to limit God's gifting to fit in with such a structure. One may, in fact, 'smell the infinite fragrance and taste the infinite sweetness of the divinity' in mid-morning! Philip Endean made the important point: 'Secondly, the three styles of prayer recommended for the Ignatian day–contemplation *simpliciter*, repetition and the Application of the Senses—are much more homogeneous than the traditional accounts suggest.'[176]

James Walsh and Hugo Rahner both widened the concept of 'application of the senses' to include all the contemplations of the gospel mysteries presented by Ignatius. Walsh wrote: '... the particular recall of gospel presence, whose traditional name is *memoria Christi* and was dubbed by Ignatius 'Application of the senses', appears, on different levels of awareness or consciousness, as both the beginning and the end of the contemplative process, which structures (and is structured by) each day of the ignatian Exercises, whether in the second, third, or fourth weeks.'[177]

Hugo Rahner had a very exalted understanding of Ignatius's 'composition of place':

> Furthermore, it noted that the Application of Senses, which runs throughout the entire *Spiritual Exercises* and sets the tone for prayer, comprises everything Ignatius mentioned in regard to what he called the Composition of Place, which is to precede each individual meditation...This Composition of Place may seem trivial but it turns everywhere into a symbol of truths which are beyond visualization. It uses pictures and images to present what is otherwise beyond all conceiving; it prepares the soul for the Application of Senses to which,

---

176. P Endean, 'The Ignatian Prayer of the Senses', in *Heythrop Journal* XXXI (1990): 369.
177. Walsh, 'Application of the Senses', 61.

after a day of meditation, it must devote itself in the calm and recollection of the evening; and it paves the way for the images, symbols and dispositions whereby the senses of the soul will be enabled to touch and savour spiritual truths.[178]

Did Ignatius have in mind the possibility that from the Second Week of the Spiritual Exercises on a person would be beginning to 'use the spiritual senses'? We saw that Marechal, while admitting that the Application of the Senses approaches 'contemplation strictly so called', at the same time denied that there was any involvement of the spiritual senses. Ultimately, it is not possible to conclude from the text of *The Spiritual Exercises* precisely what Ignatius had in mind.

Philip Endean rightly summed up the situation regarding the exegesis of the ignatian text when he wrote: 'There can be no question here of solving all the exegetical problems arising from Ignatius's elliptical text—indeed, a conclusive exegesis may be impossible ... It may be that Ignatius simply never articulated what he meant in a way that could be fully intelligible to later generations, especially since, in any case the process of the Exercises normally engages both retreat-giver and exercitant at levels deeper than that of their fully reflective awareness.'[179] Perhaps, in his wisdom, Ignatius wrote a text that was so open to the fundamental principles of flexibility and adaptation that it was able to be used for beginners and for the very advanced.

At the same time, there is ample evidence that many of the early companions of Ignatius were very clear that he was well aware of the tradition of the spiritual senses, and in the fifth exercise was alluding to them in his usual understated fashion. Chief among these is the witness of Juan Polanco, who wrote in his Directory of the Spiritual Exercises:

> The fifth exercise which is the Application of the Senses can be understood as applying to the imaginary senses. As such, it is suitable for those less used to meditation, to whom the Exercises are principally given. Or it can be understood to apply to the inner senses of higher reason. In this mode it is

---

178. Rahner, *Ignatius the Theologian*, 188-9
179. Endean, 'The Ignatian Prayer of the Senses', 398.

more suitable for the proficient who are more used to the contemplative life.'[180]

Later Polanco continued:

> If we interpret the Application of Senses as belonging to the inner senses and higher reason, according to the teaching of Blessed Bonaventure in the fourth chapter of *The Soul's Journey into God*, these senses can be explained as belonging to a soul in which the image of God is refashioned through the grace of God by faith, hope and charity. When through faith we believe in Christ, through him, as through the uncreated Word, which is the splendour of the Father and the radiance of eternal light, we recover and exercise spiritual vision. We consider the splendours of that light, and so Christ is for us the truth. When through faith we believe in Christ who is the incarnate Word, teaching what belongs to our salvation and perfection, through him we recover and exercise hearing, to accept his teaching, and so Christ is the way. Through hope we yearn to receive Christ as the inspired Word, dwelling in us through his gifts, and inviting us to his share his greater charisms, and eventually the full enjoyment of himself. Through the movement of desire and hope we recapture the spiritual sense of smell which we exercise by seeking the odour of the anointing of Christ, who is the life. When, through charity, we are united to Christ who is the incarnate Word, we receive delight from him on our pilgrim journey, we taste how sweet the Lord is, and we recover and exercise the spiritual sense of taste. Through pure love we embrace him and we pass over into him who transforms us. He never allows us to be separated from him; nor does he allow us to think of anything but him or love anything but him, except in him and for him. So we recover and exercise the spiritual sense of touch.[181]

---

180. MHSI 76, 300: 'Exercitium quintum, quod est applicatio sensuum, vel potest accipi de sensibus imaginariis (et sic convenit *in meditatione minus exercitatis*, quibus haec Exercitia potissimum proponuntur), vel de sensibus superioris rationis aut mentalibus, et sic proficientibus et versatis in via contemplativa magis quadrant.'
181. MHSI 76, 302-303: 'Si de sensibus mentalibus et ad rationem superiorem pertinentibus interpretamur, iuxta B. Bonaventurae doctrinam, quarto capite *Itenarrii mentis in Deum*, explicari possunt hi sensus de anima, in qua Dei

The relevant part of St Bonaventure's fourth chapter to which Polanco referred is: 'Having recovered these senses, when it sees its Spouse and hears, smells, tastes and embraces him, the soul can sing like the bride in the Canticle of Canticles, which was composed for the exercise of contemplation in this fourth stage. *No one* grasps this *except him who receives* (Apoc. 2:17), since it is more a matter of affective experience than rational consideration. For in this stage, when the inner senses are restored to see the highest beauty, to hear the highest harmony, to smell the highest fragrance, to taste the highest sweetness, to apprehend the highest delight, the soul is prepared for spiritual ecstasy through devotion, admiration and exultation according to the three exclamations of the Canticle of Canticles. The first of these flows from the fullness of devotion, by which the soul becomes *like a column* of *smoke from aromatic spices of myrrh and frankincense* (Cant 3:6). The second arises from intense admiration, by which the soul becomes *like the dawn, the moon and the sun* (Cant. 6:10), according to the progressive stages of the enlightenment that lift up the soul to gaze in admiration upon its Spouse. The third arises from the superabundance of exultation, by which the soul, *overflowing with delights* of the sweetest pleasure *leans* wholly *upon her beloved* (Cant 8:5).'[182]

---

imago per gratiam Dei, fide, spe et charitate, reformata est. Dum enim per fidem credit in Christum, per eum tanquam per Verbum increatum, quod est splendor Patris et candor lucis aeternae, recuperat et exercet spiritualem visum ad considerandum ipsius lucis splendores, et sic Christus est ei veritas. Dum per fidem credit in Christum, ut Verbum incarnatum *quae ad salutem et perfectionem nostram pertinent docentem*, recuperat per eum et exercet auditum, ad eius sermones suscipiendos, et sic Christum suscipiendum ut Verbum inspiratum, *per sua dona in nobis habitantem et ad potiora charismata et demum ad plenam sui fruitionem Invitentem, per desiderii et spei affectum*, recuperat homo spiritualem olfactum, quem exercet currens in odorem unguentorum Christi, qui ei hoc modo est vita. Dum charitate coniungitur Christo ut Verbo incarnato, tanquam suscipiens ab ipso delectationem *etiam in hac peregrinatione, gustans quam suavis est Dominus*, recuperat et exercet gustum spiritualem. Dum eumdem complectitur et in eum transit per purum amorem in *eum transformantem, qui ab eo divelli non permittit*, nec aliud quam ipsum cogitare nec amare sinit, nisi propter ipsum et *in ipso*, recuperat et exercet spiritualem tactum.'

182. St Bonaventure, *The Soul's Journey into God*, chapter 4. 3, in *Bonaventure* (New York: Paulist Press, 1978), 89–90.

Nadal too was well aware of the spiritual senses, and wrote about them very contemplatively: 'The principal spiritual senses are extensions of the three theological virtues. From the conviction of faith comes the faculty of hearing; from the understanding of faith comes vision. From hope comes the sense of smell. From the union of charity comes touch; and from the joy of charity comes taste. These senses are helps towards the greater graces that Jesus Christ, our Lord gives to those he loves. The one who receives them knows what they are.'[183]

Two of the classic expressions of the spiritual senses in operation, from Origen and from Augustine, are cited by Hugo Rahner in *Ignatius the Theologian*. First, from Origen's *Commentary on the Canticle*, 2: 'Christ is the source, and streams of loving water flow out of him. He is bread and gives life. And thus he is also spikenard and gives forth fragrance, ointment which turns us into the anointed *(christoi)*. He is something for each particular sense of the soul. He is called Light so that the soul may have eyes. Word, so that it may have ears to hear. Bread, so that it may savour him. Oil of anointing, so that it may breathe in the fragrance of the Word. And he has become flesh, so that the inward hand of the soul may be able touch something of the Word of life, which fashions itself to correspond with the various manifestations of prayer and which leaves no sense of the soul untouched by his grace.'[184]

Secondly, Rahner quotes from the *Confessions* of St Augustine, X, 6: 'But what do I love when I love my God? Not material beauty or beauty of a temporal order; not the brilliance of earthly light, so welcome to our eyes; not the sweet melody of harmony and song; not the fragrance of flowers, perfumes, and spices; not manna or honey; not limbs such as the body delights to embrace. It is not these that I love when I love my God. And yet, when I love him, it is true that I love a light of a certain kind, a voice, a perfume, a food, an embrace; but they are of the kind that I love in my inner self, when my soul is

---

183. MHSI 27, 677-8: 'Los sentimientos spirituales principales son las extensiones de las tres virtudes theologales. De la persuasion de la fe viene el audito; y de la intelection de la viene el viso. De la esparanca viene el odorato. De la vnion de la charidad viene el tacto; y del gozo de la misma viene el gusto. Son estos sentimientos adminiculos para mayores gracias que Jesus Christo nuestro Senor da a sus queridos, las quales conoce el que las tiene.'
184. H Rahner, *Ignatius the Theologian*, 200.

bathed in light that is not bound by space; when it listens to sound that never dies away; when it breathes fragrance that is not borne away on the wind; when it tastes food that is never consumed by eating; when it clings to an embrace from which it is not severed by fulfilment of desire. This is what I love when I love my God.[185]

Ignatius himself, as was his style, did not write directly about the tradition of spiritual senses. But in the light of the writings of his companions, it is impossible to think that he was ignorant of that tradition, In his *Spiritual Diary* Ignatius wrote repeatedly about gifts of visions received from God, which clearly go beyond the mode of ordinary prayer to the mode of the spiritual senses. Similarly, there is his occasional, powerful reference to his experience of the divine *loquela*. An expression of this which can only be understood in terms of the spiritual senses of hearing and taste is given in his Diary for 12 May 1544, where he wrote: 'Monday, May 12th—I stayed with the same, with many tears, and afterwards with tears again. All of these were like those of the preceding day, with such a great taste of the interior *loquela*. It was an assimilating or remembering of the *loquela* or heavenly music, increasing my devotion, and my affection with tears in the intimate understanding that I was experiencing or learning all this from God.'[186]

At the height of his exposition of mystical union in *The Living Flame of Love*, it is to the language of the senses that John of the Cross has recourse, in the form of the senses of hearing and taste. Commenting on the first stanza of his poem *The Living Flame* he wrote: 'This is the language and these the words God speaks in souls that are purged, cleansed, and all enkindled; as David exclaimed: *Your word is exceedingly enkindled* (Ps 119:139); and the prophet: *Are not* my *words, perchance, like a fire?* (Jer 23:29). As God himself says through St John, these words are spirit and life (Jn 6:63). These words are perceived by souls who have ears to hear them, those souls, as I say, that are cleansed and enamoured. Those who have a sound

---

185. H Rahner, *Igantius the Theologian*, 200.
186. MHSI 63, 137: '47.1. d. Lunes (*12 Maji*) - En la misma con muchas lagrimas, y despues della con ellas. Todas estas eran como el dia pasado, y con el tanto gusto de la loquela interior vn asimillar o recordar de la loquela o musics celeste, crecsendo la deuocion, y afecto con lagrimas en sentir que sentia o aprendia diuinitus.'

palate, but seek other tastes, cannot taste the spirit and life of God's words; his words, rather, are distasteful to them.'[187]

Later John continued:

> 'Those who do not relish this language God speaks within them must not think on this account that others do not taste it. St Peter tasted it in his soul when he said to Christ: *Lord, where shall we go? You have the words* of *eternal life* (Jn. 6: 68). And the Samaritan woman forgot the water and the water jar for the sweetness of God's words (Jn. 4:28).
>
> Since this soul is so close to God that it is transformed into a flame of love in which the Father, the Son, and the Holy Spirit are communicated to it, how can it be thought incredible that it enjoys a foretaste of eternal life? Yet it does not enjoy eternal life perfectly since the conditions of this life do not allow it. But the delight that the flaring of the Holy Spirit generates in the soul is so sublime that it makes it know that which savours of eternal life . . . David mentions: My *heart and my flesh rejoiced in the living God* (Ps 84:2). David did not refer to God as living because of a necessity to do so, for God is always living, but in order to manifest that the spirit and the senses, transformed in God, enjoy him in a living way, which is to taste the living God - that is, God's life, eternal life. Nor did David call him the living God other than because he enjoyed him in a living way, though not perfectly, but as though by a glimpse of eternal life. Thus in this flame the soul experiences God so vividly and tastes him with such delight and sweetness that it exclaims:
>
> O living flame of love!
> that tenderly wounds my soul.[188]

While Ignatius was loath to write much about the deepest things of the spiritual life, his letter to Teresa Rejadell of June 18th, 1536 became famous as a classic expression of some of these deeper realities. It included the following paragraph:

> It remains now to talk of what we feel as we learn from God our Lord how we are to understand it, and how, once it is understood, we are to take advantage of it. It often happens

---

187. St John of the Cross, *The Living Flame of Love. 1, 5, in The Collected Works*, 642.
188. St John of the Cross, *The Living Flame of Love. 1, 6, in The Collected Works*, 642

> that our Lord moves and forces us interiorly to one action or another by opening up our mind and heart, i.e. speaking inside us without any noise of voices, raising us entirely to His divine love, without our being able to resist His purpose, even if we wanted. Any purpose of His that we then adopt is such that of necessity we conform with the commandments, with the precepts of the Church and with obedience to our superiors, and it is full of complete humility because the same divine Spirit is in everything.[189]

Here the language Ignatius uses is that of the Application of Senses, in the form of hearing, and also that of 'consolation without preceding cause' (SE 330). It is one of the few occasions when he writes in his letters with a clearly mystical mode of expression.

Following our methodology in the treatment of the Application of the Senses of ascending from the lowest interpretations of this exercise to the highest, the last word belongs to Hans Holstein. While Holstein's ideal can hardly be deduced from the text of *The Spiritual Exercises*, there is no doubting that the reality was often experienced, and is still is experienced to this day by those making the Exercises. Holstein, as we saw above, declared that 'in this, it seems to us contemplation is distinguished from the application of the senses, where the higher faculties experience a quasi-mystical silence.'

Contemplation and the goal of the Spiritual Exercises

In the first Annotation of *The Spiritual Exercises* Ignatius outlined their goal as being 'preparing and disposing the soul to rid itself of all inordinate attachments; and, after their removal, of seeking and finding the will of God in the disposition of our life for the salvation of our souls.'[190] Our purpose here is to examine the light that the fulfilment of that twofold goal throws upon the nature of the prayer which leads to it.

First of all, how is the twofold goal fulfilled? The first part is principally the work of the First Week, though the work of conversion

---

189. J Munitiz (ed and trans), *Inigo: Letters Personal and Spiritual* (Inigo Enterprises, Hurstpierpoint, 1995), 26
190. SE 1

will continue through each of the following weeks, especially the Third Week, and indeed throughout one's lifetime. The second part of the goal has proven more problematic. Does it refer only to the election of a state of life? Clearly not. From the start, Ignatius and his companions frequently gave the Spiritual' Exercises to many whose state of life was already definitely fixed. In 1536 in Venice Ignatius gave the Exercises to Pietro Contarini, and in 1538 journeyed to Monte Cassino to give them for a month to Dr Pedro Ortiz.[191] For neither of these could there be an election of a new state of life. On the giving of the Exercises to those in a fixed state of life Jerome Nadal commented: 'To other women give almost all the exercises of the first week and little more, without the elections. However, to nuns more exercises can be given, with circumspection, however, and without the elections, at least of a state of life.'[192]

There are those who regard the election as being in some way essential to the making of the Spiritual Exercises. In treating of 'the essence of the Spiritual Exercises' in giving a preached retreat to young Jesuits which was reproduced in the book *Spiritual Exercises*, Karl Rahner declared: 'The Spiritual Exercises are not a theological system. From a theological point of view, the Spiritual Exercises are nothing, but an election or choice: the choice of the means and the concrete way in which Christianity can become a living reality in us. St Ignatius is only interested in this: that a man places himself before the Lord of the 'Kingdom of Christ' and the 'Two Standards' and asks: What should I do? What do You want from me according to the sovereignty of Your divine will?'[193] Rahner goes on to say: 'In our annual retreat, therefore, instead of choosing a way of life, we will ask ourselves with regard to some concrete point: What does God want from me now? Is He pleased by the, way I make my meditation, choose my reading material, and so forth? What about my determination to make progress in the spiritual life? We only really begin to make a retreat when we have found such an Archimedean point in our lives.'[194]

---

191. J de Guibert, *The Jesuits Their Spiritual Doctrine and Practice*, 125.
192. MHSI 27, Instructiones 61, 597: 'Et aliis quidem mulieribus dantur fere primae hebdomadae paulo amplius sine electionibus. Monialibus autem plura etiam, cum iudicio tamen et sine electionibus, saltem status.'
193. K Rahner, *Spiritual Exercises*, 11–12
194. K Rahner, *Spiritual Exercises*, 12

We are concerned here with a rather delicate point of spirituality. On the one hand, the approach of Rahner could be interpreted as overly oriented towards externals and observable results, with the concomitant danger evident in the not too distant past of making in prayer 'here and now' voluntaristic resolutions. The same is true of remarks like that of Brou (p 60, above), in writing about the prayer of Jesuits: 'But, discursive, affective or contemplative, it should be practical. It does not have its goal in itself.' On the other hand, there is a very important truth here. The way that God leads every person is truly human, and therefore eminently practical. The text of Matthew 7:6 is always applicable: 'It is by their fruits that you will know them.' Gonçalvez da Câmara, writing in his *Memoriale* about the occasion when Ignatius strongly rebuked Nadal for allowing Spanish Jesuits to lengthen the prescribed time for prayer, recorded these observations of Ignatius: 'He (Ignatius) said in conclusion: "For a truly mortified person a quarter of an hour is sufficient to unite oneself to God in prayer". And I do not know now whether he added then with regard to that matter or it is just that on many other occasions I heard him say that of 100 persons who are much given to prayer, 90 will be deluded. And I remember this clearly, though I am doubtful whether he may have said 99.'[195] The avoidance of illusion, the 'practicality' that Brou insisted on in Jesuit prayer, the need for an election in every retreat that Rahner spoke of, can all be seen as expressions of the need to apply continually the touchstone of reality to ensure that one's prayer is authentic.

One could say that the prayer of Ignatius, the 'contemplative in action' is aimed at reaching a degree of integration where there is no contradiction between being totally practical and being totally contemplative. Nadal, well aware of the essentially apostolic orientation of Jesuit prayer, was able to write: 'From this understanding of our end we can appreciate that the Society embraces both ways of life, the contemplative and the particular active life: because we practise

---

195. MHSI 66, L Gonçsalves da Câmara, *Memoriale*, (196) 644-45: 'Enfim concluyou: Un verdaderamente morteficado bastale un quarto de hora para se unir con Dios en oracion'. E nao sey se ao mesmo proposito ajuntou entao oque outras muitas vezes Ine ouvi dizer; que del 100 pessoas muito dadas a oracao as 90 seriao illusas. Edisto me lembro muito clara mente, ainda que duvido se dizia 99.'

both among ourselves, but we must practise the contemplative more intensely, and, to speak frankly, we must primarily be contemplative and dedicated to prayer; still, this is not the distinctive mark of our vocation and institute, but rather that we live that life which is called *the higher active,* in which we receive from Christ and practise in Christ the power to be able to help our neighbours, to assist one to be active and another to be a contemplative.'[196] To be a 'contemplative in action' it is certainly necessary first to be a contemplative.

Prayer is not to be judged by the feelings experienced or any other psychological criteria, but by the fruit of union with God lived out in the practice of virtue. Teresa insisted in her imagery of the different kinds of supplies of water for the garden that the goal is not water (the experience of prayer), but the flowers in the garden (the virtues).[197]

At the depth of contemplative purification in the second book of *The Dark Night* John of the Cross makes no distinction between contemplative purgation and nakedness or poverty of spirit, declaring that they are 'all about the same'.[198] But Ignatius yields nothing to John in asking for 'the highest spiritual poverty,[199] and is surpassed by nobody in proposing the Third Degree of Humility. Such gifts of poverty and humility are only possible if the prayer that Ignatius proposes, the contemplation of Christ in his mysteries, is authentic contemplative prayer.

---

196. MHSI 90, J Nadal, *Annotationes in Examen,* c. II, (31) 144: 'Ex hac finis ratione illud quoque intelligimus, Societatem utramque complecti vitam tum contemplativam tum activam particularem: utramque enim in nobis exercemus, sed contemplativam impensius et, ut aperte dicam, primarie debemus et quasi unice esse contemplativi atque orationi dediti; sed tamen haec non est proprietas nostrae vocationis et instituti, sed ut eam vivamus, quae *activa superior* dicitur, in qua facultatem a Christo accipiamus atque in Christo exerceamus, qua facultate iuvare proximos possimus, et alium ut activus fiat, alium ut contemplativus evadat iuvare.'
197. St Teresa of Avila, *The Book of Her Life,* chapter 11, in *The Collected Works,* volume 1, 113. St Teresa of Avila, *The Interior Castle,* 3. 1, in *The Collected Works,* volume 2, 308.
198. St John of the Cross, *The Dark Night,* 2.4.1, in *The Collected Works,* 400.
199. SE 147.

Conclusion

God enters into relationship with every human person through the gift of creation. From the human side this relationship will always be shrouded in mystery. There is a fundamental mystery within the human situation which must be continually responded to. In the face of mystery the appropriate attitude is what is normally called 'contemplative'. Every human person is gifted with an ability to contemplate the mystery of life, and is invited to develop their own personal gift. There is a natural mysticism of which every person is capable.

All grace is the grace of Christ. It is through the mystery of Christ that the natural gift of contemplation is received. It is through awareness of that mystery that the gift is developed through explicitly contemplative prayer. Those who have been privileged to receive the fullness of divine revelation in Christ, set forth within the Church, know that the natural gift of contemplation and mysticism is to be developed especially through prayer. The explicit development of the gift is primarily a communitarian activity. It is through union with Christ in the Church that the possibility of individual, personal growth in union with God is fully opened up. Persevering, personal prayer becomes the means of drawing on the grace present in the Church and its sacraments, in order to grow to the fullness of the possibilities of each one's life in Christ.

Throughout history God has gifted particular individuals with charisms for the building up of the Body of Christ. One of the most evident examples of such charisms is the gift of a highly developed life of personal contemplation that can be communicated to others. In every age of the Church's life there have been men and women outstanding for their gifts of personal holiness and of contemplation and their ability to communicate those gifts to others.

There is no doubting the advanced degree of holiness and of contemplative and mystical life enjoyed by Ignatius of Loyola. Along with these gifts, Ignatius was also able to communicate to others the way in which God had led him, and something of the universalism of God's dealing with people who entered seriously upon growth in personal relationship with this loving God. Ignatius set this down in writing, principally in the book of *The Spiritual Exercises*. Through the making of the Exercises the opportunity is presented for each person to develop their own personal relationship with God. Just as this led Ignatius to a highly developed life of mystical and contemplative prayer, each one has the possibility of growing in these gifts, in so far as they are given by God, The growth in contemplation and mysticism is not to be understood in the restrictive sense of withdrawal from active involvement with the world, Each person must discern their own particular vocation in this regard. Ignatius provided in *The Spiritual Exercises* a powerful help for discerning each one's personal call to service. Such service is not to be seen as the enemy of contemplation or mysticism, but rather as their appropriate expression.

From the start, Ignatius and his way of proceeding, principally through the Spiritual Exerclses, were often misunderstood. The whole style of life of an 'active' order like the Society of Jesus was so different from the monastic that there seemed little room for contemplation. Through his opposition to lengthy prayer for those called to the apostolate and his rational and practical approach to organising the things of the heart Ignatius was seen by some as the enemy of contemplation. Too much emphasis on the rational and practical led to a diminishing of the true role and importance of contemplation in the life of followers of Ignatius. The word 'contemplation' tended to be dropped, in favour of the more rational 'meditation'. Right up to the end of the twentieth century the problem of recapturing the primitive contemplative thrust in the life of Ignatius and in his book of *The Spiritual Exercises* has remained alive.

The great figure of John of the Cross, with his profound theological and psychological analysis of contemplative prayer, dominated Catholic thinking to such an extent that other ways of contemplation tended to be thought of as not quite so authentic. In the latter half of the twentieth century openness to Eastern, non-Christian religions and their ways of prayer, together with a renewed interest in historic, Christian ways of apophatic contemplation has, to some extent led to a lessening of appreciation for the very different approach of a practical, contemplative work like *The Spiritual Exercises*. The adjectives 'ignatian' and 'imaginative' used by writers about contemplation in the Exercises have carried with them a connotation of distinguishing this kind of contemplation from true contemplation.

It has been the aim of this work to show that contemplation the Second Week of *The Spiritual Exercises* is truly deserving of the name. It was presented by a man who had been gifted by God with extraordinary degrees of contemplative experience and personal holiness. He had been profoundly influenced, especially through the Carthusian, by the great Christian, contemplative tradition of *lectio divina*. Ignatius brought to the time of his conversion outstanding natural gifts of concentration, determination, single-mindedness, clarity of thought and ability to sense a goal and apply the appropriate means to pursue it. When he was, in fact, converted, he was clearly a person likely to reach the heights of sanctity. He was then gifted by God with mystical experiences which his own personal gifts enabled him to translate into practical outcomes. One of the most far-reaching of these outcomes was the writing of *The Spiritual Exercises* in which Ignatius tried to capture and share with others all the best of what he had received from God.

As a result, the Spiritual Exercises provide an entry into a way of Christian life that is both contemplative and eminently practical. The contemplative aspect of the work draws upon all the best that Ignatius could distil from the traditions of the Christian world of late medievalism into which he was born. He was the inheritor of the powerful contemplative thrust of the Benedictine, Cistercian, Franciscan, Carthusian and Dominican traditions. He did not abandon these traditions, but adapted them to his particular charism of an apostolic vocation. The traditions both shaped his own contemplative experience and enabled him to translate that experience into a spirituality that was relevant to the needs of the Church and the world of his time, and has proven to be of lasting value for the next five centuries. Till the end of the twentieth century the Spiritual Exercises have proven to be able to respond to the desire of discerning people of prayer to find an authentic way to deepen their relationship with God and place their lives at the service of people and of the coming of the Kingdom.

In the book of *The Spiritual Exercises* Ignatius both remained faithful to his own mystical experience and produced a text that could be adapted to the spiritual needs of a vast array of people. This has been borne out in recent history. The enormous advances in psychology, anthropology and scripture scholarship of the twentieth century have not only not proved a threat to *The Spiritual Exercises'* but have affirmed the authenticity flexibility and adaptability of Ignatius's approach. The renewal and updating called for by Vatican II saw a new impetus in the apostolate of the Spiritual Exercises, which were found by people of a vast array of traditions to be a most suitable instrument at the service of renewal. New ways of adapting the Exercises to individuals and groups have continued to flourish. The movement that has continued since the time of Vatican II has been embraced not only by Catholics, but by Christians from many different traditions. Non-Christians too have found in the Spiritual Exercises valuable help in their personal growth, their decision making, and their relationship with the 'higher power' that guides their lives. Such adaptations and uses of the Exercises are not unknown. In his *apologia* for the Spiritual Exercises Nadal had proclaimed in the sixteenth century the desirability of adapting them always through the goal of God's call to all persons to respond to the gift of creation, to the needs of 'heretics and infidels'.

In the text of *The Spiritual Exercises* Ignatius insisted repeatedly on the principles of flexibility and adaptation. He produced a text that was faithful to his own mystical experience of God, and contained 'all the best that I have been able to think out experience and understand in this life'. At the same time this text was to be used even for those who desired only a certain degree of peace of mind, in the satisfaction of knowing themselves as loved and forgiven (SE 18).

The danger arises through the desire to be accommodating to all who wish to 'have the experience of making the Spiritual Exercises' of losing sight in the adapting of the sublime possibilities to which the Exercises can lead. They are a school of contemplative and mystical experience, and a means to the most profound union with God. To achieve these ends it is necessary to acknowledge and affirm the truly contemplative character of the prayer which Ignatius proposes for those who have a radical experience of conversion of heart in the First Week, and wish to follow Christ in total self-gift through discipleship in the Second, Third and Fourth Weeks. It has been the scope of this work to recognise and affirm that from the Second Week on the exercises on the mysteries of the gospels are to be regarded as contemplation in the strict and authentic meaning of that word.

Index of Biblical References

Old Testament

Genesis
28:12	108

Psalms
4:9	97
33:16	109
84:2	223

Proverbs
2:4	112

Isaiah
6:10	194

Zechariah
3:3f	194

Ecclesiastes
31:9	113

Song of Songs
3:6	220
6:10	220
8:5	220

New Testament

Matthew
1:23	206
5:8	109
9:22	156
11:28	85
13:44	112
15:28	156
21:1–11	208
21:1–4	208
26:6–13	208
28:20	206

Mark
1:21–28	161,
2:5	156
5:1–20	161
5:34	156
7:24–30	161
8:17–18	175
9:14–29	161
10:52	156

Luke
3:10	168
7:50	156
8:48	156
17:19	156
18:42	156
19:47–48	208

John

1:18	148
1:39	xv
1:40	x
4:28	223
5:40	xv
6:37	xv
6:44	xv
6:65	xv
6:68	223
7:37	xv
8:12	121
8:59	208
12:1–8	208
12:2	208
12:3	208
12:20–22	xii
12:26	121
14:5–6	157
14:6	200
14:7	xv
14:9–20	157
14:9	xv, 201
14:18	xv
14:19	xv
14:23	xv
14:26	121
14:56	157
15:4–10	x
16:13	121
16:14	121
16:32	xvi

Acts

2:37	168
8:27–38	165
9:1–19	165
9:5	xviii
16:30	168

Romans

1:18—2:21	152.
2:11	152
3:21–22	153
3:24–25	152
4:22–25	152

5:5	194
6:3	194, 195
6:6	191
8:9	194
8:10	194
8:11	194
8:29	177, 190, 191
13:11–14	195
13:14	194, 195

1 Corinthians

1:31	84
2:2	xviii
2:10	192
6:9–11	195
9:1	192
11:1	189
12:13	194
14:15	132
14:30	192
15:8	192
15:49–54	195

2 Corinthians

4:16—5:5	195
4:6	192
5:3	95
5:16	xviii
8:9	198
13:5	194

Galatians

1:15	xviii
1:16	192
1:17	192
2:19	193
2:20	192, 193
3:26	195
3:27	191, 192, 194, 195

Ephesians

2:16	191
3:17	194
4:24	195
4:25	191

Philippians
2:5   191
3:10   xviii
3:15   192

Colossians
1:27   189, 194
3:10–22   191
3:10–13   195

1 Timothy
2:5   xvii

Hebrews
1:2   98

1 Peter
3:12   10

1 John
1:1–4   xvi
1:26   x
1:27   x
1:38   x
1:39   x
2:20   75
2:27   111
3:2   196

Apocalypse
2:17   220

Index of Names and Authors

A
Abbott, W, 101, 114.
Ambrose, Saint, 114.
Ambruzzi, A, 30, 164.
Arrupe, P, 123
Aquinas, T, 175, 200
Aschenbrenner, G, 158.
Ashton, J, 184.
Avila, T, 15, 49, 65, 68, 69, 70, 80, 81, 164, 203, 204, 205, 227.

B
Bangert, W, 4.
Barry, N, 163, 164.
Bermejo, L, 14.
Bernard, C, 61.
Bernard, Saint, 54, 86, 95, 102, 103, 105, 205.
Berulle, P, 202.
Biondolini, P, 30.
Bonaventure, Saint, 220.
Borgia, F, 18, 66, 67, 119, 161, 201.
Brou, A, 22, 28, 32, 33, 60, 143, 162, 163, 226.
Butler, C, 50, 68.
Byrne, B, 26, 27.

C
Canisius, P, 119, 161,
Caesarius of Arles, 107.

Coathelem, H, 21, 22.
Colledge, E, 87, 108.
Corbishley, T, 30.
Courel, F, 29.
Cusson, G, 28, 62, 88, 89, 116, 118, 120, 121, 122, 123.

D
da Câmara, L, 37.
Dalmases, C, 53, 54.
Dalton, W, 187.
Davila, G, 209
de Caulibus, J, 87.
de Gasperis,F, 103, 104.
de Guibert, J, 27, 28, 32, 59, 61, 63, 70, 71, 79, 80, 81, 117, 119, 120, 125, 127, 128, 161, 225,
de Mello, A, 29.
de Maumigny, R, 215.
de Sotto, P, 11.
Declouz, S, 134, 135, 136, 137, 138, 139, 140, 141, 142, 143, 144, 145, 146, 147, .
Delmage, L, 30.
Denzinger, H, 65.
Dulles, A, 48.
Dunn, J, 192, 193, 194, 195.

E
Ebling, G, 195.
Echarte, I, 31, 35, 186.
Egan, H, 11, 49, 66, 72.

Endean, P, 30, 52, 53, 84, 99, 123, 124, 125, 126, 127, 128, 129, 133, 135, 166, 217, 218.
English, J, 23, 24, 25, 164, 165.

F
Fitzmyer, J, 116.
Fung, R, 192, 194

G
Gagliardi, A, 216.
Gallus, T, 203
Ganss, G, 19, 20, 21, 30, 58, 59.
Garrigou-Lagrange, R, 50, 51.
Gregory, Saint, 108, 175.
Guigo II, 108, 109, 110, 111.

H
Häring, B, 67.
Helyar, John, 9.
Holstein, H, 165, 166, 167, 169, 170, 171, 172, 175, 176, 187, 188, 190.
Houdek, F, 16, 17, 18.

I
Ivens, M, 106, 153, 179.

J
Johnston, W, 49, 50, 61, 62.
John of the Cross, 39, 61, 66, 73, 77, 78, 81, 142, 222, 223, 227, 230.
John of Gorze, 107.

K
Kavanaugh, K, 78.
Kempis, T, 83.
Kolvenbach, P, 37.

L
Leclerq, J, 107.
Leo the Great, Saint, 174.
Lonergan, B, 50.
Luther, M, 190.

M
Mansfield, D, 18, 19.
Maréchal, J, 213, 216.
Merton, T, 185.
Minge, J, 103, 107.
McCoog, TM, 4.
Mollat, D, 117, 118, 119, 122.
Moo, D, 190, 191
Morris, J, 30.
Mottola, A, 30.
Munitiz, J, 30, 52, 53, 84, 99, 100, 123, 124, 125, 126, 127, 128, 129, 133, 135, 148, 166, 224.

N
Nadal, J, 4, 53, 63, 119, 122, 129, 130, 132, 133, 134, 140, 159, 161, 163, 162, 214, 221, 225, 226, 227, 232.
Nicolau, M,161.
Nober, P, 102, 103, 104.

O
O'Brien, P, 191.
Onuphrius, Saint, 123

P
Peeters, L, 33, 38.
Peter the Venerable, 107.
Peters, W, 34, 34, 35, 36, 54, 110, 111, 117, 178, 179, 207, 208, 209.
Pius XII, Pope, 185
Polanco, J, 36, 52, 54,128, 147, 214, 215, 218, 219, 220.
Puhl, L, v, 30, 31.

R

Rahner, H, 11, 28, 38, 39, 148, 190, 217, 218, 221, 222.
Rahner, K, 48, 49, 50, 158, 159, 178, 189, 201, 225, 226.
Rejadell, T, 12.
Riley, M, 115.
Rodriguez, O, 78.
Roothaan, J, 63, 654, 65, 120, 216.
Ruppert, F, 108.

S

Saxony, Ludolph of, 83ff, 166.
Schiavone, P, 29, 30, 106, 168.
Schonmetzer, A, 65.
Seager, C, 30
Stanley, D, 100, 101, 102, 104, 117, 156, 181, 182, 183, 183, 188, 189.

T

Tetlow, J, 31
Tinsley, E, 190, 196, 197

V

Veale, J, 16.
von Balthasar, H, 30, 49.
Voulet, P, 44, 165, 169, 171, 172, 173, 174, 175, 176, 177, 178, 179, 180, 181, 190.

W

Walsh, J, 99, 100, 150, 203, 217.
Wickham J, 167
Wulf, F, 48, 133.

Y

Young, W, 11, 134.